D1400299

WE REMEMBER THE CHILDREN

Edited by

Jack Salzman
and
Zelda Marbell Fuksman

IGI Publishing • Minneapolis, MN

"inSIGHT Through Education"

FIGHTING PREJUDICE THROUGH EDUCATION

The reprinting of this book was funded
by a generous grant from
"inSIGHT" who support Holocaust and Genocide Education
These memoirs remind the reader
to fight bigotry and hatred
and to strive for a safe and peaceful world.

Child Survivors/Hidden Children of the Holocaust
Palm Beach County, Florida

This book serves as a Memorial to the Six Million
Murdered in the Holocaust
of which One and a Half Million were Children.
Our hope is that it will allow the reader
to fully understand that all people
deserve to live in peace and with justice.

[handwritten inscription:] e remember / So that you will / remember! / Zelda Marbell Fussman

WE REMEMBER THE CHILDREN

This book speaks for us
For those who were silenced and
To those who will fight for equality

The Child Survivors/Hidden Children
of the Holocaust
Palm Beach County, Florida

IGI Publishing
A division of Lerner Publishing Group, Inc.
241 First Avenue North
Minneapolis, MN 55401 U.S.A.

Library of Congress Cataloging-in-Publication Data

We remember the children / edited by Jack Salzman and Zelda Marbell Fuksman.
    p.   cm.
    ISBN 978–0–9825503–9–7
    1. Jewish children in the Holocaust—Biography. 2. Holocaust survivors—Biography. 3. Jews—Biography. 4. Holocaust, Jewish (1939–1945)—Personal narratives. 5. World War, 1939–1945—Children. 6. World War, 1939–1945—Jews. 7. Europe—History—1918–1945—Biography.
    I. Salzman, Jack. II. Fuksman, Zelda Marbell.
    D804.48.W4 2011
    940.53'180922—dc22   2010033178

Manufactured in the United States of America
4-42952-3000473-9/21/2016

Since its inception eighteen years ago, The Child Survivors/Hidden Children of the Holocaust, Palm Beach County, Florida, has contributed to Holocaust education, which has had an impact on thousands of students.

Through the years, our past and present leaders have guided and cared for our child survivors with dedication, always mindful of our lost families and painful memories.

Frieda Jaffe
Rosette Goldstein
Dr. Pierre Chanover
Alex Moskovic
Blanche Feinberg
Norman Frajman

This book is the result of the emotional and hard-fought efforts of the many contributors who have told their stories, as well as the diligent efforts of the editorial staff and the book committee.

ACKNOWLEDGEMENT

We extend our gratitude and appreciation to Professor Jack Salzman who has guided us with heart and thoughtful input in every way.

Edited by
Dr. Jack Salzman
Zelda Marbell Fuksman

Editorial Assistant
Cecily Salzman

Project Advisor
Judith Evan Goldstein

Front Cover Art, "Faces of the Past," by Judith Evan Goldstein

Book Committee
Dr. Pierre Chanover
Mary Eckstein
Norman Frajman
Leon Ginsburg
Rosette Goldstein
Frieda Jaffe
Benno Lindenberg
Max Markowitz
Richard Weilheimer
Hershel Fuksman, Photography

Our Dedicated Teachers
Cynthia Glazier
Maureen Marullo

Contents

Introduction

Sometimes you get lucky. I did. I was born in Germany in December 1937. In March of 1938 my mother and I left Germany for the United States. I do not know the exact date of our departure, nor am I sure of the city from which we embarked. I do know that I was three months old and my mother was about eighteen. I was told that the journey was "difficult," that my mother was frequently ill, and that a woman we would never see again often took care of me on the journey to the United States. Although I know little of what took place before the departure or on the ship, I do know that my mother and I arrived in New York on April 1, 1938. It was an easy date to remember, and from time to time I would be reminded that I arrived in New York on April Fool's Day.

It may have been April Fool's Day, but how lucky I was. After all, in 1933, just four years before I was born, Adolf Hitler became chancellor of Germany and the first concentration camp, Dachau, was opened. Two years later Germany adopted the notorious Nuremberg Laws. While I was safe in New York, *Kristallnacht*—the Night of Broken Glass—took place on November 9 and 10, 1938. Less than a year later, on September 1, 1939, Germany invaded Poland, and World War II was under way. In his poem, "September 1, 1939," W.H.Auden wrote, "We must love one another or die." Many millions would die—six million Jews and millions of others. How lucky I was not to be among them.

But numbers—six million and more—tell us only a part of what we need to know or, more strikingly, what we do not want to know. Not knowing is so much easier than knowing and understanding. So, for example, when my mother and I arrived in New York on that April Fool's Day, we were met by my father, who had left Germany within days after I was born. We went to Washington Heights, which for some years had been home to a large number of German Jews. There, I was told, we stayed for a short time with relatives who had left Germany in the early thirties and were responsible for bringing us to the United States. Not long after, we moved to the Williamsburg section of Brooklyn, where I remained for the first twenty years of my life. Though much of my time was spent the same way as most boys growing up in

Brooklyn—playing ball on the streets, going to school—my earliest memory is sitting alone on the fire escape in the back of our apartment. Alone is what I most remember: being alone, despite the friends, the schools, the sports. Being alone came from the silence in the house, from what was not said but at times could all too readily be felt.

Brief breaks in the silence were usually accidental rather than intentional. What I knew—what I was told—was that we had "gotten out just in time." That was a phrase I would hear often. Sometimes it would come with a line about being on the last boat or next to the last boat "to leave." Though I later would come to realize that that was hardly the case, what was true is that most members of my family whom I would know only through photographs and my imagination, did not "get out" on time. They waited too long. They did not believe that their lives would be turned into nightmares. They were not the lucky ones.

Occasionally my mother would softly say something about how much she missed her mother. My father's silence was even more profound than my mother's. I was told that almost all my family had been killed in the "camps," but I knew little more than that. His silence intensified when, in 1946, he learned that his mother, who had survived Auschwitz and whom he was trying to bring to New York, had been pulled from her house in Poland and shot to death. His tears soon gave way to anger, and his fear of "it happening in America" became irrational. When I wondered aloud how God could allow all this horror to take place, he would simply tell me to stop asking such foolish questions. There were so many questions to be asked, but how could they ever be answered? I came to understand that it might not be possible to have a rational conversation with someone whose fear has made him irrational, but it does not make the fear less real because it is irrational. Nor does such understanding help to make sense of either the past or the present. How was I to know, in a world of silence, what demons my parents—the lucky ones—carried within them? More importantly, how could I not know?

That question begets another question: What was there to know? Numbers, yes. Six million is overwhelming. But numbers do not tell us about the people who made up the six million; nor does it tell us about those who survived or about the "lucky ones." For all too long, the pain and suffering of survivors and their children were bound by a wall of silence. There were occasional memorials, letters, even museums; works by Anne Frank, Elie Wiesel, and Primo Levi were published. But if memory defines who we are—if it is our past, our history—it was essential that there be more than a few representative voices. "No one would believe me, so what's the point of talking?" some would say; others would comment, "I don't want to know, don't tell me." But slowly, memory began to flow; stories were told; a history took shape. That history has been created not just by the work of professional historians, but by the written memoirs, oral interviews, personal reflections, novels, poetry, photographs, film, and paintings of the survivors.

The thirty-six memoirs that make up this volume are by members of the Child Survivors/Hidden Children of the Holocaust of Palm Beach County, Florida. Their accounts provide us with invaluable information about and insights into their struggle to survive in nine countries: Austria, Belgium, Czechoslovakia, France, Germany, Holland, Hungary, Poland, and the Ukraine. Each account adds to our memory and understanding of a time whose horrors and suffering often seem beyond our imagination. In so doing, they provide us with a legacy that both addresses the suffering of humanity and the extraordinary strength of people to survive and rebuild their lives. And in doing so they not only help us understand the past, but make it possible to think hopefully about the future. "*We Remember the Children*" is meant not only as a memorial for those who died in the Shoah and for the lost childhood of the children who did survive; it is a volume that reminds us of what happens when we remain silent in the face of hate and forget the importance of compassion and human decency. The memoirs that follow may tell stories of fear and loss. But, just as importantly, they are accounts of survival and belonging.

Jack Salzman
New York University

My Survival Story

by Rachelle Bashe

I was born on June 22, 1935, in Brussels, Belgium. Ours was a warm and loving household and my first years were happy and carefree. I felt loved and pampered by my parents and two older sisters, Tauba and Catherina, who often looked after me while my mother, Perla, and father, Israel, manufactured handbags in our apartment. Our family observed many Jewish customs including the lighting of the Sabbath candles and festive Friday night dinners.

All that came to an end when Germany invaded Belgium on May 10, 1940. My parents, afraid to remain in Belgium, packed up personal belongings for the family and fled to France with my grandmother and us. Our safety in France was short-lived because France soon collapsed under the advancing German armies. My parents decided to return to Belgium, but grandmother was not allowed to return because she was considered a stateless person. (She had entered Belgium illegally in 1936 and did not have an identity card.) She was arrested and interned in a camp for displaced people. With heartbreaking and tearful good-byes, we returned to Belgium just in time for my sister, Mimi, to be born.

For the next year or so, we lived with constant apprehension. Many edicts were decreed to the Jewish community. We were issued food ration cards and were forced to wear a yellow star in public (even little children had to do so). Our travels were restricted to certain hours and we had strict curfews. Jews were no longer allowed to work or to own property. Jewish children were barred from attending school and could no longer go to a park or playground.

In July 1942, we received an order from the Belgian police that my two older sisters had to report to work for the Germans. The police said my sisters would get paid but they would have to live away during the week and return

4

home on the weekends. Tauba was barely 16 at the time. After agonizing over what to do, my parents and Tauba decided that if she went the Germans would forget about Catherina, who was only 14.

With a small suitcase filled with personal belongings, Tauba presented herself to the Belgian police. Within the week the German police came to our apartment and arrested Catherina for failing to appear at their request. She was sent to the same place as Tauba, the armory Dossin in Malines, which was not a work camp but a holding place for prisoners. Their stay in that camp was short. In August 1942, my sisters were sent to Auschwitz in a cattle car with the first convoy to leave Belgium. They were gassed to death immediately upon arrival. I know this from information provided by the International Red Cross and verified in Serge Klarsfeld's book, *Memorial de la Deportation Des Juifs de Belgique*.

Rumors started spreading like wildfire about the fate of the people who had been sent to the armory. No one was coming back from there. We could no longer live openly as Jews. We had to go into hiding. An underground network of resistance fighters, consisting of Jews and Christians, soon took shape. Many institutions and private families opened their homes to hide children. Mimi and I were brought to a convent, but not by our parents; it was too dangerous for them to venture into the streets. We were brought there by a stranger.

We were left sobbing and calling for our mother and father. My baby sister would not eat and refused to go to sleep. She was terrified of the nuns. Little by little the nuns quieted our fears and gained our confidence. After a few more days, we settled into our new life. The nuns were very kind, but warned us never to tell anyone who we really were and gave us new names.

Mine was Raymonde Freres; my sister's name was Marie Freres. We were given non-Jewish identities. This was done in case the convent was checked by the German police. Officially, we were Belgian orphans. I did not know it then, but my parents had abandoned all their belongings and also had gone into hiding.

By September 1942, all fifteen beds in the convent were occupied by girls 20 months to 12 years old. Because we needed an adult to supervise us while the sisters were busy with their charity work, they brought in another Jewish woman, Gutki Stolnecki. She was 19 and is the person I remember most from that time. She was like a mother to us, and for many years after the war I searched for her.

For nine months we lived contentedly in the convent, learning catechism, going to the chapel, and doing chores. My responsibility was peeling potatoes, shelling peas, and making up the beds for the younger children. We were never allowed outside the convent. We were cut off from the outside world and from our families. Not long after, I learned from the mother superior that my father, during a rare outing in search of some news of the war's progress, had been caught in the street by the Gestapo.

We lived in perpetual fear of being discovered, and that fatal day eventually arrived. On May 20, 1943, between 9 and 10 a.m., the Gestapo arrived at the convent. There were three of them: a German officer, an interpreter, and a collaborator. The collaborator identified us to the German officer. When confronted with the threat of losing us, mother superior begged the officer to give her enough time to feed and prepare us for the journey, but the officer would not relent. While examining our ration cards, the officer realized that three of the children were missing. The three had been baptized and were allowed to attend classes with the nuns. When told why these children were missing, the German officer replied: "We don't care about religion, we want all the Jews." He told the nuns they would come back the following morning and wanted all 15 children present or they would take one nun for each missing child.

The nuns were frantic. What to do? Sister Marie Aurelie, the mother superior, got on the phone and started calling everyone she knew. She reached a priest in the community, who in turn called the cardinal, but he wouldn't get involved. The priest then called the queen of Belgium. She promised to intervene on our behalf, but to no avail. She couldn't persuade the German authorities to spare us.

With each passing hour and no sign of hope, we gathered in the chapel to pray. Mimi was brought to the door of the tabernacle by the mother superior and told to knock on the door. Mimi asked in her baby French, "*Petit Jesus, sauve nous*" ("little Jesus save us"). People from the neighborhood who had witnessed the raid came to see us and tried to give us hope, but they had no answers or help. Night came, and the sisters got us ready for bed and prepared small packages of food and a change of clothes for each to take along on the journey the next day. Unknown to us, mother superior had received a call from the Jewish underground that gave her a glimmer of hope. At 10 that night, a young woman, Andree Ermel, and a young man came to the convent, spoke in secrecy to mother superior, and hurriedly left. No more than 15 minutes later, there was a pounding on the door. One of the nuns hesitatingly opened the door and was shocked to see five young people holding guns. They pushed their way into the courtyard and locked the nuns up in a room. The mother superior, who was ill, was locked in her own room. The men then cut the phone lines and proceeded to wake us and get us dressed. We grabbed the small bundles the nuns had prepared while one of the men went to the office to retrieve the food cards that the mother superior had conveniently left on her desk earlier, and within minutes we were out the back door and into the street.

Under the cover of night, we ran silently through the streets to a safe house—the older children holding the hands of the younger ones, ready to quiet them if they cried. That was the last time I saw my baby sister until the end of the war. I didn't know it then, but Andree Ermel, the woman rescuer, was so overcome by emotion while carrying Mimi, who was crying, that she went straight to her own mother and told her to raise Mimi as if she was her own child. Madame Celine Ermel became Mimi's grandmother and Mimi called her "Bobonne." Mimi stayed there until the collapse of Germany.

By 11:30 that night, assured that we had reached our destination, the sisters called for help and were rescued by a neighbor to whom they threw a key to the front door. The police came, then the Gestapo. The nuns were interrogated for days, but managed to convince the authorities that they were not accomplices to the kidnapping and were spared.

Because I had come down with a high fever, I was the last one to leave the safe house, which was a tailor shop. Two days later, a little boy and I were placed in a home in Brussels with a widow who had nine children of her own. Life was very harsh there. We never had enough to eat. We had to take turns wearing underwear and socks. I developed skin sores and looked emaciated. I felt insecure and threatened by the presence of a German headquarters on the same street just diagonally across from the house.

Once, while playing in the street, a soldier approached me and asked my name. I replied that my name was Raymonde Freres, the name I had been given at the convent. He then remarked that I looked different than the other children, to which I replied that I was an orphan and that I lived with my aunt and my cousins. He seemed satisfied with my answers, gave me a piece of candy and left. I had learned my lesson well. I was 8 years old, but I knew how to lie in order to survive.

When the English and the Americans started to bomb Brussels, the sirens woke us in the middle of the night. We ran in our pajamas for several blocks into the basement of a nearby church. Sometimes we would come out and nothing was the same. Buildings were demolished; the smell of fire and broken concrete was everywhere. The memory of it stayed with me for a long time after the war. For many years I could not walk in front of new construction without remembering the smell of the bombed buildings.

One day, while playing in the street, I noticed at a distance a lady who looked vaguely familiar. As she got closer, I realized it was my mother. When she saw that I recognized her, she shook her head signaling me with her eyes to keep quiet. I stood frozen in place with tears welling up in my eyes and watched her as she passed me by. I had not seen her in over a year and I could not even run into her arms, for fear of attracting the attention of the Germans across the street.

Shortly after that episode, I was moved into a home in the south of Belgium. My new godparents were elderly, loving, and kind. They were poor, but they shared what they had. I stayed in touch with them until they passed away.

The war ended in May 1945, and soon after I was returned to my mother, who also had been in hiding. Mimi stayed with Madame Celine Ermel, the mother of the rescuer Andree Ermel, until we emigrated to the United States in 1951. I learned much later that my father died during a death march sometime in April 1945. My maternal grandmother, Chana Bornkind, was repatriated after the war ended. She had survived after spending five years in a camp in France.

In 1991 there was a conference of "hidden children" in New York. Although I could not attend that first meeting, at a second meeting almost a year later, I subsequently was able to locate four children who were hidden with me in the convent, as well as the young woman, Gutki Stolnecki Milliband, who had been our mentor and temporary mother. In 1995, the Hidden Children Organization of Belgium sponsored a conference in Brussels, which Mimi and I attended. It was there that Mimi and I finally met our rescuers and had a chance to say "thank you for saving our lives." In Belgium, 4,000 children were saved by gentiles who, at peril to their own lives, stood up against racism and prejudice and performed acts of heroism. These special people are known as "The Righteous Among the Nations."

Mimi lives in California and we are very close. We visit each other once or twice each year, and speak two or three times a week. In total the Frydland (Fridland) family lost 15 members in the Holocaust. All were murdered simply because they were Jews.

Remembering the Innocence of a Child

by Riva Kaganovicz Bernstein

My hometown, Novogrudok, Poland, was a graceful and picturesque county seat surrounded by hills and castles, and was the destination of many vacationers. It had a Jewish presence dating to 1484. This is where my twin brother, Calke, and I were born in 1928. We had two other brothers, Iche Meier (1923), and Shimon (1925). Iche Meier and Shimon were my father and mother's pride and joy. Much was invested to provide them with the best possible education by sending them to private schools.

My father, Aron Dovid, was a modern and freethinking man who valued education and spent every opportunity in the library or reading about current events in the newspapers (including the *"Velt Shpigel"*—the *World Mirror*). He provided a decent living for the family by producing shoes and sandals for the local people and harnesses for horses. My mother, Chaike Angelchik, was from a rabbinical family and tried to maintain a Jewish influence, but without much success. She spent most of her time at my father's side helping in the business.

A Polish woman, Alexandra, cared for me and Calke with affection and protection. She treated us as her own and on many occasions took us along to visit her brother's family in a distant farm settlement where we were given fresh farm produce and enjoyed the clacking of the farmyard animals.

Although life at first was basically peaceful, there were occasional outbursts of anti-Semitic expressions against the Jews. Then, during the Depression years, my father's machinery was seized and I heard cries of "To Hell with the Jews." Life became harder, and with neither protection nor support from the Polish government, the Jewish citizenry was left to exist in suffering and uncertainties.

After Germany invaded Poland on September 1, 1939, Novogrudok and the surrounding areas were taken over by the Soviet Red Army on September 17 (as was agreed by the Molotov-Ribbentrop Pact of August 1939). Many Jewish "capitalists" and political leaders, together with their families, were deported deep into Soviet territory. Most Jews welcomed the Red Army. We looked at the USSR as the protector who had awakened in us hope for equality and safety. Slogans and songs proclaimed, "One for all and all for one," while the posters of Stalin and Lenin became the new icons. I was just 10 at the time, and the promise of safety to the sound of the rhythmic music and uniforms was intoxicating to all the people, especially the young. My father was glad that he was able to give a decent education to his children in the free public schools. He encouraged us to excel in our studies based on his own thirst and search for knowledge.

This hope of a peaceful, just life did not last long. The Nazis occupied Novogrudok [now in Belarus] on July 3, 1941. German tanks, troops on motorcycles, and planes flying overhead replaced the retreating Soviets. The bombing continued for two weeks. My older brother, Itche Meier, and my twin were urged to run into Russia to escape the rumored danger under the Germans. But Calke returned because he could not endure to be away from the family.

The German army declared military rule and established a police force of Poles and Belarusans. Almost immediately, anti-Jewish laws were introduced. Yellow stars had to be worn on the front and back of all clothing. Jews were no longer allowed to walk on the sidewalk. Jews lost their right of citizenship. All valuables—gold, silver, copper, fur coats—had to be given to the authorities. Every Jew from age 12 to 60 had to report for work. In the first week of occupation, the authorities demanded that the *Judenrat* (Jewish Council) provide Jews for a work detail. When those selected were assembled in the center of the market place, 52 professional men were taken out of the crowd and shot on the spot. In the background, a German Army band was playing music by Johann Strauss.

The reality of this action was observed with shock. The limp bodies were carted away with a trail of blood staining the road. The abuse continued. Sometimes the Germans confiscated clothing, bedding, household goods, radios, furniture and other property. The second week, the *Judenrat* was ordered to present 200 able-bodied men to work for the army. These men, we learned, were taken and shot at the edge of a ditch; their bodies tumbled into the ditch and were not buried. These actions made everyone aware that we were in the hands of the devil himself. Murder continued. The SS entered the city in canvas-covered trucks, collected Jews, put them on trucks, and took them out of the city where they were murdered.

In November 1941, Novogrudok's Jews were ransomed for gold, jewelry and stock certificates. The *Judenrat* had to list all men and women over 18, who then were issued work papers. The first mass murder committed by the *Einsatzkommando 8*, aided by local police and others, occurred in December 1941. The first efforts to escape happened after the second mass murder at the end of 1942, and were motivated by the messengers from the Bielski brothers—Jewish partisans who sheltered most of the runaways and saved more than 1,200 Jews. (The young people who were able to reach Russian partisans often met up with anti-Semitic units. Many were robbed and murdered by these units in the forests.)

By September 1942 the Jews from the surrounding towns were brought to our ghetto, where all were gathered in three buildings. Two thousand people from the first two buildings were taken to ditches and shot. As luck would have it, my family and I were in the third building, where we survived for a year under the most dreadful conditions. Any hint of an Aktion—a selection— would chase us into hiding in the cellars. Many parents with tiny babies would discover that they had asphyxiated their own child in an effort to keep him quiet. The scenes were shocking but no one was shocked any more. The pain was great but one did not cry out.

During this time in the ghetto, Alexandra occasionally came to the barbed-wire fence and was able to hand us some food. Regardless of the danger, I was able to smuggle in a potato or other meager food item when I went out to get water. On one occasion I was caught and beaten mercilessly with 25 lashes. I don't remember my own tears, but seeing my mother cry over my distress broke my heart.

The fourth mass murder happened on May 7, 1943. Three hundred and seventy-five people, mostly women and children of the work camp, were killed. Four days earlier, Storm Troopers and Lithuanian guards rounded up everyone and herded us into a building. All knew that it would be the end of our existence. Two hundred men that the Germans needed for work were separated and led away into the adjoining building.

Seeing the forlorn despair in everyone's face with no hope of escape, I searched out my mother's eyes, which seemed to be saying to me: "survive." I wanted to hit back and kill somebody, but all I could do was shirk away into the building where the 200 men were kept. I was one of about four girls among the chosen workers and knew that we would immediately be spotted. I searched until I found the roof and hid there, not knowing what my next move should be or how to save myself.

From my hiding place, I heard people—my parents and brothers included—shouting in desperation. My soul was torn. I existed in a daze, as if out of my own body. I realized that I was all alone. From that day on, my actions were driven by an inner strength. My life source was my mother's lessons and my father's message.

The 200 men and few girls were permitted to live and work by producing things for the Germans and the guards in the workshops. Knowing our existence was limited, we started to build an escape tunnel 200 meters long. It was finished after three months of digging. On September 26, 1943, more than 200 Jews succeeded in escaping to the forest. Most of them joined the Bielski brothers' units, while a few went to other partisan units. I was among the first to get through the tunnel and into the stormy, thunderous, windy night.

As dogs barked in the distance and lights flickered from the village, I ran in the direction of the dark forest. I did not look back and soon discovered that I was all alone. I spied a hut in a small clearing and hid in the outhouse. I knew that I was not safe there. After a rest, I continued into the depth of the thick forest. As if led by an unknown force, I arrived at a farmhouse that seemed familiar. It turned out to be the home of Alexandra's brother and family I had visited so many years ago. They greeted me with recognition and gave me some food. But they said they could not house me, and told me to continue into the forests where the partisans were stationed.

With no alternatives, I continued in that direction. I was soon accosted by two men who questioned and treated me roughly. When I finally admitted to being a Jew they declared themselves partisans and took me to join their group. The Zorin *Otriad*—military unit—was composed mostly of Russian Jews. There I was deposited in the family camp, where I met Rozel and her daughter, Reizke. Rozel's legs were frostbitten and she could hardly walk, but she took me in and treated me like a daughter.

After about three months, Rozel, Reizke, and I were transferred to the family camp of the Bielski's Jewish *Otriad*. Here some support and food were doled out to the unattached, non-fighting members; but mostly each woman had a man of her own who protected her and supplied her with food, clothing, and needs for survival. The daily danger of being discovered by the incursions into the forest of Germans and their collaborators, made life precarious, and one lived just for the day. I later discovered that out of 200 men and the few women, only 42 managed to escape through the tunnel before the rest were discovered and shot.

The Bielski unit was known for its fierce offensive fighting and demolition work, which made the unit's presence notorious throughout the region.

Everyone—Poles, Belarusans, Lithuanians, Ukrainians and the Germans—felt the long arm of revenge of this brave unit of men and women.

When the Eastern Front was moving back by the push of the Red Army, many German troops were going through the woods and they had to find safety in the tangled depths of the forests. During this time, when the camp inhabitants ran to hide, Rozel was unable to walk and remained hidden in a dugout shelter. She was discovered and shot by the retreating Germans.

On July 9, 1944, the Russians liberated us. Reizke and I returned to Novogrudok to try to begin a normal life. Remembering that my father hid a stash of leather goods under the house, which was now in a demolished state, I enlisted Alexandra's help and retrieved this treasure. I was able to sell this much-needed commodity, which helped me live and continue my education under the Russians.

After I found out that my oldest brother was killed fighting with the Russian army, I had nothing to keep me in Novogrudok and decided to join the many survivors in their flight to the West and to Palestine. I joined *Hashomer Hatzair*, a youth organization, and eventually was taken out illegally from Poland and wound up in Italy.

I remembered my father's curiosity of the meaning of life and his constant pursuit of the thoughts of the great thinkers and made them my own quest. With financial help from my grandparents, who had arrived in America much earlier in the century, I had the freedom to continue my education. I spent four years in Italy and finally immigrated to the United States in December 1949.

Again, education was uppermost on my mind. I continued my studies, became a teacher, and taught high school for 18 years in the New York school system. I married Bernie (Irving) Bernstein, a talented young man whose career as art director for an ad agency satisfied his artistic endeavors. We have two children, a son, Alan, who is a surveyor, and a daughter, Eve, a chiropractor and a mother of three children.

In retrospect, I often wonder how it was possible for me to survive and to live my life with purity and dignity. I believe that this was the inheritance that I received from my mother: that no matter what the circumstances, "A righteous life saves the soul".

My Story

by Marcelle Bock

I remember the Germans marching into Paris in 1940. I was 9 years old. I remember the air raids, the foul smell of the gas masks, the run on sugar, flour and other staples, the rationing, the rumors. Worry began to hang in the air like a fog.

First the Jews were ordered to register at the police station. Not long after, we were told to turn in our radios. Then we were issued yellow Stars of David to wear on our clothes. Then came a myriad of restrictions.

The first raids to grab up Jews took place in 1941, and several of my uncles were arrested and sent to so-called work camps. On July 16, 1942, the Big Raid, "Grande Rafle," took place. Thirteen thousand Jews were arrested over a period of two days. Because we had heard rumors that there may be a raid, father managed to escape by staying at my aunt's apartment since my uncle had already been arrested and the police would not be searching there. The possibility that women and children would be arrested was not considered; that was simply unthinkable. But on that terrible morning the unthinkable became a reality.

It was very early when I awoke to the sound of strange voices. Two uniformed policemen and a man in plain clothes were questioning my mother in angry voices, wanting to know my father's whereabouts. She told them that she did not know where he was. They ordered us to get dressed, pack enough clothes and food for two days, and follow them. They rushed us along, not giving us time to think. Mother grabbed this and that, and suddenly we were on the street walking.

There was an eerie feeling about the familiar street. The morning sun casting long shadows, and the deserted streets, emphasized the voices of the other families who were also being marched off. The neighbors' windows were all tightly shuttered. It was as though the city was empty, and there was no one to see or hear us.

The police did appear at my aunt's apartment where father was hiding. When they began to pound on her door she clamped her hand across my little cousin's mouth to muffle his cries and did not answer. Luckily the police did not break down the door. Years later, I learned that my father, in his distress, watched us being marched off from my aunt's apartment window.

They took us to the Velodrome d'Hiver, a stadium used to hold bicycle races. It's hard to find words to describe the few days I spent there. The place was a madhouse. Over 7,000 people, of whom 4,000 were children, were held with little food, no bathrooms nor any form of hygiene. People were in shock, and a number threw themselves from the bleachers.

A volunteer nurse who we knew somehow got me transferred to the Rothschild Hospital (by then a prison hospital). She was the first of a number of my rescuers without whom I would not have survived.

I was at the hospital for a couple of weeks. It was there that I met Simon, who was 13. He and I had passes to leave the building and would meet on the hospital grounds. We fell in love, as only kids that age do. The last time I saw him, he had a plan to escape and asked me to go with him. I refused, fearing that we would be caught. We separated as usual that day, Simon going back to his hospital ward first. I waited a few minutes before going to mine, not wanting anyone to suspect that we had been together. When I got to the point where I could see the building I was headed for, I stopped dead in my tracks. German soldiers, carrying guns, surrounded the area. They were quickly loading patients one by one into a truck parked at the entrance. Suddenly I realized what it meant. They were transporting us somewhere and we knew that it would be to the same atrocious conditions as at Velodrome d'Hiver. I was dazed, everything went dark. I don't remember anything after that moment. I know I must have escaped, but to this day I cannot recall how. The next thing I recollect was walking down the street with my father. We spent one night sleeping on the bedroom floor of the empty apartment that had been our home. The Germans had commandeered the furniture, and the apartment door had been sealed. Father broke the seal; he had not yet found a better place to hide.

Hiding and hiding places were the main preoccupation from then on. My father went into hiding in Paris while I was sent into hiding in the countryside, where I remained for nearly a year with one family and with another for the remainder of the war. Those years were harsh and severe, especially after father was denounced and arrested on June 1, 1944, just six days before the Allies landed in Normandy. I was not quite 13 at that time.

Eventually, the war ended. A few survivors returned, but none from my family. My father Vevech, mother Chana, and eight year-old twin sisters, Berthe and Jenny, were murdered in Auschwitz. And so was my Aunt Chipah, who left behind three young children under the age of six, who eventually also were murdered. So too were Aunt Sourcha, Aunt Cinka, Uncle Avrum, Uncle Shimon, cousins Bernard, who was only five years old, and Rachel just a year older than me. In Poland, my mother's older sister, her husband, seven children—many of them married—were wiped off the face of the earth. Only one person survived, my cousin Malka.

I no longer am a child.

I know what anti-Semitism is: *It is a killer, a killer that kills Jews.*

Marcelle Bock passed away in the fall of 2005.

Safe Pass–Safe House

by George Bodrogi

My name is George Bodrogi (Gyorgy). My father, Kalman, my mother, Julia, and our extended family lived in Budapest, where the Jewish population numbered more than 200, 000. I was the youngest of three children, and in 1939 was only four years old when the openly anti-Semitic sentiments spilled out against the Jewish citizens of Hungary.

My father was a plain man, lacking formal education; nevertheless, he developed a successful textile business, which provided a luxurious life for us, with a live-in maid, chauffeur-driven cars, ownership of our own apartment, summer home, sailboat, horses, and vineyards. My father's success enabled him to share his good fortune with charities and synagogues.

I attended the Jewish Parochial School, where both secular and religious studies were taught. Even though my family lived a life of integration into the Hungarian life style, their commitment to their Jewish ancestry was required of me, with full involvement in the Jewish community.

After the Anschluss, in March 1938—and the annexing of Austria by Germany—Hungary passed discriminatory laws limiting Jewish participation in its economy and society. Factories were required to discharge their Jewish employees. In May 1939, the Hungarian government further limited Jewish involvement in economic activities and designated Jews as a "racial" rather than religious group. The government also created a new type of labor-service draft, which Jewish men of military age were forced to join. My brother, Tibor, was conscripted along with many Jewish men for forced labor. Tibor was killed when he and others were used as human mine sweepers to remove mines from the fields.

As anti-Jewish laws were being passed, the Hungarian authorities formed an alliance with Germany and its agenda. In October 1940, Hungary joined Germany, Italy, and Japan in the Axis alliance. In March 1941, despite its alliance with the Yugoslav government, Hungary joined Germany in invading and splitting up Yugoslavia. By that time, with all its new territories, the Jewish population in Greater Hungary had reached 725,000, not including about 100,000 Jews who had converted to Christianity but racially were considered to be Jews.

In June 1941, Hungary decided to join Germany in its war against the Soviet Union. Most of the Jews of Hungary lived in relative safety for much of the war. However, in the summer of 1941, 18,000 Hungarian Jews were randomly designated as "Jewish foreign nationals," were kicked out of their homes, and were deported to Kamenets-Podolski in the Ukraine, where most were murdered.

During this time I attended the Jewish school and even attended synagogue on the sly. Being a cherished youngest child, I was shielded from all difficulties and shortages. Still, I recall a difficult, fearful scene as a child of seven. My family was roused out of bed by Arrow-Cross thugs who burst into our apartment and other Jewish apartments in the building, brandishing their whips and clubs, ordering all to dress, pack for a three-day journey, and assemble in the courtyard.

About 100 people, young and old, were gathered and waited throughout the night huddled together against the fall chill. In the morning, we were herded into the middle of the street, Kiraly Utca, with hands raised above our heads as our neighbors, who had lined up on either side of the street, screamed out: "*Jo szappant csinalunk beloletek*"—"We'll make good soap out of you."

My family and the weary, abused Jews were marched to another building courtyard and were held there for about three days, in the open, without any facilities or food. After three days, we unexpectedly were told to return to our flats. Apparently they could not get transport for deportation.

After Germany's defeat at Stalingrad and other battles in which Hungary lost tens of thousands of its soldiers, the regent of Hungary, Miklos Horthy, began an effort to disengage from the alliance with Germany. This move was not acceptable to Hitler, and in March 1944, German troops invaded Hungary to keep the country loyal. Accompanying the occupation forces was a *Sonderkommando* unit headed by Adolf Eichmann, whose job was to begin implementing the "Final Solution" within Hungary.

Many more anti-Jewish decrees were immediately passed. The Germans isolated the Jews from the outside world by restricting their movement and confiscating their telephones and radios. The Jews were forced to wear the Jewish Star of David for easy identification. Their property and businesses were seized, and from mid-to-late April, the Jews of Hungary were forced into ghettos. On June 30, 1944, all Jews in Budapest were quarantined in specific buildings in the city. All luxuries were taken away, and they were forced to abandon their apartments and businesses and give up all possessions. My family moved into my maternal grandmother's apartment, where the extended family was cramped beyond belief—sleeping on mattresses that were stacked against the walls during the day. We did not know what to do. All the oppressions and decrees were enforced. Freedom of movement was restricted. We could only shop for food for two hours each afternoon. Pretty soon, Jews weren't allowed to be on the streets. After two to six weeks the Jews of each ghetto were put on trains and deported. About 430,000 Hungarian Jews were deported, mainly to Auschwitz, where half were gassed on arrival.

As rumors of deportation threatened our family, my father and uncles explored the possibility of getting a *Schutzpass*—a "safe pass"—that was being issued by Raoul Wallenberg of the Swedish government. They seized this opportunity and relocated into a safe house, flying Swedish flags. These buildings were located on the banks of the Pest side of the Danube. They stood in the first line of fire from air or artillery attacks by the Allies.

My family brought what each of us could carry and settled into the designated overcrowded safe house. Life was difficult, but we hoped that the safe pass and safe house would be the safe haven for our existence. Our first-floor dwelling, with a large picture window, provided a view to some of the military actions and maneuvers. On one occasion, as I was called away by mother, the explosion of a bomb across the street shattered the glass window.

As a child, I found ways to satisfy my curiosity and to entertain myself. One day, as I was playing outside the building, a German soldier spotted me and shouted for me to halt. Instead I ran; when I did, the German fired his rifle and shot me on my right thigh. To this day the scar brings forth the scene of pain and fright.

In early July, all of Hungary was "Jew-free," except for the capital, Budapest. The Jews of Budapest lived in relative safety. However, on October 15, Horthy announced that he was going to make peace with the Allies. The Germans blocked this move, and simply toppled Horthy's government, giving power to Ferenc Szalasi and his Fascist, violently anti-Semitic Arrow Cross Party. They immediately introduced a reign of terror in Budapest.

Nearly 80,000 Jews were killed in Budapest. Many were shot on the banks of the Danube and thrown into the river. Thousands more were forced on death marches to the Austrian border. In December, during the Soviet siege of the city, 70,000 Jews were forced into a ghetto; thousands died of cold, disease, and starvation.

Tens of thousands of Jews in Budapest were saved during the Arrow Cross reign by members of the Relief and Rescue Committee and other Jewish activists, especially Zionist youth-movement members, who forged identity documents and provided food. Those Jews worked together with foreign diplomats, the Swedish Raoul Wallenberg, the Swiss Carl Lutz, and others who provided many Jews with international protection. Lutz established 76 Swiss safe houses throughout Budapest, and with the help of his wife, Gertrud, liberated Jews from deportation centers and death marches. By the end of the war, close to 124,000 Hungarian Jews survived. Nearly half of these owed their life to the courageous actions of Lutz, whose name, until recently, had largely been forgotten by the Jewish people and the world at large. Perhaps this is so because, despite such courageous action on the part of some individuals, up to 568,000 Hungarian Jews were murdered during the Holocaust.

In March 1945, the Soviets liberated Budapest and freed the city from the Germans and the Arrow Cross power. The retributions against the enemy and collaborators were swift and without trials. Lynching of the oppressors was common and carried out on the street-lamp posts by the avenging Hungarians.

The liberation freed me and all the ensconced Jews from the safe house. We returned home to our apartment where we found it ransacked of all valuables—only some furniture remained. We discovered that many of our relations and friends had been sent to the killing camps, never to return. We also learned of the cruel end of my dear grandmother. When the family found shelter in a safe house, my 96-year-old, tiny paternal grandmother, too frail to be moved, was left behind under the care of a gentile man who was well paid and was promised additional rewards after liberation. But, we learned from another neighbor that on Christmas Eve, he carted my grandmother to the shores of the Danube and pushed her in, saying that no Jew should spoil his Christmas. After the war, charges of this evil deed were brought against this man who was jailed and died in prison.

When the war was over, Hungary came under the control of the Soviet Union, and, of course, the Communist power eventually took possession of the country and all properties. The economy collapsed in 1948. All businesses that had restarted after the war were nationalized and my father was thrown out of his startup enterprise. Life was a struggle to meet the daily needs, but we adjusted and continued. I returned to school, earned a bachelor's degree in liberal arts in 1952, and went on to become an electrical engineer.

In 1955, I was drafted into the Hungarian Air Force and served for one year. In 1956, the Hungarian uprising offered an opportunity to escape. I said a sad goodbye to my father (my mother had passed away in 1950), thinking that I would never see him again, in view of the fact that I was a deserter from the Air Force. (Sixteen years later I was able to return and visit with my father, then 85 years old, a year before he died.) I crossed over to Vienna on November 20, 1956. Here I applied for political asylum with the American embassy, where I worked for a while as an English translator for the displaced Hungarians. After a few weeks, I was permitted to enter the United States, where I was welcomed by some relatives. I was 21 years old. Because of my acceptable English, I acclimatized to American life speedily and was able to get a position with IBM, where I had a successful career for 35 years.

Except for the American relatives, all of my family that survived the Holocaust remained in Hungary. There was a longing to revive my family in this country and rebuild a life, yet I could never forget the evil that I had to live through as a youngster and then as a young adult under the Communist rule.

In 1959 I married Sabina Roosa. We have two sons, Peter and Michael, and three grandchildren, Adam, Ian and Hannah. The family has filled my heart with love and has enabled me to celebrate a better life than my own in Hungary.

Joining the Child Survivors/Hidden Children of the Holocaust not only has appealed to my need to remember, but the solidarity with survivors and their cause, the commonality of backgrounds and experiences, has enhanced and enlarged my family.

I Was a Hidden Child

by Pierre Chanover

My father Jacques and mother Helene came to France from Poland in their teens. There, they enjoyed a life of opportunity, as opposed to the oppressed life in Poland. They obtained their French citizenship, which was immediately revoked when the Germans occupied France. They married and I was born on December 10, 1932 in Paris in the Rothschild Hospital, where almost every French Jewish child was born.

The Chanover family established a home in Paris in a large apartment on Boulevard St. Martin, where father used part of the apartment as a design studio for his fine tailoring business, which was at another location. He designed all of my mother's and my clothing and I was probably the best-dressed little child on the block.

As an only child, I was exposed to the best that Paris offered and was treasured and pampered by my kind and gentle father, who always stepped forward to shield me from my strict mother's censure. Our fishing excursion to the countryside lakes and launching of sailboats in the basins of such Paris gardens as the Jardin des Tuileries and le Jardin du Luxembourg left me with pleasant and grateful memories. Many of my relatives who resided in Paris enriched my young years with play and holiday celebrations.

Tragically, none survived. I had many cousins with whom I played on weekends and holidays. None of them are alive today. All were killed in concentration camps.

My pre-war years were happy ones. Our way of life was mostly modern, but we did follow a Jewish identity; we attended synagogue on High Holy

Days and on other special occasions. Sadly and painfully, I witnessed the anti-Semitism directed at Jews. To blend in and not be conspicuous, I was told at an early age to be quiet, to be polite, to assimilate. Never volunteer information. Never speak about your parents or relatives. Never be an arrogant No. 1. Never be a loud loser. Don't complain, even if it hurts. Be stoic. Be humble.

My first school was Ecole Communale de Garcons, an elementary school for boys. There were many incidents of anti-Semitism that I didn't understand at that time. I was called Youpin (Jew). Was it because I had more or better toys then the rest of the boys on the block? The usual chemistry that exists between boys between the age of eight and 18 was shattered by name calling, the destruction of my belongings, and, at times, painful physical confrontations. I went home with a bloody nose many times.

When Europe was plunged into the Second World War against Germany, men, including my father, were drafted in haste into the French Army. He was assigned to a Jewish battalion. At the very beginning of the war the battalion was disbanded. Once again father became a civilian and returned to Paris. His stay was very brief because soon after there was a roundup of Jewish men, and in early 1941 he was interned in the camp of Beaune-la-Rolande, Barrack 18. From there he was sent to Auschwitz.

> *I learned of this only 12 years ago. Even though I knew there were mass exterminations, there is always that little light of hope that shines in your heart thinking that he may still be alive somewhere in the world. It was in the Yad Vashem Museum in Israel that I saw his name appear on the computerized list of the Holocaust victims. There was his name; the boxcar number 930 that took him to Auschwitz; his number, 43706; date of departure, June 30, 1942, from France and date of extermination, July 3, 1942.*

I was eight years old when the war broke out. I was not even aware what the word "war" meant. Yes, I knew all the war dates from French history, but I just recited them. Now I was seeing war in its true dimensions. My first experience was the bombings by the Germans of the Renault factory. Glass was flying; people were killed and wounded from the bombs, which were falling randomly.

I stopped attending school when the Germans invaded, and I eventually kept out of sight by staying indoors and learning not to be seen. My mother and I remained in Paris, where we were required to wear the infamous yellow star inscribed *JUIF*, which I still own. We had to face and endure imposed indignities and depravations, which made our daily existence strenuous and fearful since we never knew what was coming next.

It was not long before another roundup of Jews was in the planning and this time it was going to be women and children. The warnings coming from a variety of sources compelled mother and me into hiding. We spent several nights staying out of harm's way in cellars with rats running about in darkness, and without food. A strict observance of silence was necessary since the Germans and their French aides searched all the apartments.

I remained in Paris with my mother, and by a decree of the occupied French government she had to go to city hall to have her ID card stamped in red ink JUIF. That star had to be worn at all times and if it was not properly sewn or not worn that meant automatic death. The first time I wore it I cried because it made me feel ashamed, different, inferior. I was a target for mockery. I wore scarves, jackets that I turned inside out, anything to hide that star. Hide. Hide. Hide.

Before long there were mass gathering of Jewish women and children. We got word that the Germans would search every apartment where it was known that Jewish people resided. After all, these records were easily available at the city hall of Paris and the French authorities were not hesitant to give names to the German commandants.

My mother was told that the Germans were going to be at our house at a certain time so we went to the cellar to hide. The French word for cellar is cave and that was exactly what it was: a *cave*, for the sole purpose of storing coal and nothing else. It was damp, dark, smelly and full of rats. Whatever morsels of food we had lasted two days and we did not eat for another day. We did have a candle, but it was hardly used because we did not want to draw attention with a glow of a light for fear we would be discovered. On the third day, a school friend came to the cellar for some coal and discovered us. He ran upstairs to the sixth floor where he lived and told his mother that we were hiding in the cellar. Our biggest fear was that he would denounce us to the German authorities. We were bewildered when in the early evening the boy's mother appeared and told us to come upstairs to her apartment where she gave us some food and allowed us to wash. My friend's mother could not keep us in her apartment for more than another day but made arrangements for us to leave Paris.

I learned later on that my friend's grandfather was killed by
the Germans in WWI, thus collaboration was out of the question.
I noticed that throughout the war, people who helped me one way
or another had bad memories from WWI.

Realizing that our stay in Paris was precarious, mother decided that we should leave and go south to safety in Vichy-controlled France, Free France, which remained under French control.

Leaving Paris was an ordeal. I was instructed by mother to always walk by her side, never utter a word, walk straight and erect, never look backwards, never ask questions, follow all her commands, and never question the motives.

We did not wear the star, which meant that if we were caught it would mean immediate death. We took the subway to the house of a Protestant pastor who gave us a bible, some money for the train, and a false ID card with which to board the train and to be destroyed once on the train. We were offered a small lunch and again traveled by subway to the train station—Gare d'Orleans—where we boarded a train heading south. My mother told me that if we were to be separated, in the lining of the right leg of my pants was the address of our final destination in Bordeaux. How my mother knew about this pastor is still not clear to me.

We boarded a train that was heading to a destination as far south as possible. The train ride was long and tedious. It chugged along at a snail's pace. The two-day voyage was about to end as an inspection of all passengers was carried out by German soldiers. Mother, sensing the danger of being captured since her identity card had the word JUIF stamped in red, made a brave decision to save me. This strategy was rehearsed very carefully earlier should she not be able to continue with me. As the train was slowing down, entering a station, mother told me very firmly that we were close to the demarcation line and that I should jump from the moving train, and run for safety to the barbed wire fences. I obeyed mother's command, struggling with my secret pain that I would never see her again. I jumped from the train, fortunately landing without major injury, and ran as fast as I could, trying to reach the predetermined destination alone. Mother was detained and sent off to a local jail. I was nine years old.

My objective was to get to Vichy France where it would be safe. I knew I had to cross that demarcation point at all costs. I asked farmers which way to go and was given varied answers. The last farmer told me to take a small road, which I did, and it lead me right back into the hands of the Germans. Germans were shooting in all directions as they unleashed a big vicious dog to chase me. Just separated from my mother, and now encountering a gigantic dog barking and pulling on me while the bullets were getting more intense, caused me to become extremely frightened. In desperation, I picked up a log, and hit the dog with it. I do not know if I hurt him or killed it, but the barking stopped. As I crawled away from the area I noticed that my left thigh was bleeding; the dog had started to get his teeth into me. To this day I still have the scar. I ran away from the loud yelling German voices and noticed other people running. I followed them, hoping that they were going in the direction of the demarcation line. All of a sudden I saw barbed wires and I froze. As I approached and squeezed under the wires the bullets flew in my vicinity. With a pounding heart and panic, I managed to reach the other side with only minor scrapes.

Stumbling on a local small farm flying a French flag, which indicated that I was in free France, gave me hope that I was safe. The farmer was sheltering many people who had crossed the barbed wires. He was making a fortune from all the desperate people who were trying to enter Vichy. I approached the door slowly and appealed for shelter. He looked at me quizzically, seeing a little boy alone, hurt and crying. I was fearful that he would take me back to the Germans to be shot. He asked me for a large sum of money, which of course I did not have. Apparently taking pity on my sorry plight he gave me some soup and bread which I devoured in a second. This little reprieve in safety rejuvenated me and I was determined to continue to my destination.

A priest stopped at the farm for a drink of wine and proceeded to ask me questions that I answered with half false information. I insisted that I wanted to be in Bordeaux, as my mother had instructed me before I was separated from her. He looked at me with fluid eyes and decided to help me. He let me sit on the back wheel of his bicycle. Not seeing any German soldiers during the entire trip reassured me that indeed I was in Vichy France. After a few days of walking and with the help of this kind man, I was able to reach Bordeaux, where I had a contact, the pastor, whose name and address was sewn in my clothes. The pastor determined that it would be safer for me to be in the country than a large city. This selfless, godly man saved my life.

I was taken to Sainte-Foy-la-Grande where I stayed on a farm tending to small animals. This was a new world for me; never experiencing farm life before and being away from mother depressed and confused me. To lift my spirits, the lady of the farm told me that my mother would join me soon. Later, I put together that this woman never knew where my mother was. I couldn't ask too many questions and whatever I heard or saw I had to keep to myself. I worked the fields for a while, but the chickens, rabbits and pigs were my domain.

By 1942, France was completely occupied and German soldiers were everywhere. The sound of a motor was a German plane, a German tank, a German truck, or the famous German motorcycles with sidecars. Guns, revolvers, swastikas, green uniforms and spit-polished boots of the SS were now the local scenery, and the danger of again being caught was a real threat.

The people on the farm did not want to hide me for fear that they would be denounced and shot. I was told to leave the farm and head south towards the Pyrenees Mountains and maybe, if I was lucky, I could go to Spain. Naturally, at that age I did not know the reason for such rejection but I left the area with a heavy heart since I was getting comfortable with my little animals.

I wandered on the road for three days not knowing where I was going. I saw signs telling me where the next towns were but they did not mean anything to me. I did notice that the nights were getting cooler and I realized that I must be close to the Pyrenees.

One morning, while I was walking, I heard a motorcycle in the back of me. I became frightened and ran to hide in the ditch. The motorcycle stopped and in perfect French a German soldier asked me for directions. I told him that I did not know and he asked me where my parents were. I told him that my father was in the army and my mother was with him. This last comment caused suspicion and he told me to drop my pants, which I obeyed. At that time I still did not understand the meaning of such a request. He yelled to the other soldier, "Hier ist eine Jude"—he is a Jew—as he yanked me onto his motorcycle and took me to the small town of Oloron-Sainte-Marie in the Department of

Basses Pyrenees in the south of France.

I was questioned by the Gestapo and then a few hours later, in the pouring rain I was loaded onto an open truck with other refugees of all ages. A sign posted on the road said Camp de Concentration—Gurs—15 km. There were other children my age on the truck and I soon discovered that they too had entered Vichy France through the demarcation line and were caught sooner or later.

Camp de Gurs housed Spanish men, women, and children; it was built by and for the Spanish refugee internees from the Spanish Civil War. How ironic: Here were people who had fought for freedom now interned in the traditional land of asylum. In this mix of camp populations were also non-Jewish German political prisoners and deserters and, of course, Jews of many nationalities.

When we entered the camp, we noticed that it was surrounded by barbed-wire fences. An administration building was at the entrance along with a small hospital building, which was only for the chronically ill—such as TB or those in need of emergency surgery. I learned later on never to enter that hospital because most people never came out from there. A paved road about a mile and a half long ran through the center of the camp. On each side of the road the camp was divided into blocks with about 25 barracks each, which also were fenced with barbed wire. Ditches separated the blocks from one another. At the entrance of each block was a small guardhouse with an armed guard—sometimes a Frenchman and sometimes a German.

The camp barracks were built with wooden boards and covered with tarpaper. At either end was a door and a small light bulb barely illuminating the darkness of the barrack. In the middle stood a stove, totally useless because there was no wood to burn. There was also a table with two benches, which was the only place to sit. There were no windows, only hatches that were kept open with whatever would prop them up. When open, there was a bit of daylight and fresh air, but when it rained—and in winter it rains almost daily in that part of France—water would constantly seep in. The rainwater dripped on us mercilessly from the leaky roof. There were no cots or mattresses of any sort. There was not nearly enough straw and most people, including myself, had to sleep on the bare floor There were about 60 people to a barrack, with about 2 feet of space for each person. Very soon, we all made the acquaintance of rats and mice and not too long after, fleas, bedbugs, and lice.

The camp food consisted of some hot brown water, which was meant to be coffee in the morning. At noon we received a watery soup with a few bits of vegetables and turnips, turnips and more turnips. We were given the same watery concoction in the evening. The daily ration of bread was about 250 grams a person. Since the loaf had to be divided in the barracks, it created a number of fights. We soon learned who were the takers, the sharers, the thieves; we did whatever we could to survive.

At the beginning of my internment, aside from trying to adjust to the miserable conditions, I worried that my mother, father, and relatives did not know what had happened to me. How would my family know? How, if ever, would I get out of that place? Would I be able to write letters? Would I receive mail? Where would any help come to me?

All the days were alike. Work seemed senseless, as they had us move one big pile of dirt to one location and upon completion bring it back to its original location. Another chore was peeling turnips under the watchful eye of a guard. After all, the crude knife we had in our hands was a weapon. No one spoke and we were all eyes and ears. We watched the trucks come in, either with more refugees or taking away refugees. We did not know where they were being taken, but many of them were never seen again. I suspect they were sent to Auschwitz because this camp did not have a crematorium or a gas chamber. Those who died in the camp were transported out to where I still do not know.

Six thousand Jewish prisoners were deported from Gurs to Auschwitz. The first transport left Gurs on Aug, 6, 1942 and the last in the fall of 1943.

I am not quite sure how long I was in this camp; I could only calculate that I was there one winter and one summer. I did not know the day of the week, the month or what time it was; we had no watches. All I know is that we listened and responded to the soldiers like puppets. There was a constant blasting of German music coming from a building; there were no other programs, not even propaganda indoctrination. Frequently, we heard shots, and we knew that anyone was a target for murder.

Life was monotonous. We just waited and were afraid of what was coming next. Would we be transported to another better place or a worse place? Would we die in the camp because food was getting worse and less and less? Would we be liberated? At that time I knew nothing about American and British armies. It was total isolation from the rest of the world. I often wondered if anyone knew that this camp existed and that that was why we were not freed.

There were many children in the camp but we spoke to each other very sparingly, if at all. Our minds forgot how to be children; all we knew was how to pass another day without being picked for some sort of abuse. I learned from one of the boys that a boy had been tortured because the Germans wanted information concerning his family. Another boy went to the hospital and we never saw him again. Our minds were numb, and yet, being a child, I learned to observe and absorb anything that could help me have another day of life.

There was a youngster, about my height and build, who was a refugee from the Spanish Civil War, who told me that somebody had escaped by hanging underneath a truck and when he was outside the barbed wire had dropped and ran. He boasted that he was going to repeat this feat. At that age, or at any age, there is always the element among peers to dare each other to do something

drastic. I suggested that he should hide inside the truck when it is full of potatoes, turnips or anything. He told me that before a truck leaves the camp, two
Germans go in the back and use their bayonets to make sure that nobody is
underneath a load. Several people have been killed in that manner. Several
days later, I did not see that Spanish boy again and I concluded that he escaped.
I watched the trucks coming in and out of the camp and I wondered if I should
do the same: hide underneath the truck and hang on for dear life.

On a rainy day, as the soldiers were becoming more and more nonchalant,
I approached a truck with the motor running. I made a drastic decision and hid
myself underneath and waited for the truck to move. I did not know if the truck
was going around the camp or park somewhere; I was frozen with fear because
if discovered I would be beaten to death or just shot. Because it was pouring,
the truck moved slowly and as soon as I saw the barbed wires behind me I let
go of my hold, which was just in time because I could not hang on much longer. I presume because of the heavy rain, the driver and his companion were
concentrating hard on the road and paid no attention to the rear and there was
no one in the back of the truck. No guards, no dogs, no detainees to be witness.
I rolled into a ditch and stayed there for a while to get my bearings.

Not to see barbed wires was a relief, which was unfortunately replaced by
fear and uncertainty. I did not know where I was or where the next town was.
I was hungry and ate raw potatoes from the nearby field. Removing myself
from the road, which was dangerous any time of the day or night, I went deep
into a field which had a clump of trees and I cried and cried.

Looking back, I recall that my senses had become very tuned and were always on guard, trying to interpret any danger any sound. I heard in the distance
a truck that was slowly chugging along. I raised my head to see its origin and
to my surprise and fright, the truck stopped very close to where I was concealed. I thought I was spotted and the end of me had arrived. One man with a
rifle and revolver, in civilian clothes, asked me what I was doing here. Sheer
terror prevented me from saying a word. The man said to his friend. "This kid
must be from the camp, look at the rags he is wearing, he must be starved."
They pulled me onto the truck, blindfolded me and we were on our way, to
where I did not know. All this time I did not hear the German language and I
was wondering why, but when I heard that they were planning to blow up a
small German installation nearby, then I realized that these men were the good
guys. This was my first encounter with the French underground.

My stay was very short and every day I was riding either in an old car or an
old truck but always blindfolded. I was told that I was going to be taken to a
much safer area and be with a lady who had a daughter my age and there I would
be fed and sheltered. This is how I reached the city of Bergerac in the state of
Bordogne, but actually stayed in the suburb of that city called LaForce.

The lady, Madame Alice Constantin, who was my guardian angel for over a year and a half and her daughter, Arlette, took me in. Madame knew that I was Jewish, and again I had to change my name. But I was told to say that I had been born in Paris, since my Parisian accent was evident immediately. I was introduced as Madame's nephew, whose father was in the army, and because of all the severe bombings up north, it was best for me to be with my aunt. That worked for quite a while and indeed I was treated as one of the family.

I soon found that the climate was different, the food a little more abundant, and the people more outgoing. But more than anything else, I saw very few German soldiers. They were entrenched in the city of Bergerac, which had a large Gestapo headquarters.

I was puzzled why each night there was a package with clothes and food on the table, and one day I discovered the answer. I was awakened and asked not speak and carry one package of clothes and food and run with the family to the nearest woodland. I learned that the Germans were coming to every home to take whatever their needs were: food, clothes, furniture, bicycles. Since the house was locked and we were not on the premises, the neighbor told the marauders that the family was staying in the city overnight and so our house escaped being pilfered, although the bicycle was taken, which was an important means of transportation and was greatly valued by its owner.

And so here I was, ensconced with these lovely, kind people when suddenly Madame Constantin started to yell at me with great anger and told me that I had to leave her house that very moment and that I was to go to Bergerac. I cried because I had grown to love this woman who was so tender to me and I could not understand why I was being chased out of the house. I had not done anything wrong; all this was most confusing to me.

> *Later on, I discovered that she had been denounced by a neighbor who said she was hiding a Jewish boy. If I was found by the Germans, the entire family would have been shot. As is expected in time of crisis, weak people denounce others for a favor of some sort; many times, they were shot themselves. I kept in touch with this savior, Madame Constantin, until her death in 1992. I still speak by phone with her daughter.*

Fortunately, I found shelter in a restaurant in the city with Madame Rosier, who detested the Germans because they killed her husband during World War I. The restaurant was in the middle of the city of Bergerac with Germans swarming everywhere. But since I had a false name I had to make sure I responded quickly with the correct information if asked. Madame Rosier's son, Robert, who was in his 20s, came and left the restaurant at very odd hours. I was treated kindly, but had to contribute by helping with washing dishes, peeling potatoes, and in general doing any chores that needed to be done. She never asked me any questions and I am sure she knew all about me.

It was ironic to be in a restaurant that served almost no food but since this was the wine country of France, wine was available. Many people stopped for a drink, and a good number of them did not pay a cent; apparently there was a silent agreement that said: Don't bother me and I will give you wine when you want it. German officers came by, as did the police commissioner as well as priests.

One priest noticed me and told Madame Rosier that he wanted me to be in the choir of the cathedral. She was hesitant at first, but then, since she apparently knew all about me, she thought that total assimilation would be best for me. I learned to cross myself, to genuflect, and to recite all my prayers and I was given the garb of a choirboy. The priest asked me a few questions that I was hesitant to answer, but he stopped quickly after he realized who I really was. What I loved most was the singing; it made me feel that I belonged, which I needed so desperately. I sang for all the masses and services. At least when I was singing, hope awakened in my heart. It was a way of begging a God to listen. Our voices harmonized and I did not feel alone or scared. The priest always put his arms around me and told me what a beautiful voice I had. The other boys in the choir noticed this favoritism and teased me no end. One day, when we were outside, a boy told me that my zizi, as they call it in France (since I was circumcised), was different from his. Not knowing what he meant and how to respond, we got into a fight. The boy told his parents, who confronted Madame Rosier. From that time, I was forbidden to go outside.

Years later I learned that the parents reported the priest to
the Germans, who shot the priest for having me in his choir.

One day there were about 20 Germans who came into the restaurant for a meal and there was very little to be served. I was horrified when I saw Madame Rosier kill two cats and make a wine sauce and other things to go with it and feed it all to the Germans. She then told me that her husband was killed in WW I and her hatred for the Germans was so strong that she sought revenge whenever possible.

In the fall I was told that I had to take the bicycle with a little trailer hooked on the back and go to a relative outside Bergerac to transport a huge flask covered with straw to be filled with wine and bring it back for consumption in the restaurant. This meant that I had to cross guarded check points each time. It meant that each time I was subject to search and questioning. When I reached my destination, the huge flask covered with straw was exchanged for one that was full of wine. I also had an opened bottle of wine to give to the guards, who made sure that this wine was the same as in the flask. The guards seemed satisfied and I had a feeling that after the third time, they were looking forward to my crossing as they enjoyed a free bottle of wine. The flask was very heavy and I pedaled laboriously arriving near collapse when I reached the restaurant. I was hugged each time I delivered the flask, which was stored in the cellar in a locked compartment. I never saw exactly what was in that compartment.

Looking back now, I realize that Madame Rosier's son Robert was a leader in the underground and the flasks had false bottoms. Without knowing it, I was carrying guns into the restaurant. As time went on, I saw less and less of Robert because he was outside the city doing sabotage work.

News travels fast, even without radios. There was a horrible story that frightened all of us, which happened in the town of Oradour-sur-Glane, not too far from Bergerac. The Germans, needing hostages, brought the entire population into the church. A baby was crucified at the main door of the church, then the church was set on fire with the entire town in it. Whoever escaped was shot. Then the town was burned down. Atrocities were escalating and so was sabotage.

It was 1944 and the Allied bombings were taking place all over France. Bergerac was no exception, since it had a very big ammunition factory that was bombed one night and destroyed many houses nearby and killed many people. When I heard the planes, I ran upstairs and saw reddish pink flares illuminating the city. The explosive sound of the antiaircraft guns was deafening. Madame Rosier ran upstairs and yanked me to the floor as bombs shook the entire area. Glass was flying and some walls crumbled. Had I not been on the floor away from the window, I probably would have been killed. The next day I saw open trucks carrying bodies, with blood dripping on the pavement.

From that moment on there was more and more sabotage. I did not move from the restaurant. And as months passed by, I heard of more and more killings by Germans; things were escalating to a point of danger for everyone. Ammunition was being parachuted into the countryside and now Madame Rosier's son was never home.

Parts of France were liberated either by the underground or the American soldiers. The landing of Allied soldiers on the soil of France was rejoiced by all but we were far from the north of France. How long would it take to be freed? Now that the underground was doing more damages to the German Army, we all hoped that we would not be affected by retaliation. One day, I saw trucks and cars packed with underground men. They were waving French flags, wearing their arm band with the three letters FFI, for Force Francaise de l'Interieur (French Force of the Interior). Bergerac was liberated, and a week later the Americans, who had landed in the south, passed through. Freedom at last! The women who had collaborated had their heads shaved and were paraded through the city and in front of the Palace of Justice; then they were shot.

The Red Cross passed through the city and Madame Rosier made arrangements that I be taken to Paris. I thought that I was being thrown out again, and I could not understand the rationale, especially now that we were liberated. I was reassured that if there was no one in Paris for me, I could come right back. The two-day trip to Paris by Jeep, riding with a representative woman from the

American Red Cross and an American soldier, made me feel that I was safe and in good hands.

In Paris, I gave my address and tried to recollect and identify neighborhoods. Paris appeared different to me. Of course it was; I was four years younger when the war started. We found the street where I had lived, and I walked up the stairs to my apartment on the third floor. With dread, I knocked on the door not knowing what to expect or who would answer. I was almost faint with joy when mother answered. Our reunion was expressed with flowing tears as we looked at each other, trying to recognize some likeness of the person we were when we parted.

The apartment had been completely ransacked by the French and Germans. Nothing of value was to be found, so our life continued with depravation and hardship. Because life right after liberation was still difficult, suffering shortages of money and food, we were resigned to appeal to the Joint Distribution Committee, whose answer to our plight was to place me in an orphanage in the Chateau de Corbeville outside of Paris. This would alleviate the dire conditions with mother. The Oeuvres de Secours aux Enfants had several places designated to rehabilitate and educate Jewish children. It was an orphanage and for the first time in my life I was taught some Yiddishkeit (Jewishness) and was able to revive my emaciated body and renew the school studies. It was both a fearful and awesome experience to return to normalcy and rejuvenate the curiosity and a love of learning. After all, most of the Jewish children had not seen a classroom for four years or more.

As more areas of Europe were freed, we learned of the atrocities perpetrated by the Germans and collaborators. We were fearful that father must have been a part of that tragedy. It was not until I went to Israel for my daughter's Bat Mitzvah many years later that I discovered my father's records of deportation to Auschwitz listed at Yad Vashem.

In the late 1940s, a cousin who resided in the United States came to Paris and urged me to go to the States. This opportunity was a blessing and I immigrated right away, although without mother, who followed about a year and a half later.

New York opened opportunities and difficulties for me in my new life. At the beginning, life was difficult as I was also known as "*der greener kind*" the green (newcomer) child. I lived with cousins who were extremely Orthodox, which was a great culture shock and most difficult to adjust to. I struggled to achieve normalcy, continued my education, and succeeded in becoming a Ph.D.

I am blessed with two children and grandchildren. Nancy is an astrophysicist and Michael is a computer graphic designer. I reside in Boynton Beach with my wife, Marianne Sinacori, and devote my energies to my career and Holocaust education.

A Game of Survival

by Joseph Eckstein

The flames of the five chimneys shooting 10 to 20 feet in the air greeted the tormented arrivals on the dark night of June 19, 1944. Three days riding in packed cattle cars with up to 100 people in a car only helped to disorient and confuse the new arrivals at Auschwitz/Birkenau.

I was only 15. I descended the train together with my parents and sister; I was amazed to see that my mother's hair had turned white during the torturous ride. The German soldiers greeted us with shouts, clubs and growling dogs. The bright lights on the platform blinded us and made the dark distant horizon only darker.

The shouts and commands pointed me and my sister, Eva, to the left—life—while our parents and the rest of my extended family were marched to the right—death—into the darkness never to be seen again. To this day I cannot erase that vision. To this day, lines of people take me back to those horrible hours and my memories of my childhood.

I was born in April 1929, in Etyek, Hungary, a small town of 2,000, mostly *Schwab Deutsche*. There were only five Jewish families. It was located just 30 kilometers from Budapest. My father, Meyer, and uncles ran our family business, established and handed down by my grandfather. The general store, cement factory, and grain exchange were part of our courtyard, where our large home was located; the vineyards, in nearby acreages, added to our family wealth and provided more than a comfortable living.

My parents were introduced by a matchmaker, and as it turned out, they had a good and loving relationship. My mother Sofia (Schwartz) came from Czechoslovakia. She was ultra-Orthodox, wearing a *sheitel* (wig), and availed herself of the ritual bath (*mikvah*) in Budapest every month. She ran a kosher home following the commandments of the Torah.

Our household was full of life and activity. As the youngest of four siblings—sisters Eva (1925) and Yucy (1928) and brother Rezso (Reuven, 1924)—I was spoiled by all and had a happy environment.

I attended the public state school, which included Catholic teachings. Being the only Jewish child, I experienced many confrontations on a daily basis, even though the same boys would show friendship at other times.

Summers, father hired a *Yeshiva* (Hebrew religious school) student to live with us and teach us Hebrew, religious studies, prayers, and history. *Shabes* the Sabbath, was the highlight of the family and Jewish community. The tables set in finery, the candles lit, the Sabbath ritual prayers chanted in each home since there weren't ten men to form a *Minyan* to pray together. The special foods and happy feelings were continued on the following day by a delicious *cholent* (like a crock-pot oven dish), which each of the five families baked and retrieved on Saturday to be eaten at each home hot, since we were not allowed to cook on the sacred day. This heavy meal was followed by a leisurely stroll to the town square where the Jewish families gathered to discuss politics and just spend time together after a week of work. Life was good and no one had any fear of their future in Hungary. They felt themselves to be devoted citizens.

When Hitler came to power in Germany, the mood and restrictions against the Jews were picked up in Hungary. My father was drafted into the Hungarian Army and after about a half a year was dismissed. Between the years of 1938 to 1941, the Hungarian government put into effect three anti-Semitic laws, not unlike the Nuremberg laws in Germany. The first two laws restricted the economic prosperity and livelihood, while the third was a blatant racial law that stipulated "race-protective" orders. On March 29, 1941, the Hungarian Council of Ministers also formed the three aforementioned anti-Semitic decrees that stripped the Jews of whatever they had left. The laws excluded Jews from all basic necessities of living. They forbade them from the professions of law, the press, motion picture and theater. We could no longer ride in cars, taxis, trains, buses and ships; the only mode of transportation left to us was the streetcar. Eventually, even telephones and radios disappeared from Jewish households. Because the government froze or restricted our bank accounts, the Jews could only have a nominal amount of money, which made even buying a meal nearly impossible. Suddenly Jews no longer cared about such simple pleasures as listening to the radio; they were now more concerned with staying alive.

In March 1939, Germany seized Czechoslovakia and on September 1 invaded Poland. The Hungarian Labor Service System was established that March. Hungarian Jewish men, age 20 to 48, were drafted into forced-labor camps where conditions were brutal.

Admiral Horthy, the leader of Hungary, Slovakia and Transylvania, did not follow all the Nazi edicts and was sympathetic to the Jews. Yet he was mindful of Hitler's demands. Annexation of parts of Czechoslovakia and Transylvania increased "Great Hungary's" Jewish population to over 800,000. The Jewish population tried to adjust to the new conditions, waiting for a change and hoping for help from the outside world.

We started to hear from the local German population about Hitler's rise and rough treatment of all who stood in his way. In 1939, this was confirmed on a personal level when my family hid some Austrian Jews who had escaped Hitler's reach. In 1940, my mother's family in Czechoslovakia wrote that 11 young cousins had been sent to Theresienstadt and their letters hinted at trouble. The Hungarian Jews, including my family, could not believe what they heard; we could not comprehend such a reality and did not seek nor know what choices to make.

The local German-Schwab youths were induced to join the SS and homeland neighbors turned against their Jewish neighbors. By the end of 1943, Jewish businesses were not allowed to exist and our family store inventory was carted away. The adjustment to hardships and precarious life again was the norm. The yellow Star of David was added to all edicts.

On March 18, 1944, Hungary came under the German sphere of evil. Jews, including our family, (except my brother Reuven and sister Yucy, who were taken into the forced-labor camps) were brought together from all villages, hamlets and small towns, were put on trucks and horse and buggies, and transported to Biczke, a gathering of over a thousand people. The Hungarian gendarmes ran this place and took opportunity to enrich themselves by choosing known wealthy Jews to extract valuables from them, through coercion or beating. My Uncle Sam was beaten to death.

Beginning in May 1944, the ghetto population was marched to the railroad station with instruction to take only what we could carry. We were transported about 60 kilometers to an ancient army fort where we were housed in underground cellar rooms in Komárom. No food, no beds, no facilities were provided for the gathered. All slept on the floors, on the blankets that we managed to bring along. When our own meager food ran out, the only access to food was when it was thrown over the wall by the Jewish members of the forced labor. On June 13, 1944, the gendarmes turned their captives over to the Germans, who packed us into cattle cars. We traveled for three days and three nights, without water or food. People began to die. "We are in big trouble," one of my uncles said when he realized that we were being transported to Poland.

When we arrived at Auschwitz, the scene was one of confusion. The screaming both from the German SS and the population that was forcibly being separated was deafening and heartbreaking. There was no time to absorb anything. One moved with the throng, not fully grasping the reality of this place.

My sister, Eva, and I were pointed to the left. We were led into rooms where we were told to undress for showers. All hair, including body hair, was shaved; we were sent into the showers, followed by a delousing process; were given striped uniforms, a cap and wooden clogs (although I somehow managed to save my own shoes). The scene of being transformed into images of prisoners was shocking.

This was June 19, 1944. As I exited, the total cleansing of all personal possessions and dignity, I noticed the huge flames jumping into the skies from the tall stack chimneys. I asked a Polish Jewish inmate, "What are those chimneys? What kind of factories are these? What are they making there?" His answer reverberated in my being for the rest of my life, "Those are not factories, that is where your mother and father are burning." This statement did not penetrate even a clear-thinking mind, and after going through the trauma of Auschwitz, I could not fathom this; my existence became mechanical, only looking for ways to survive.

I was assigned to Lager D—Birkenau—Barrack 20 for a couple of weeks along with other young boys. The unsanitary, harsh and overcrowded conditions brought on an epidemic of scarlet fever where about 100 sick boys were removed; rather than being treated, they were gassed and sent to the crematorium.

After this epidemic, I was assigned to Barrack 5 with adults. There, the daily survival became almost a game. After the morning *Appell* (roll call), I often found ways to hide and together with about 25 other youngsters we avoided the cruelty of the work selections and beatings that were meted out. But at times, I was trapped and had to work on roads and do physical labor. The aggressive, heartless beatings still burn in my memory.

One day, Josef Mengele ordered a surprise *Appell*, choosing many from among the men standing lined up 10 deep. They were taken away to the gas chambers. On another occasion, while we were sitting in the barrack, soldiers with dogs appeared to chase the inmates out. Along with a few others, I climbed up to the high windows, broke the windows and escaped a selection. As I remember these scenes, my eyes are burning with tears and shake my being. I recall my friend escaping this daily tortured existence by running to the electrified wire fences, which killed him instantly.

By October and November 1944, ghettos were being emptied and sent to Auschwitz. The chimneys were aglow with a constant flame dancing in the sky, day and night. The smell of burning flesh was a continuous state; one became hardened.

During this time, a revolt by Jewish slave laborers at Auschwitz-Birkenau resulted in the destruction of Crematory Four. The men were apprehended and hanged in the *Appell* field for all to see. I cannot explain why, when I became sick with pneumonia in November 1944, and was sent to the hospital where I contracted typhus and was cared for three weeks, that I was not carted away to the gas chambers. Luck? I don't know. While I was in the hospital I heard a voice calling my name, "Eckstein, Sofia Eckstein?" I was startled to hear my mother's name. I looked at the man and after searching the face I recognized my uncle George. I washed and cared for him, but I was not able to keep him alive.

In January 1945, everyone in the Birkenau camp was ordered to walk the three miles to Auschwitz or be killed. At Auschwitz, thousands of men were loaded onto trucks, given a loaf of bread and a liverwurst sausage, to be shared by four men. I was convinced that our existence was precarious as I overheard that we were going to the next camp and that stragglers would be shot if they could not continue the march. The game of survival was learned well. I, along with five Jewish doctors and couple of kids, hid in the attic of the warehouse where the clothes were sorted. We stayed there for about three days. Being the youngest, I was then asked to go down and investigate the scene below. I found that the camp was deserted except for 14 sets of twins (upon whom Mengele performed medical experiments). The survivors, finding freedom, broke into the SS headquarters and camp, found food and even a live pig, which they slaughtered and cooked.

On January 27, 1945 the Soviet army appeared and we were transported to Krakow. In Krakow, we discovered that the Soviets wanted us to fight on the front. By this time, all I cared about was surviving, returning to my hometown, and searching for my family. We found the Joint Distribution Committee, which was already helping survivors. We also were shocked that here, after being liberated, the Polish population would not even sell any food to a "*Zhyd*" (Jew).

The twins from Hungary and I got on the first train. We huddled to keep warm on the ride to to Slovakia, where we again found the Joint providing assistance to survivors.

In February 1945, I decided to go to Budapest rather than to my hometown. I was lost emotionally and could not make a decision in what direction to continue and how to pick up the pieces of my life. I settled in a youth home near Budapest, where the *Shlichim*, (representatives from Israel) were helping the youngsters to find their spirit and a return to a childhood.

Eventually, I found that my sister, Eva, and my brother had survived, and that Rezso had returned and was living in our home in Etyek. When I arrived in town to be reunited with my brother, a Schwab neighbor, with a caustic, almost jeering voice said, "Where did you materialize from? And where are your parents?" All that I could do was to walk past them without a word. Soon these neighbors appeared at our door with the looted fine linen and silverware taken from our home, hoping that we would help them remain in town rather than be repatriated to Germany since they were Schwab.

After liberation, Hungary was taken over by the Communist government under the wing of the Soviet army. After much searching, I decided to learn a trade and became a mechanic. I was active in the Zionist Movement. In 1949,

I was drafted into the service and served for two and a half years as a gunsmith.

Under Communism, one had to find ways and means either to earn money or barter for goods. I became expert at this and found a way to live a good life even under this system. I was determined to survive and succeed.

In 1955, I married Marika Feldmann, who was an optician. Together, we established a comfortable home and eventually had a son, Peter. When the revolution against Soviet dominance was fought in Hungary, Mary, Peter, and I, along with 250,000 refugees, fled Communism and anti-Semitism. We first went to Austria, and then emigrated to Syracuse, N.Y., where my sister, Eva, and her newly established family had settled. We had a second son, Jack, who passed away in 1993.

My survival has taught me to appreciate my life, my family, and my love for my fellow Jews. I find ways to help the needy elderly and although I see the world with distrust, I have not lost the capacity to smile, feel strongly, and love even more strongly.

My Auschwitz tattoo on my left arm—B-14777—is my badge of courage and sacrifice. I lost my parents, sister, and extended family of over 70 members. I had to grow old at age 14 and learn how to survive.

In 1986, Mary and I moved to Florida. We live close to our son, Peter (who is the education and program director of Temple David in Palm Beach Gardens) his wife, Carol, and our two granddaughters, Ma'ayan 17 and Keren 14, who have brought us joy, pleasure, and love overflowing.

Living Dangerously in a Safe House

by Mary (Marika Feldmann) Eckstein

I can almost hear my mother's voice calling me from the upper floors of the apartment building complex where we lived in Budapest. I was born in 1936, and as an only child, I was doted on by my mother, Boris (Stem), my father, Jozsef Feldmann, and the large extended family that enhanced my youngest years. My parents were a loving couple, and mother often claimed that father was the love of her life. This happy pair extended their warmth and love to me and to the entire family.

I cannot recall being deprived of anything, even though both my parents had to work to support us and help my grandmother—my father's mother—who was widowed. This was a large burden for my father, but my parents never complained.

We observed Orthodox Jewish traditions, keeping kosher and observing the Sabbath, although father was clean-shaven and lived in the modern way. He worked as a head clerk for a retail/wholesale textile goods store where he was known as Jozsef Faludi. It was normal for Jews with Jewish sounding names to adopt a non-identifiable name in the workplace. Mother worked as a dressmaker and made the burden of caring for the extended family easier for my father.

My mother's parents, my grandparents, lived and worked in the town of Eger, a town that had a long history of resistance against the Turks because of its massive and powerful castle-fortress, which served as an army base in modern times. Grandfather ran a canteen-tavern there, and when he died in 1912, grandmother took over this enterprise in order to support her children. This was a bold act on her part—a woman in the midst of soldiers. Nevertheless, she overcame all hesitation and made a living for her family. She provided a tutor for a basic education for her children, one of whom was my mother, and even gave them the opportunity to learn the piano. In all, 55 family members resided in this town. Not one survived the Holocaust.

We resided in a mostly Jewish section of Budapest. My contact with non-Jews was limited, and I did not experience anti-Semitism except once when I wanted to buy ice cream in a nearby store and was refused because I was a Jew. I remember standing on the sidewalk crying, both from the disappointment of not having the treat and trying to understand why I was so discriminated against. A passerby noticed my tears and asked why I was crying. When I told her, she took my money and bought me the ice cream. This incident, both the discrimination and the kind deed of the lady, has remained in my memory.

Because Hungary cooperated with the Nazi powers as Allies and had its own Nazi party, the Arrow Cross, edicts against Jews began in the 1930s. There were quotas for Jewish students to enter medical school and universities, and all opportunities which had been guaranteed as of the 1890s were now limited for Jews. The regime of Miklos Horthy carried out its gradual barring of Jews by a series of laws passed after 1938. The first two laws made our economic situation more and more difficult; the third law, which was passed in 1941, was a real Nuremberg-type racial law introducing "race-protective" orders. The laws limited Jewish participation in all aspects of society and many Jews were dismissed from their jobs.

Upon joining the alliance of Germany, Italy and Japan, Hungary adopted an aggressive anti-Jewish policy. During the period from 1941 to March 1944, more than 15,000 Jews from Budapest were killed in labor camps and deportation occurred even before the German occupation. In 1941, Jewish men were conscripted into forced-labor camps, which at that time still allowed furloughs for them to come home to their families. As the pro-Nazi sentiment was unleashed in Hungary, the army used the Jewish laborers in the front positions of the battlefields to march through mined areas in order to clear those dangers with their bodies. The laborers also were used to work in the depth of the coal mines under the most dire conditions. They were never permitted to come above ground and most succumbed to this brutal treatment. (Jews who had converted were given less arduous labors, but they did not escape the anti-Semitism.)

I was able to begin public school and attended until the middle of 1942, at which point I was halfway through second grade. Soon more edicts were implemented against the Jews. They had to turn in all electric appliances, radios, and telephones. Jews were not allowed to work for non-Jewish shop owners or transact any business with non-Jews.

Since Hungary was cooperating with and was an ally of the Nazi government, it was not occupied until March 1944. The entry of the Germans was without violence. But orders were immediately issued that all Jews were to wear yellow Jewish stars on their outer clothing. The stitches were to be sewn so close that a pencil could not be inserted between the star and the jacket. Not passing such a test would result in punishment and/or arrest. The Jewish ghetto was formed in June 1944; a month later, 200,000 Jews were moved to 2,000 "Jew-homes" in Budapest.

Horthy put an end to the deportations of the Jews on July, 6, 1944; however, by that time, all of Hungary's Jews living outside of Budapest had been deported. Horthy apparently discerned that the Allies and Red Army were making strides against Germany, and he was afraid that the capital would be destroyed by carpet bombing if the Jews were deported.

After Horthy appealed for a cease-fire and stated that he would not cooperate with the deportations, the Nazis took over the government on October 15, 1944. Ferenc Szalasi, the leader of the Arrow-Cross Party, came to power with the help of the Germans and the danger for the Jews became more dire. Violent attacks were committed against Jews, many of whom were shot and thrown into the Danube River.

Our building consisted of 24 apartments and was designated a "Jew House;" a large yellow Star of David was affixed at the street gate to the building and locked. My two aunts and cousin moved into our apartment, while grandmother and my extended family relocated into other apartments in the building. As a child of eight, my life was full of fun and play with this increased population of children to play with. I could not understand why we had such overcrowded conditions but for me it was a boon of playmates.

The "Jew Houses", for all intents and purposes, were separate little ghettoes where the Jewish people were confined in crowded conditions and were easy to find for future selections and deportations. One day the Arrow Cross militia came to our building and selected all the women for the debarkation point. Among them was a very beautiful woman who, it was thought, convinced a guard to let the women escape. Among them were my mother and two aunts.

It was not long before Adolf Eichmann ordered Hungarian Jews to be sent to dig fortifications against the approaching Soviet army. Fifty thousand men marched on that particular Death March. We heard that Raoul Wallenberg and the Swiss consul, Charles Lutz, as well as Portuguese and Spanish legations, were creating "protected" houses and a "protected" ghetto to house the Jews with international identity papers. Our people lined up by the thousands to get these *shutzpasses*. Thousands were handed papers. The crush of people was so great that the embassies were throwing the *schutzpasses* from the windows to the gathered crowd. They knew it would be impossible to process all in a timely manner. Some people were even taken into the Swiss Embassy and kept there till the end of the war.

On October 15, 1944, we had to find a safe house to live in. Mother, an aunt and I tried to get on a streetcar where mother and I were apprehended by the Arrow Cross. We were marched in the rainy and cold day to the brick factory ghetto, where we were kept for one week. I was separated from my mother and was grouped with other unfortunate children. We were taken to the Red Cross center. Just then, an air raid siren blasted the air. Pandemonium broke out. I was overwhelmed with fear, especially because I had been separated from my mother. I already knew that Jews were being killed and thrown into the Danube. I thought that we would be marched to the river and killed. Instead, we were taken, two by two, to our apartments, where I learned that my aunt had found a temporary shelter for us. A German woman took me to join my aunt.

In the meantime, mother and the other women were taken to the Nazi headquarters, where many were tortured and shot. Suddenly, as if by miracle, a German officer appeared and ordered the Arrow Cross to free the women. Mother was lucky to get away and located us in the temporary shelter. A week later we found an apartment in a Swiss safe house, where we had to share the congested space with 40 people. We slept on the floor, wall to wall. We brought with us whatever food we had, and when we ran out of food, the eight- to ten-year-old children stripped off their yellow stars and snuck out to get bread. By the time our confinement was over, every stitch of furniture was broken apart to make wood kindling to keep us warm.

Our family was saved from starvation by the wife of our apartment building superintendent who proclaimed herself a Nazi, and actually had been openly anti-Semitic. But she apparently took pity on us and every week she brought us a basket of food. I still cannot explain her kindness.

Now, more and more bombings by the Allies were taking place. The Allies flew over nightly, trying to break the will of the Nazis. My mother said she would not run to the basement to hide. She said if she were to die, she would prefer to die from an American bomb. On December 5, 1944 the Arrow Cross selected all the young women, including my aunt, to be deported. To this day I cannot understand why mother was left behind. Maybe they had some sympathy that there would be no one to care for me.

Soon after, the Nazis came back and took most of the Budapest Jews to the ghetto, where they surrounded the entire area with mines and explosives and planned to blow up the ghetto. The speedy advance of the Russian army stopped this action and we were liberated by them near the end of January 1945. In all, 550,000 Hungarian Jews were murdered during the Holocaust, of whom 100,000 were from Budapest.

We were among the lucky ones and were now free to try to make a new life. But how does one create a feeling of stability and how does one learn to trust neighbors and leaders who had more than 500,000 Jews deported and killed?

Mother, who was small of stature but strong of will, got us back to our original apartment, which we found was occupied by others and we were forced to once again reside in one of the safe houses. In a short time, however, mother was able to have the squatters vacate our apartment, which had been emptied of our own furniture. Slowly, like a detective, she traced who took our furniture and we were able to get most of it back.

Life took on a jumbled meaning and struggle. All shortages and interruption of services were a great hardship to try to reestablish one's life. But my mother had a will that would not let us give up. And, miraculously, father appeared a few days later. Emaciated, worn out and without strength of mind to deal with new challenges, he convinced mother that it would be best for us to move to a small village east of Budapest. He loaded our luggage and a few necessary possessions on a sled and placed me on top of the bundles wrapped in a down comforter. Father harnessed himself to the sled and pulled it for about a week, while mother walked behind. We slept in barns and stayed out of sight of the Russian soldiers, not knowing how we would be treated if they saw us. When we arrived in Nagykoros, we rented a house and settled down for a couple of months. We then moved to my grandmother's house in Eger, where father looked for buried valuables he had hidden there. During his search and digging, he cut his hand on some rusty object and developed blood poisoning that killed him within three weeks. He died on May 24, 1945.

Our shock at the loss of father was difficult to deal with. We had to overcome our emotional upheaval and regain strength to continue on—now just mother and I. We remained in my grandmother's house for about a year, where we reclaimed our emotional strength.

Mother especially felt very much alone. But, eventually, she met a man and they married and established a home for me. We returned to Budapest to our old apartment, but life took on a somber atmosphere because mother suffered terribly from bouts of depression. I had to become the strong one to almost nurture myself. I continued my education and eventually become an optician.

Our life under the Communist government was one of always being cautious and careful, never trusting anyone. We managed to keep ourselves out of sight of "big brother" observers who were ready to punish anyone who did not fall into step with the Communist ideals.

In 1953 I met my husband Joe, who was a kind and cheerful young man and brought to my life optimism and security. We were married in May 1955, and our first son, Peter, was born the following year, when the uprising in Hungary motivated many to flee the country. We, too, escaped, going to Vienna, Austria, seeking asylum, and hoping to come to America. We were approved to immigrate to the States within four weeks. We joined an aunt and uncle who had come to Syracuse in 1948. There, we finally established our life with freedom and without fear. We were blessed with a second son, Jack, who passed away in 1993. Now, our wonderful family—Peter, his wife, Carol, and our terrific granddaughters, Ma'ayan and Keren, who live near-by—are our joy.

When I think back on our life and the life that the Jewish people had to endure and survive, I shudder that again, our unstable world is trembling under the hateful expressions against the Jews and Israel. If you think it can never happen again and here, think again: It can!

A Child's Survival Life Story

by Norman Frajman

Warsaw, the capital of Poland, is situated on either bank of the Vistula River. Before the outbreak of World War II it had a population of about 1.3 million, of which 400,000 were Jewish—one third of the total population. This was my family's hometown, where I was born on September 11, 1929. Eighteen months later my sister, Renia, was born. She was a striking, blue-eyed blond girl with a sweet disposition, who at times got in the way of my activities with the boys.

My father, Leon, together with my grandmother, had a number of business enterprises that provided a comfortable life for our families. My mother, Hela (Trysk), an attractive and determined lady, established a home of refinement, appointed with fine furniture, family heirlooms, silver candelabra, and wine cups, which mother kept almost as a shrine in respect of the generations past. Although we lived in step with the modern times, we observed kashrut and father supported charitable causes and a small synagogue of the neighborhood.

Father was the one who demanded obedience; yet he was a most attentive parent, who indulged me with outings to soccer matches, ice cream parlors, and attractions that appealed to a young boy. On a few occasions I felt his anger, but along with his stern words he left me feeling that I was the apple of his eye. My family was my safe haven; I enjoyed being loved and was given opportunities to attend a Jewish private school where Hebrew studies were part of the curriculum.

Our neighborhood was comprised of a Jewish majority, and there were not many anti-Semitic expressions. The few gentiles who lived in our neighborhood, however, did often look for Jewish boys and adults to beat up. When these attacks happened I could not understand why. The victims were always innocent of any wrongdoing; they were just picked to express hatred for Jews.

I recall that before Germany invaded Poland, there were hysterical, abusive voices against Jews on the radio. Hate was infecting the Polish population. On September 1, 1939, when I was 10, Germany attacked Poland. Our city was bombed and the Polish government ordered the evacuation of the city.

Securing our apartment, my parents, sister and I and several members of our family gathered some meager belongings that could fit into a horse-drawn wagon and proceeded out of the city along with the throng of refugees. Overnight we were reduced to beggars. Father ran around trying to secure food for the family. It was not only a day-to-day existence, but survival from minute to minute. Our destination was Bialystok in the eastern part of Poland, which was now under Soviet occupation. After traveling for several weeks, we arrived in Kovel, a small town near Bialystok, where we settled for the winter of 1939-40 and where we hardly kept body and soul together.

When we heard that life in Warsaw, under the German control, was bearable, we decided to return. We tried to smuggle through the border at the demarcation boundary between Russian and German forces, where we were caught, jailed, and detained for a few days by the Russians. My mother, sister and I were sent back to the German side of Poland; my father was sent off to a Russian prison, and eventually was incarcerated in Siberia.

On our return trip to Warsaw, we boarded a train designated for Jews only. It seemed odd that we were segregated from the general population. We did not understand what this meant, but a sense of uneasiness was felt without recognizing what was happening. Arriving back home, we found the conditions in Warsaw crowded, but tolerable. Our apartment had been plundered of our beautiful furniture and possessions. It was occupied by Jewish refugees who had been deported from Germany. Mother had to argue and demand entry and finally we were given one room for our use. We found that our family business had been confiscated and given to a *Volksdeutsch* (Pole of German descent). We were issued ration cards, which qualified us for a meager food allotment. In general, the city of Warsaw was in despair. Our extended family shared what we had. Life had come to a standstill; we could do little but seek ways to survive.

As of November 12, 1939, every Jew 12 or older was compelled to wear on his right arm a white arm-band with the blue Star of David imprinted on it. The Nazis immediately started their assault against the Jews. They appointed a *Judenrat* (Jewish council), to run a census, which indicated about 359,000 Jews living in Warsaw. To keep the Jewish people off balance and controlled, the Germans announced that they were establishing educational camps for all Jews. They then stated that all assets except for 2,000 Polish zloty per family must be turned over to them. With short intervals of adjustment, they began to enforce a multitude of prohibitive rules and ordinances. Jews were forbidden to work in key industries or in government institutions. They were not allowed to bake bread, earn more than 500 zloty a month, buy from or sell to "Aryans," seek treatment at Aryan doctors' offices, help the Aryan sick, ride on trains and trolley cars, leave the city limits without special permits, or possess gold and jewelry. Conditions deteriorated daily.

The abused population was demoralized. Killings occurred without rhyme or reason. To disobey a decree meant instant death. Any individual rebellion would bring on collective punishment, which caused the people to worry not only about the guards, but what a heroic Jew might decide to do.

In April 1940, construction of the ghetto walls began, and on Yom Kippur— October 12—1940, the Nazis revealed the creation of a Jewish residential quarters, a tiny section of the city where Jews from Warsaw and those brought in from other places throughout Western Europe were ordered to move to, while 113,000 Christians were moved out of the area. Any Jew found outside of this area after the deadline would be shot. Mother ran from place to place trying to find a shelter for us. Finally we switched places with a gentile woman whose apartment was in the designated area. Of course the trade was far from equal. Her rooms were like a chicken coop, but we were very happy to find a place and have a roof over our heads, especially with winter approaching.

I was 11 when we moved into the ghetto. My grandparents, my aunts and uncles, all lived in the ghetto. We were a very closely knit family and we helped one another as best we could; we all starved together there, too. As time passed, the conditions became torturous. People were in tatters, suffering from malnutrition with swollen bellies. That bitter winter, typhus spread like wildfire and people were dying in great numbers.

The ghetto was divided into a small ghetto at the south end and a larger one at the north end. German and Polish police guarded its outside entrance, and a Jewish militia was formed to police the inside. Warsaw had 1,800 streets, and only 73 were consigned to the ghetto. The overall boundary was 11 miles long; the walls were 10 feet high with barbed wire and broken glass on the top. All this was paid for by the *Judenrat*.

The population of the ghetto reached more than half a million people. Unemployment was a major problem. Clandestine workshops manufactured goods that were sold illegally on the outside and raw goods were smuggled in. Children became couriers and smugglers.

Everyone was assigned work. Mother worked in a factory, Transavia on Stawki Street, which produced airplane parts. I worked as a messenger at the Umschlagplatz for the Transferstelle, the exchange center. This is where food was brought into the ghetto, which consisted of rotten potatoes and vegetables that were originally destined for the garbage. Later, the Umschlagplatz became the gathering place for the selections from which the Jews were sent off in cattle cars to the extermination camps: Treblinka, Auschwitz and Majdanek.

We were terrified every moment of our lives. Without reason, just as a whim, we were beaten; we were constantly in terror of being murdered or maimed. This was the purpose of the Nazis. Life meant nothing to them, especially Jewish lives. Often, German patrols on motorcycles with side cars and mounted heavy machine guns, came into the ghetto and just shot, indiscriminately, because whomever they hit would be Jewish. Being caught outside the ghetto after curfew, no matter the reason, resulted in instant death. This happened to my cousin, Lolek, who was delayed in disposing of the ghetto garbage and was not able to return to the ghetto at the designated time.

At eleven and a half years of age I had to be a big boy and take on responsibilities that should not have been a youngster's job. I became involved in smuggling food from the Aryan side into the ghetto through the cemetery and a hole in the ghetto wall.

By 1942, the Nazis forced more and more people from the surrounding towns into the ghetto, while at the same time making the area of the ghetto smaller, creating even more unbearable conditions.

The first mass deportations of Jews to Treblinka began in the summer of 1942, numbering 300,000. About 5,000 to 7,000 people, reaching a high of 13,000 people, were deported daily. At first, the selections were actually fulfilled by asking for volunteers. The Germans promised the volunteers to relocate to a better life and gave them bread and marmalade as enticements. Many people believed the Germans and volunteered. It was deception.

We did not hear what happened to them, but eventually some letters did arrive which we learned later were written under duress describing utopian conditions in order to quell any fears and encourage more volunteers to be transported out of the ghetto. Before long, the volunteering stopped, so the Germans started to kidnap people off the streets and from their jobs and forcibly brought them to the Umschlagplatz to be taken out of the ghetto.

In July 1942, when I was 12, the Nazis had one of these selections and culled people from where I was working. I was among those to be taken to the Umschlagplatz. Nearby the Umschlagplatz was a building that was formerly a hospital. It stood very close to other buildings where we were being held. I was asked by some adults if I would place a plank connecting the two buildings, walk across and open a window so that we all could save ourselves. I found a narrow board and placed it between the windows of the two buildings and began to cross over. I was spotted by the German police, who began to shoot at me. I managed to escape the bullets and hid in a credenza that was part of a Nazi stash of confiscated furniture that was taken from the transported Jews. The furniture was destined for shipment to Germany. No one else managed to save themselves; they all were shipped off on the next transport.

I stayed in the credenza until nightfall. I was in a state of fear and indecision; I didn't know whether to continue hiding or get out. I waited and waited and no one came. Trembling, I got out and went back into the ghetto. I did not return to my Umschlagplatz job but managed to find some other work and stayed with my mother for a while. My sister was too young to work and would have been killed immediately, so she stayed hidden behind a false wall in the daytime. Mother shared her starvation rations with my little sister.

At first, ghetto factory workers, Jewish police, *Judenrat* members, hospital workers and their families were spared, but they were also periodically subject to deportation. Another wave of deportations to Treblinka began in January 1943, during which many factory workers and hospital personnel were selected, too. Unexpected Jewish armed resistance, however, forced the Nazis to retreat from the ghetto after four days of deportations.

By this time information had reached the ghetto about what the final destination would be and what the Germans were doing to the Jewish people. We now knew that every one of us who was still alive was not going to make it; we were all going to die. The young people organized an underground. They smuggled themselves outside the ghetto to purchase arms from the Polish underground. Only a handful of Poles helped and the meager arms bought cost great sums of money. We had experienced anti-Semitism in Poland for ages, and at this time with the help of the Germans, most Poles were happy to see Poland free of Jews. The Warsaw Ghetto uprising started several months before the final liquidation of the ghetto. The uprising was led by Mordechai Anielewicz, a 23-year-old leader of other young men.

They knew that it was a suicide mission; they knew they were going to die, but they didn't want to die without a struggle. They gathered their will and their resources and killed many Jewish collaborators who worked with the Germans. We all knew we were going to die, so what better way to die than with a weapon in your hands? We were not typical teens. My desire to join the resistance overwhelmed me, but I was too young. These young fighters were the symbol of what our future struggles, as a Jewish people, would have to be to reclaim a homeland.

To state that it was a battle of even might would be absurd. The tattered Jewish fighters fought with inadequate arms and homemade Molotov cocktails and whatever else they could scrounge to stop the final transport of the remaining Jews of the ghetto. They ran from rooftop to rooftop, fighting. But they could not save themselves. Some of them ran through sewers, but in some cases, when they came out on the Polish side, they were denounced by some Poles who took them back to the Germans, for which the Poles got five pounds of sugar in exchange for a Jewish life. Very few of the resistance fighters who managed to escape to the forest survived. Some of them, who did survive went to Israel and founded the *kibbutz*, Lohamei Haghetaot. This kibbutz was founded solely by the survivors of the Warsaw Ghetto.

On April 29, 1943, the night before Passover, which coincided with Hitler's birthday, the Germans wanted to give Hitler a gift of making Warsaw free of Jews. They called it *Judenrein*. That night, troops—made up mainly of Ukrainians, Lithuanians, Latvians, Croatians and Estonians, as well as German peasants who were indoctrinated in their churches with libels that Jews killed Christ and killed Christian boys for their blood to be used in the baking of matzah—were given weapons and a free hand to kill the Jews. They did their job very well.

It took the Germans only three weeks to conquer the entire country of Poland. It took them only three weeks to conquer France and Belgium. But the ghetto partisans resisted for six weeks. The Nazis were afraid to come into the ghetto! During this period, my mother, my sister and I hid behind the false wall. All the while the Germans brought in heavy artillery and soldiers, and bombarded us from the air. It was a battlefield against a bunch of desperate Jewish boys and girls. The ghetto was aflame, burning on all sides. At the end of it all, there were 70,000 people left. The tattered survivors, included my mother, sister and I, were searched out, smoked out, and forced into boxcars for the torturous ride to the concentration camp.

Without warning, on May 1, 1943, we were rounded up with the help of the Polish police while the ghetto was surrounded by Lithuanian, Latvian, and Ukrainian troops. The cattle cars, which normally held eight horses and two men, were now packed with 120 human beings; there was no room to sit or crouch. We all had to stand. The floors of the cars were sprayed with a chlorine disinfectant, supposedly to cleanse the cars, but in fact the fumes made it difficult to breath and resulted in our becoming extremely thirsty. Many people died or became crazed by the inhuman conditions. This journey, which should have taken six to eight hours, took three days. There was not a drop of water to drink. I had to resort to drinking my own urine. Twelve people from our car did not survive the journey.

We arrived in Lublin [Poland] on May 3, 1943, where we were greeted with hysterical shouts. Machine-gun emplacements, German guards, Lithuanians and criminal inmates of the concentration camp surrounded us. With prodding, beatings, and snapping of the vicious dogs, we were ordered to disembark and line up in columns, five abreast, and commanded to march to an unknown destination, which turned out to be the concentration camp Majdanek, four kilometers from Lublin.

I was marching next to an elderly man who started to recite the *Vidui*, the prayer that one says on his deathbed, as the smell of burning flesh burned our nostrils. They brought us to an open field—several thousand of us—where we spent the night huddled together to shield ourselves from the cold. In the morning, the selection and division of men from the women and children began, as an SS officer pointed his thumb to the left or right. Left meant life. Right meant death—for anyone who wore glasses, anyone who did not walk straight, had gray hair, pregnant women, older women and men, children, anyone the SS considered unable to work or be useful. My mother and sister were selected to survive, but that was the last time we saw each other. They were torn from me and I had no time to even say goodbye.

I was pointed to what turned out to be the life side and was marched off together with about 1,000 men. We were surrounded, prodded, and beaten by psychotic Kapos, who guided us into the concentration camp. Next, we were lined up single file and stripped of all clothing. We were shaved of all hair, including the body hair, and were speedily herded to the showers. Without having time to even process why and what was happening to us, I thought that this was the end—that the gas chambers were our destination.

With disbelief, I realized that water was spewing from the showerheads. We were pushed along to the next station where creosote, a disinfectant, was applied with a large paintbrush to all shaved areas, including the head. The smell and a burning pain entered every pore, but we had no time or senses left to feel. The process continued. We were tossed striped uniforms that were either too big or small, consisting of a thin jacket, pants and wooden clogs, and each of us was assigned a number. I looked at the men around me and could not place myself among them, but I was one of them, a clown appearance, in shock and lost of all dignity or semblance of a human being.

We were prodded to the third field. This field was for newcomers, but we were treated even harsher because we were considered criminals from the Warsaw uprising. We were marked and treated even worse than the other inmates. Nearby, the conspicuous gallows were standing at ready.

Majdanek was surrounded with high-voltage electrified fences. The five fields had watchtowers between them. The general latrine had holes as seats and one was allowed to stay no longer than three minutes. Overstaying the time brought a vicious clubbing. There were some cases where people were thrown into the latrine and drowned. Finally, we were led into Barrack 21. The three-high, shelf-like bunks that accommodate three men in each section and level, which was designed for about 100 inmates, now had 400 men. When the red light was on, no one could go outside because they would be shot. Each was given a lice-infested blanket and a bag, which we filled with straw for a mattress. Then we had to sew on the number that became our identity on the jacket.

After this process we were finally permitted to rest. Our complete exhaustion and disorientation was escaped in sleep, but this too was cut short. At 3:30 in the morning we were torn from sleep, with shouting, prodding and beatings, to line up for a body count in the yard. The dead, who passed away during the night, were piled up and added to the count. At last we were given tools and wheelbarrows and marched off in groups of 30 to 40 men to work at a running pace, loading bricks, under the supervision of sadistic Kapos.

At noon we were marched back to camp for lunch. We were again lined up for a body count. We were given a boiling hot, smelly slop/soup, which we had to sip because we did not have any spoons. Before one could consume this burning liquid, the whistle blew and we had to dump the soup and run back to work. At 6 o'clock we were brought back to camp. Again we were counted and given our rations, which consisted of a 2-pound loaf of bread for 16 people; once a week, we got a quarter-pound of margarine for 20 people. I never ate my margarine; instead I smeared it on my body because I had eczema and my skin became cracked and dry.

At night, matters became even worse. It was then that the Kapos displayed their sadism with a vengeance. The blankets on the bunks had to be made up straight without a wrinkle. Anyone not meeting the inspection was given 20 blows with a club on his back or bottom. These beatings left one unable to move. We were assigned work for the following day and were finally permitted to lie down. The barracks were both our jails and comfort from exhaustion. And so each day began at 3:30 in the morning with a lineup and head count and a breakfast of burned wheat coffee and taken to some useless work just to wear down the prisoners. I witnessed many atrocities carried out against individuals; one had to become invisible to get out of the sight of the Kapos.

I spent several months in this camp. It was Hell on earth. Every minute was a death sentence. Majdanek was considered one of the worst extermination camps in existence. The only way out was through the chimneys. Prisoners of the concentration camps had to fill the shortage of laborers in Germany, so when a transport of laborers was being taken away, I managed to get myself onto it. First and foremost, I wanted to get away from Majdanek. But I also hoped that I would meet my mother and sister who may have been on the same transport. I soon learned that my family had been gassed and sent to the crematoriums after they arrived. I never learned when they died nor where their ashes were scattered along with the thousands of other innocent people. The loss of my dear ones broke my spirit even further, and I just dragged along in a robot-like existence at this camp.

The transport ended up in a camp called Skarzysko, where we were assigned to work in an ammunition factory. Here I worked at *Werke A*, in an ammunition factory that produced grenades and bullets. We were driven hard in our work, but this was a luxury compared to the assignment that I was given, with two other men, of painting a watchtower with creosote for many days. We were suspended on ropes in the bitter cold in only our threadbare clothes. The wind, freezing exposure, and irritation of the creosote punished our bodies.

Shortly after this work, I came down with typhus. A fellow inmate hid me under wood shavings to avoid the selection. Since this camp had no head count, it was easier to keep the sick hidden. He saved my life that day. I definitely would have been selected to die.

I was interned in Camp Skarzysko till late 1944 when we were evacuated to Buchenwald on August 5, 1944, and was registered as prisoner No. 68616. I was soon transferred to Schlieben, a satellite camp of Buchenwald. Here again I was assigned to work in an ammunition factory where we made bazookas. Buchenwald handed out the same cruelty as in the other camps, with sadistic supervision of beatings, disease, hunger and a daily threat of death.

One night, after I had been there for a few months, an explosion tore the place apart and several hundred people were killed. You could see human parts strewn all over the place. The remains were cleaned up as just a bunch of rubbish. No tears were shed; no one had any left. An SS contingent was sent in; none looked older than 20 years. They supervised the reconstruction of the factory and railroad tracks. Within a week and a half we were driven with urgency and blows, in the grueling labor, forced to work day and night until it was finished. In the bitter cold, without gloves, our hands froze to the rails, and to this day I suffer from the frostbitten hands.

As the Russians were getting closer, the Germans took us away in freight cars, dropping off groups of men along the way. My group was dropped and marched from town to town under SS guard and was made to dig anti-tank ditches. Men were dying from exhaustion, hunger, and exposure; some were just pushed aside and shot.

Finally we stopped in a small town called Nixdorf, which was at the German Czech border. On the morning of May 8,1945, we discovered that all the guards disappeared. We didn't know what this meant and were afraid that it was some kind of trick. But when we saw the first Russian tank, we knew we were free. The Soviet soldiers greeted us and shared their field rations. They were full of compassion for us, especially those who were Jewish. We devoured the little bit of food they were able to give us.

We were so happy! Immediately I felt the wall of the Nazi evil prison collapse and I began to think of my family, wondering where they were, if they were alive, yearning to see them again. I felt alive for the first time in a long time, and to this day, I consider May 8 my second birthday, the day I was liberated. The first thing I did was to go into a German home and get civilian clothing. I also took a bicycle. No one dared to stop us. We spent the next week or two just going into homes and eating and sleeping.

After years of complete submission and having no self-value, what does one do? I was 15 ½ years old and had lost all sense of proportion or trust. My family and home were gone, my childhood stolen. Soon, under the security of the Russians, I found a will to live and survive. But what was normal? For the first few months of freedom, I worked as an interpreter for the Russians. Then, following the example of many survivors, I crossed to the American Sector of Berlin to a displaced persons camp. From here I made my way to the United States to an uncle in New York in March 1948.

Our reunion was emotional. I learned that my father was alive. He survived in a Russian prison and when the Polish citizens were permitted out of Russia after the war, he was released and eventually immigrated to Israel.

This is my story in brief. How does one remember and not cry? How does one understand? Are there any words that allow one to describe the Holocaust? I know I try. I share my survival story, but it pains me and yet I do it. I want to remember, I must remember for my mother, sister, my large extended family, and the six million who were murdered with such cruelty.

I Survived to Speak for Them

by Judith (Beitscher) Freeman

The city of Uzhorod, Czechoslovakia [now in Ukraine], which came under the Hungarian rule in March 1939, is close to the Polish border. This is where my entire family was born and lived. Until the takeover we enjoyed a comfortable, secure life.

Influenced by Germany and under Hungarian dictate, all media were censored. At first, we had some sense of safety when only the Polish, Russian, and other European Jews of our area were shipped away. In March 1944, the German army occupied my hometown, and that is when our lives changed. I was 15 years old.

Within a day, all Jews were ordered to wear yellow stars on the front and back of their outer clothing. A curfew was imposed. Then, an edict was issued that all Jews had to turn in all their valuables to a central headquarters. Finally, all families were ordered for relocation and were ordered to bring only those personal belongings that each person could carry. A lumberyard in town became our living space, a ghetto. Thousands of us were moved into this very small area. We were crowded together in buildings with sides open to the weather. After a little more than a week, the real deportation started. We assumed that our destination would be a place to work and that somehow we would survive.

My family and I, along with thousands of other people, were ordered to march to the train station, where we were packed into cattle cars with 70 to 80 people in one car. An empty bucket served as a latrine. The door was slid shut and padlocked. The clink of the key triggered an inner fear, a premonition that we were being taken to a miserable and dangerous existence. The trains slipped

56

away from the station on a journey that lasted several days and nights; we soon lost track of time.

So many people were crowded together. People moaned, babies cried; there was no air to breathe. The meager food that we brought along was soon gone. Periodically, the train stopped and we were permitted to empty the latrine buckets. But these stops also became robbing stops. German soldiers would board the cars and demand jewelry, gold, and watches. I recall that when they could not get any valuables, they began to shoot at random. My friend's grandmother, who was sitting next to me, was hit by a soldier's bullet, which shattered her skull. The shock of seeing this cruel death brought me to hysterical tears. My father comforted me by saying, "It will be all right; don't be scared. That was a mean person."

After several days of this horrible journey, we arrived at our destination: Auschwitz. As soon as the train stopped, the doors were opened with shouts of "*Raus! Raus!*"—Out! Out! We were ordered to leave our belongings on the train. Men in striped uniforms were milling about; I later learned they were Polish Jewish prisoners. Numerous SS guards with vicious German shepherd dogs, rifles on their shoulders, and guns in their holsters, glared at us with disgust.

The infamous Dr. Josef Mengele—"Dr. Death"—sat at a long table and observed the disorientated, helpless crowd. The soldiers prodded us closer to the table, separating men from women. Mengele simply waved his hand, designating that one should go to the right or the left. Waiting for my turn, I saw that older people, babies with their mothers, pregnant women, and people who looked sickly were sent to the left side. My mother and my 12-year-old sister were pointed to the left.

As I approached the table, Mengele asked how old I was. I answered that I was 15, and he waved me to the right. Everything was happening so quickly; I felt as if I were in a daze. As I turned around searching for my parents and sister, I spotted them being taken away into another direction; I could not follow them.

Along with other women and girls, I was taken to a building where we were told to undress and file in front of women in striped uniforms, who proceeded to shave all our body hair and heads. We were prodded into another room, a great big room with showerheads in the ceiling. The hot-water shower, even without soap or towels to dry off, refreshed us after the long journey. Somehow my intuition made me grab my own shoes, which was fortunate because they were sturdy and would serve me well in the future. Many who left their shoes behind had to survive for the next several cold, rainy months in bare feet.

We continued being prodded into another room, where each of us was thrown a dress—no underwear, no stockings, nothing else. The sizes never matched our bodies. We quickly traded amongst ourselves and continued to the next processing stop where big buckets of red paint were used to put a large red stripe down the middle of the dress as a precaution against our escaping. But there was no escape. The entire camp was surrounded by an electrified barbed-wire fence, and every few hundred feet a watchtower with soldiers and powerful guns guarded the camp.

Auschwitz contained several sections. I was in Camp C, which consisted of 32 low barracks. Each wooden barrack housed 1,000 inmates. Camp C held 32,000 women. The bunks, built in three levels, were about four by eight feet. They served as sleeping places for 10 people on each bunk. The sleeping arrangements were to lie down five in one direction and five in the other—packed in like sardines—everyone on her side. The only way I could turn around was if everyone was agreeable. If not, tough luck. The occupants in my barrack were between 15 and 16 years old. Living in these cramped conditions, people had to become friends very quickly or expect terrible trouble.

I was there from May 1944 to about November 1944—six months in Hell. I wore the same dress the whole time, never taking it off. There was no way that it could be washed or exchanged for a fresh one. At night, I did take off my shoes and put them underneath my head so no one would take them from me. There were no utensils with which to eat. No one had her own dish, towel, blanket, toothbrush, or comb. We had nothing, absolutely nothing.

Each day before the sun rose, we were roused by the sound of a gong. Thirty-two thousand women and girls emptied out of the barracks for roll call into the open space, lining up for hours no matter what the weather was like. Even people who were sick—people who subsequently died—had to line up. This happened twice a day. Dressed in boots, hats, and coats against the weather, German personnel, SS women and men, counted us and made notes in a ledger.

After roll call we were allowed to go to the latrine, a low building with cutout holes as toilets in wooden benches. The stench was overwhelming. Speedily, I tried to get to a washroom where the water spigots trickled meager droplets, and with a bit of maneuvering and haste I was able to wash my hands and face.

Returning back to the barracks and assigned bunks, the Germans came around with what they called coffee. It was a sweetish tasting warm liquid. A bowlful was given to each bunk, where the ten of us had to sip, taking careful turns, until it was all gone. The rest of the day was spent in a stupor, sitting or lying down if there was room, but mostly sitting around with feet hanging over the bunk.

The afternoon roll call lasted several hours. Again we were permitted to go to the bathroom and back into the bunks, where they brought the only other meal of the day. The large containers, looking like garbage cans, were full of a vile-tasting soup. It contained turnips, pieces of potato, some greenery, which appeared like grass, and, once in a while, a smidgen of meat. The smell was so repulsive that I had to hold my nose to swallow it, but swallow I did. Also, a small piece of black bread and occasionally a little piece of margarine made up our daily routine of food. On many occasions I saved the bread, hiding it in my shoe so that I would have something to eat with the morning coffee. We were getting skinnier and skinnier, and my bones hurt when I lay down on the bare bed boards.

After several weeks of this existence, I noticed that my bunkmates were sitting about in a stupor, looking into space. A hand in front of their face would not stir them. I said, "My God, what's happening to us? Am I like that, too? I can still remember. I can still talk." What was actually happening was that the coffee/liquid we were given in the morning had tranquilizers or some sort of drugs to make us into zombies. As people became sick or demented or had breakdowns, they were taken away. At the time, I thought they were being taken to hospitals, but in reality they were taken to the gas chambers.

I began to fight the feeling, this hopeless, helpless haze-state. Deliberately, I began the exercise of recalling all the movies I had seen and books I had read and started to relate them to my bunkmates, and soon others joined the circle of listeners.

The two women in charge of our barrack were Kapos, a Jewish Slovak woman who had been in the camps for a long time, and her assistant, a Polish Jewish woman. These two, prisoners themselves, were in charge of keeping order. One evening many of the girls were crying bitterly for their mothers, which caused one of the Kapos to say to them, "I'm going to tell you what happened to your mothers, so once and for all you will stop crying for them. I'm not supposed to tell you this, but I will anyway because none of you will be able to tell anybody I told you. It won't matter because you won't live and get out of here." Without any compassion or remorse she blurted out, "A short distance from here is a camp. The huge shower rooms are not for bathing; they are gas chambers where all who enter are killed. That is where your mothers, grandmothers, sick people, and children were taken when you arrived." She continued to describe the scenes of horror: "They are packed about 2,000 to 2,500 people at a time, and instead of water, the German guards drop canisters of gas pellets through the trap doors on the roof. The gas kills them in 15 to 20 minutes. They are all gone! They are the puffs of smoke from the chimneys over there."

At first we did not believe this outrageous story, but prisoners in other buildings confirmed this horror: "Yes, it's true."

As the weeks went by, "selections" broke the monotony of the days. In Auschwitz selections meant extra roll calls, in addition to morning and afternoon lineups. With the sound of the gong or when an SS delegation went to a particular building, they demanded with shoving, kicking, and whipping at random, "Everybody out! Jew dogs get out!" We were lined up and had to undress in front of the German SS guards. Sometimes they selected people who looked very skinny and pale, who were taken away and were never seen again. When I learned that a selection was to occur, I didn't know whether to run to another building and hide or mingle in with the crowd and go through a selection and hope that I would be taken to a better camp. We soon learned that skinny and pale people were chosen; we came to the conclusion that rosy cheeks spelled health, so we pinched our cheeks to bring on a rosy, healthy look.

Later I learned that many from our group where taken to various labor camps across Germany. Toward the end of the summer of 1944, more and more selections took place, and more and more transports started coming in. The crematorium ovens never stopped. After a while we could smell the horrible odor of burning flesh. Thousands of people were still alive in Auschwitz; they couldn't kill us fast enough. One day I found myself in a selection. Along with a group of people, I was marched out of our area of the camp. I was not familiar with this place where the gagging stench was almost on top of us. We were led into a large room and told to undress.

With prodding we were then ushered into another large room that looked like a stadium where we were told to sit on benches. Looking around, I saw two huge, very heavy metal doors. Soon SS guards entered and ordered the section ahead of mine to continue through the doors. I remained on the bench waiting with trembling heart. I recognized that we were headed to the gas chamber. I was standing right there, waiting to be exterminated.

Strange things go through your mind when you are about to die. I wondered if I had been a good enough human being. Some people were reciting the *Shema*. Just as the SS guards were about to get us into the actual gas chamber section, the air-raid sirens squealed, and we were ushered out into the room where they threw the ragged clothes at us and continued to walk us back to Camp C.

My thoughts and feelings were in turmoil. I questioned: Why live? It would be better to die and stop the suffering. But my will to live was strong, and I vowed to bear witness. I said to myself, "Oh no! I want to live! The world must know of this evil place and the horrible crimes that are happening here. I want to make sure that people who know me will know of our plight and suffering and the mass murder carried out on our families, our people."

After this miraculous escape from the gas chambers, we were taken to the railroad tracks, where we were loaded into cars and transported to a labor camp, Guben, near Berlin. That camp was much smaller, with barracks that housed only 40 to 50 women. We were elated with the luxury of even being handed a blanket and a towel.

After the bitter cold ride and having escaped gassing, I fell asleep exhausted. I was soon startled by a voice asking, "Is there anyone here from Uzhorod?" I immediately got up and approached two women, who turned out to be sisters of a childhood friend from my hometown. We became close friends and found ways to help each other. And since they worked in the kitchen, I was lucky to occasionally get some extra food, which I shared with my bunkmates.

60

That same day, after all were settled into their barrack spaces, we were marched to a factory in town, which was manufacturing radio components for airplanes. The work was not physically difficult, but the 14-hour shift sapped our strength. We were marched to the factory before the sun rose and returned after darkness to avoid being seen by the city residents.

Our supervisors were German civilians. Not one of them showed any kindness to us. Not one of them ever helped with a piece of bread or a pair of stockings. Not one of them asked any questions or tried to be helpful in any way. So if you hear anybody say only Hitler and his henchmen were cruel, not caring, and sadistic, that is not so; the entire population was conditioned to think of us as subhuman.

I was fortunate to have gotten a winter coat, which was given to me by my friends who worked in the warehouse. It was pure luxury to have something warm to wear on the walk to and from the factory. Within a couple of months, a multitude of people was brought into the camp from other camps. They were skeletal, filthy, and full of lice. They told of the hundreds upon hundreds of people who died on the Death March.

We knew that any day something dreadful could happen, and, sure enough, we soon were told that the whole camp had to be evacuated. We were given half a loaf of bread per person and a piece of cheese. We had no possessions except our blanket and towel. We were marched out of camp and began what would be a long trek, our Death March. They marched us across Germany from near Berlin toward the northwest part of the country. As we marched on the main highway, more columns of inmates joined our column from many side roads. We were guarded every few feet by German guards with guns and rifles at the ready. We were warned not to stop and to keep up with the column at all times. Anyone who stopped would be shot.

We were going as slowly as we could or as fast as we were forced to march. The roads were littered with bodies. People who no longer had the strength to continue were shot on the spot. From time to time, at the end of the day, they let us go into a barn. And every so often they would cook a big batch of potatoes or turnips and pass it around.

This march lasted about two weeks, with people getting weaker all the time. The bread they gave us at Guben was long gone; the potatoes they gave us were meager. On both sides of me were my two friends. At one point, I remember saying to my friends, "Leave me here." I told them, "You keep going. I can't. I'm just going to sit down. I can't move anymore." They answered me with determination, "Oh no, while we have some strength, we are going to give some strength to you." And so they supported me under my arms and almost carried me along. They refused to let me sit down. They dragged me. This helped rejuvenate me, and I was able to continue on my own after a while.

After a time, they put us in cattle cars again and took us to another destination, Bergen-Belsen. When we arrived—it probably was February—we were led through showers and then taken to a room where the overcrowded conditions forced people to almost be on top of each other. There were no bunks, no furniture, nothing.

Another cause of suffering at this place was that the entire populace was infested with lice. Sanitary conditions were non-existent. Typhus was rampant. Every morning we found numbers of people who had died. They were dragged outside by our inmates and were piled in heaps. The mountains of dead were growing bigger and bigger every day.

My resolve to survive was at a low point. There was no way out. We were given even less food than in Auschwitz. The SS and Kapos maintained a hold on the people with cruelty and beatings. The heaps of dead bodies were daily growing higher and bigger.

When a Kapo demanded that I drag the dead body of friend who had died that night and I refused, she beat me mercilessly on the head, which made me collapse and caused me to lose my hearing for a long time. And so our daily suffering had no end.

One of the sisters, my friend, contracted typhus. The two of us who were still "healthy" tried to take care of her. The one who worked in the warehouse had stashed away some jewels that she found in the linings of clothing. She was able to trade a bracelet for two aspirins, a ring for a little cup of sugar, and a diamond for a small piece of bread. My friends shared everything with me. That is why I survived. Without them I would have been part of the heaps of corpses.

The days passed slowly. I was getting weaker and weaker and more hopeless. Seeing these enormous mountains of bodies, I said to myself, "I guess I'll die here and be one of those bodies, too." Under these conditions I turned 16. The last piece of jewelry was traded for some bread and cheese with which we celebrated my birthday. About two days later I, too, came down with typhus and was cared for by my two friends who kept me alive with all their might and resources.

One day, while I was in a delirious state, I remember someone burst into the room and announced: "All the German guards are gone. The British soldiers have entered the camp and liberated us." I did not know what day it was then, but now I know. It was April 15, 1945.

It was an incredible feeling. At first we did not believe that it was true. I was taken to the field hospital where they tried to help us and revive the half-dead. Thirteen thousand died right after liberation. Many could not be saved from the various illnesses, and others over-ate with fatal results. (Their bodies could not handle the sudden rich and plentiful diet.)

At Bergen-Belsen, many of the German guards were captured and were made to dig enormous mass graves. They carried mountains of bodies to the edge of the graves, and before they were buried, all the townspeople from

Bergen-Belsen were forced to gather, including the city officials, to view these enormous piles of bodies. They lived nearby, yet claimed they saw nothing! The bodies were bulldozed into mass graves. This was the last humiliation that was done to the people who perished in Bergen-Belsen.

I eventually recovered. I asked for a mirror and was shocked to see a stranger looking back at me. My eyes were sunken; my face was totally devoid of flesh. I was like a skeleton. A dead person was looking back at me. But knowing that I survived the horror of the camps and typhus, I felt hope, and I decided to return to my hometown.

My destination was very far from where I was liberated. I had to travel through a significant part of Germany, Austria, Slovakia, and Hungary and into the region of my hometown.

I traveled on top of trains, under seats, in lavatories, between cars, on steps—any way I could. My heart was trembling, hoping that some of my family had survived. But, as it turned out, nobody had. Later, I made a list of all my relatives; I counted 37 family members. They all had been murdered.

And so my suffering and my losses bring forth memories of horror and emotional anguish, but I have found strength and determination to bear witness to what I lived, what I saw. I feel it is my mission. Six million were murdered; most do not have even one relative to cry for them, so I will cry and speak for them.

I met my husband Lou Fried right after the war, and for two years we lived in a displaced persons camp in Germany near Munich. We were able to get to the United States in 1947, where we adopted our name "Freeman" as a symbol of being free. We rebuilt our lives and learned to live with kindness, charity, and love. We wanted our children and our grandchildren to inherit the feelings of family and of being cherished. We did not want to live our lives only with sorrow.

Our working years in Allentown, Pennsylvania, were in serving our community. Education was our calling, teaching the lesson of dignity and compassion for all.

Judy Freeman died on October 23, 2007. She was a member of the National Executive Committee of the Survivors in New York. She helped survivors receive reparations and worked in every way possible to keep the memory of the lost Six Million alive. Judy also was the originator of the idea of the Magen David "Matzeivah" grave markers to indicate a Holocaust survivor, which was adopted as a symbol of our losses and our suffering.

Liberated from Horror with Nowhere to Go

by Morris Friebaum as told to Janice Friebaum

In September 1939, when Germany invaded Poland, I was just 12 years old. I watched in fear and disbelief as Warsaw, my home, was transformed into bloody chaos. Bombs fell, tanks rolled in, and German soldiers spread out like gasoline poured on pavement. The carnage of dead horses and dead people in the streets and buildings reduced to rubble was a sight that one could never have visualized. My life would never be the same again.

I had a good, normal childhood. We weren't a wealthy family, but we never felt deprived. My father managed a cabaret and my mother was a homemaker, raising four children. My brother, Yitzhak, two years my senior, was the eldest and Chanah, my only sister, was three years my junior, followed by my little brother, Benjamin (whom we nicknamed Bentsiella), who was three years younger than Chanah. We lived in a large, two-room apartment on the second floor of an apartment building at Ulica Twarda 26.

One of Warsaw's renowned synagogues, the Nozyk Synagogue, was just blocks from our home. Instead of going there for services our family and friends prayed at home since we had two Torahs. Sabbath and holiday services were conducted right in our apartment with family and friends. I have fond memories of my uncle, Nathan Greenberg, proudly reading from the Torah my grandfather had commissioned from a scribe in Russia during World War I.

We mainly spoke Polish at home, although my family also knew Yiddish. I attended public school with a mix of Jewish and Catholic children. I recall some incidents of anti-Semitism growing up, particularly after the death of Jozef Pilsudski, leader of the Polish Socialist Party, who supported a multiethnic Poland. I saw bloody brawls where bands of drunken Poles would attack Jews in the street.

I remember hearing bits and pieces about increasingly terrible anti-Semitism in Germany. My father was a passionate Zionist and believed the message of Ze'ev Jabotinsky who, in 1937, warned that a great flame was coming to Europe and would destroy the Jewish people. My father wanted to follow his advice to immigrate to Palestine but my mother would not consider such a move. She had two younger, unmarried sisters and an elderly widowed mother in Warsaw and felt responsible to look after them.

Obviously, we never left for Palestine and that is why I am writing this story today. I am a survivor of the Holocaust, those five years and eight months of Hell that robbed me of my family, my education, and my belief in a just and compassionate world. That Hell began the day Germany invaded Poland.

The Germans quickly enacted their anti-Semitic policies against Jews. While there was no physical barrier yet around what came to be called the Warsaw Ghetto, there were restrictions as to where we could go, when we could go, and what we could do. Most schools closed after the German invasion and never reopened. Food was rationed. Jews were beaten for no reason at all. Many Jews lost their livelihoods and families; homelessness was common and a black market quickly developed for food, coal, and other essential supplies.

Everything worsened after a wall was built around a portion of the city. I'm not sure if we were lucky or unlucky, but the first part of the city to be walled in as a ghetto included our apartment building. The eleven-and-a half-foot wall was just a few blocks from our home. Later, another, much larger section of the city was enclosed by walls.

Christian Poles moved out and Jews from elsewhere in Poland began arriving in the ghetto. The new arrivals were ordered to move into apartments already crowded by families huddled together for survival. Two families moved into our apartment, and there were 16 of us living in two rooms.

The ghetto became very crowded. Most adults had no work and no way to earn income. Most children, like me, were not in school. People had nothing to do but find ways to survive. And this became harder all the time. Disease was rampant, people were starving, and dead bodies in the street were a regular sight.

Our family was forced to find food to supplement the meager rations. My parents gave me what little money we had left and I snuck out of the ghetto in search of food in the Polish (Christian) zone. Young kids were able to get around or underneath the wall if they were clever and careful. I was assigned this duty by my family, and many times I left the ghetto through a series of connected apartment-building basements. In the Christian zone, I could buy bread, potatoes, and other important staples. This was dangerous work since we children were fairly recognizable as Jews, given the poor quality of our clothing and unkempt appearance. Poles were anxious to take our money since they were not faring terribly well in wartime conditions under the oppressive Nazi regime.

One day, probably in the fall of 1941 (I really cannot remember), when my family's supply of food was nearly gone, I escaped the ghetto, determined to find food. I spent a few days looking for something, anything, and finally found some bread. But to my surprise and horror the Polish police had moved their guard posts further out in the Christian quarter. They suspected Jewish children were slipping in and out of the ghetto through building basements and they tried to cut off our access points. They succeeded. The building with my passageway was heavily guarded and I could not safely enter. I never saw my family again. I was 14 years old.

I slept in farmers' fields, haystacks, and barns. Sometimes they knew I was there and sometimes they didn't. Some Poles gave me food and some told me, "Go away, dirty Jew!" I was just a boy, on the run, trying to survive, one day at a time.

I hopped trains, riding in boxcars. I went to Lublin, but when I reached the Jewish ghetto, all the men were being sent away to work. So I continued traveling and made it to Kozienice, a small town near Lublin, where a sister of my maternal grandmother lived. There I hoped to find refuge with my great aunt and her family. But as soon as I arrived, I found out that all of Kozienice's Jews were being deported. There was no hope of safety for me in this once-thriving Jewish *shtetl*, town.

I continued to travel, by foot, heading towards Radom and trying not to fall prey to the Nazi web. It was cold. I was hungry and dirty. At some point I contracted typhus and must have fallen unconscious with high fever near a road. I was discovered by Poles and taken to a Jewish hospital in the Radom ghetto. I spent two weeks in the hospital with high fevers. When I recovered I was a prisoner of the Nazis in the Radom Jewish ghetto. My bout with typhus meant trading my freedom for my life.

I was sent to work in the Weiss munitions factory, an important Polish manufacturer of carbines, pistols, rifles and bicycles that had been in existence well before World War II. I was a slave laborer, of course, with all of the other Jewish prisoners. We worked alongside Christian Poles who were paid wages, albeit miniscule, for their work. We Jews lived in prisoner barracks and were marched under guard about one mile each way, to and from our 12-hour shifts of work. We worked seven days a week and frequently switched shifts from day to night, and night to day.

I was assigned to work on a head machine that cut the metal rims of gun barrels. It was hard work and I had to learn what to do, how to do it quickly, and without mistakes. Sometimes the machines would break and, if I could not produce 500 guns per shift, I was punished. Initially the factory was run by Ukrainians and Poles, under the direction of Nazis. Many Ukrainian and Polish guards were merciless and I was often beaten mercilessly.

At some point, the Germans took over many of the plant's operations and our camp and work conditions actually improved. We were given striped prisoner uniforms (until this point we had worn civilian clothing). The SS *Sturmfuhrer* believed that in order to get good work from his laborers they must be well nourished. This man made sure our soup was hearty and thick. He also made sure one particular Polish guard did not beat me any longer.

We were taken for showers every week or so. Food was not plentiful. Because I arrived at this slave labor camp without money or valuables, I had nothing to trade for extra food or favors. I had to do extra work, even for other inmates, in order to receive additional provisions. I also learned to steal from the Polish workers' kitchen late in the night. Many times I was caught in the act and was beaten.

Occasionally, prisoners were shot if they attempted to escape. Once, in fact, I saw 12 prisoners shot in retaliation for a different group of prisoners that tried to run away.

Many Jewish inmates knew one another from home. They were either from Radom or from the same village. I knew no one and no one knew me. I was alone in this camp for two years. It might have been longer. Time passed without accountability.

One day the Jewish prisoners at the Weiss factory were ordered to march out of the camp. It may have been the summer of 1944, when the Russians were closing in from the east. We walked a very long distance, perhaps 50 miles or so, to a town called Tomaszow. There we were loaded on boxcars and sent to Auschwitz. I don't remember the journey south except that it took several days and we were given very little food or water, if any at all.

The train doors opened when we arrived at Auschwitz-Birkenau. We stumbled onto the platform, dazed and weak. Immediately, the old, the sick, the women and the children were separated and sent in another direction. The rest of us, stronger men and teen-age boys, waited on the platform. We waited and waited. And then we were put back on the trains—and taken off again—and put back on. This happened countless times.

On the platform I witnessed the arrival of many other trains. It was always the same: the SS screamed at the Jewish prisoners, dogs barked, and selections took place where the old, sick and very young were separated from those deemed fit for work. Finally, after three days, we were put back on the train and left Auschwitz-Birkenau.

We had no idea where we were headed and at this point many of us no longer cared. The train stopped in a place we guessed to be Austria. We continued on and after a few days arrived in Vaihingen, Germany, not far from Stuttgart. A concentration camp was set up when we arrived and we went to work digging stones in order to build a factory. It was a camp just for men. It was run by the German SS and the conditions were horrible.

I spent several weeks at Vaihingen before being shipped to Hessental, another concentration camp about 50 miles away, near Schwabisch Hall. This camp was also run by the SS and the inmates were all Jewish men, mostly from Poland. Most prisoners, including myself, worked on repairing an airstrip that had been badly damaged by Allied bombings. All day long we filled the gaping craters so that airplanes could safely land and take off. Strangely, in the six months or so I was in this camp, we never saw a single plane on the runway.

Like Vaihingen, the conditions at Hessental were atrocious. There was never enough food. On our long walks to and from work (approximately two kilometers each way) we often darted off into nearby ravines to grab crabapples. Even when they were frozen they tasted good! I remember the local German people watching us march under guard. I wondered what they were thinking.

That winter, 1944–1945, was one of the coldest Germany had seen in a very long time. Because I no longer had any shoes and had to wrap my feet in burlap, I had open wounds from frostbite. I couldn't work for a period of time and was fortunate to find refuge with some prisoners who worked in a carpenter's shop. There were no showers at Hessental, at least that I remember. Lice were everywhere and many prisoners died of typhus and dysentery. There were no selections; no prisoners were executed. People either worked to death or died of illness. One man sleeping next to me died in the night and lay there in the morning, stiff as a board.

There were no crematoria in Hessental. The dead were carted off by prisoners and dumped in ravines or mass graves down the road.

We knew the end of the war was approaching with the increased frequency of Allied bombings. We enjoyed the bombings, as they provided us the opportunity to run into the fields to steal turnips or potatoes while the SS were seeking shelter. We had no concern for our own safety. At this point most of us didn't care much one way or the other about anything. We were zombies.

One day, in early April, we were ordered onto trains. Less than a mile from Hessental Allied forces bombed the area and our train was hit with shrapnel and chunks of earth blasted out of the ground. Approximately 25 prisoners were injured, including me. A piece of lime from the earth slammed into my leg. Everyone disembarked and all but the injured were marched off to Allach, a major satellite camp of Dachau. It was surely a death march and many Hessental prisoners died en route.

The group of injured prisoners waited by the damaged train for several days before the train tracks and cars were repaired. I don't remember if we received any food or water from the SS but I do remember hopping on my good leg to receive food from a German farmer.

We may have traveled on the train for one week or more. I don't remember much about the journey except that there were long waits as the tracks were constantly being repaired from Allied bombing damage.

I woke up in the Dachau dispensary. I must have passed out from the pain of my injury. The dispensary was run by Soviet prisoners of war and they tattooed my forearm with my prisoner number. I was seen by a French doctor who took a special liking to me and, although he could do nothing to help my leg, he kept me protected in the camp "hospital" until I could hobble on my own.

At some point I was sent to the camp barracks, Block 28. It was intensely crowded, and death and dying were everywhere. Very few inmates were working. Most of us just went out for roll call in the morning and in the evening, and to receive a pittance of food and liquid. Corpses were pulled out of barracks all day long, piled in heaps everywhere. I didn't know what year or day it was. I was a blank man.

One day we were given civilian clothes and a package from the Red Cross. Many prisoners got sick from eating the Red Cross food: zwieback, cheese, canned ham, and chocolate. We were taken to trains but instead we were told to march. There were hundreds and hundreds of us. The camp was being emptied and we knew this death march would be our end.

We marched under the guard of Hungarian SS. Many men died along the way. After a few days, somewhere in the mountains near Garmisch-Partenkirchen, we were ordered down into a ravine. Surely, we thought, this would be where we would be finished off. It was nighttime and very cold. A late-season storm left drifts of snow two to three feet deep. We were ordered to lie on our bellies. We stayed there many hours and heard big guns all through the night.

With the first crack of dawn some men crawled out of the ravine and shouted that the SS were gone. We emerged and saw tanks with big red stars— Russians, we presumed. We were wrong. The tanks were American and we were liberated on that day, May 2, 1945, by the Third Armored Division of the U.S. Army.

Our group of surviving prisoners was taken to a German military base in Mittenwald, near the Austrian border. The first few days after liberation were chaotic. Many did not survive after liberation; they were either too sick or indulged too quickly in eating rich foods. I did not weigh much more than 80 to 90 pounds at the end of the war and I ate my fair share of food. It was probably just dumb luck that I didn't get sick as a result of my gluttony.

I decided to head out of Mittenwald after a couple of weeks. The Red Cross package I took with me was stolen from my lap while I napped on the train. When I awoke, a passenger, a Jewish survivor from Poland, told me how my package disappeared and we became friends. He convinced me to follow him to an American army base in Marlberg to find work, and we soon became lifelong best friends.

I took a room in the house of the Marlberg *burgermeister* (mayor). I worked as a field mechanic fixing stoves in an American army kitchen. I didn't know

English but I was able to get by. I grew stronger, put on weight, and looked like a human being again.

But there was nothing left of my family or my home. I made inquiries with the Red Cross and other organizations, but no one had any information about the fate of my family. I met survivors who went back to Warsaw immediately after liberation and they reported that my apartment building had been destroyed. I lost all hope of finding any family members alive.

With no home to which I could return, I was anxious to leave Europe. Many survivors were emigrating to Palestine, Australia, and the United States. Frankly, I didn't care where I went as long as it was soon. Eventually I was able to make arrangements via HIAS (Hebrew Immigration Aid Service) to go to the United States.

I arrived in New York City on September 16, 1946. No one was at the ship terminal to meet me. I knew no one in this country. HIAS gave me $3 upon my arrival and the JDC (Joint Distribution Committee) gave me $10 a week for two weeks. HIAS sent me on factory jobs, but I was always given "pink slips" to prevent me from joining the union.

For two months, I took English lessons at night but it proved too tiring after long, arduous days working in loud factories. I basically taught myself English by watching movies and trying to read the newspapers.

With my meager paychecks it was very difficult to cover my living expenses. I borrowed money from friends. After being hospitalized for kidney problems I realized I would need to work extra jobs so I could pay back my loans. I became a waiter in hotels in the Catskill Mountains in New York during the summer and in Miami Beach, Florida, during the winter.

Though I only had my "first papers" I was still required to register for the draft during the Korean conflict. Twice my number came up and twice I was deferred (perhaps because my English was poor and I could not complete the necessary forms). But the third time I was enlisted after an army psychiatrist discovered I could speak Polish, German and some Russian.

I trained at Fort Bragg, North Carolina. My platoon was shipped to Asia, but the Berlin Blockade was established and I was rerouted to Germany, where I spent the next 19 months. Germany was the last place I wanted to be, but I honored my oath and served my new country.

On weekends and short leaves from duty, I took the train to Paris to look for an aunt I believed might have survived the Holocaust. She and her new husband had left Warsaw for Paris in 1933. It was possible, I thought, that she survived. But I did not remember her married name and this meant I could not make much progress in my search. Much later, in 1964, I did find my aunt in Paris. When I contacted her by telephone and she realized who I was, she fainted! Needless to say our reunion in person several months later was very emotional. Though she and my uncle have been dead now for over 20 years, I am still close with their children, my first cousins, and their families, who still live in France.

After military duty I returned to my "snowbird" work as a waiter in New York and Florida hotels. I met my wife Ruth in Miami Beach when she was visiting her elderly parents. We married in 1958 and I worked in a coffee shop in Manhattan, first as an assistant manager and then as manager. We had two daughters. Robyn was born in 1960 and Janice in 1962.

Today, I am a member of Holocaust survivor groups. I participate in Holocaust commemorations and I support the work of Holocaust education organizations. I do this so I will never forget, and the world will never forget about the millions who were senselessly murdered. I do this so I will never forget that my parents, brothers, sister, grandparents, aunts, uncles and cousins were among these millions. I do this so genocide will never happen again.

A Story of Escape, Struggle, and Survival

by Hershel Fuksman

Before the outbreak of World War II, there were about 3,000 Jews in Piaseczno. The Jewish community was liquidated January 22–27, 1941, when all the Jews were deported to the Warsaw Ghetto and shared the fate of that community. After the war, the Jewish community was not reestablished, as was the case with most Jewish communities in Poland.

My world, my town, Piaseczno, Poland, only 16 kilometers south of Warsaw, was where my family lived honorable lives for many generations. They worked hard and loved their families and were strongly connected to the Jewish life.

My mother, Prywa, was one of five sisters (Golde, Mechle, Blime, Feige) and two brothers (Moishe Byk and Faivel). She and her sisters were admired as great beauties of the town. My father, Leibel, had a younger brother, Munish, and two sisters, Elka and Miriam, and a large extended family of grandparents, great-grandparents and even a great great-grandmother.

Mother and father were childhood sweethearts and married with approval from both families. Father's trade as a shoemaker earned enough to supply us with all our needs. Our apartment on Warshawska, with its large windows, sparkled with cleanliness and streams of sunshine.

I was born on Feb. 28, 1933. As the first grandchild, I was a joy to both sides of the family. My parents indulged me with toys of the day and even at age three with an electric car, which I rode on the sidewalks with skill and pleasure. My memories of those days fill me with a longing for those people.

Friday outings to the town square, with its plaza surrounded by buildings and the impressive steeple of the church tower, was the focus of our day. This is where a weekly market displayed foods and goods. The air was filled with aromas and clamor. My mother and I explored the stands, taking home fruits and fresh groceries. She then prepared delicious meals and special treats to entice my finicky appetite. Saturdays, after attending synagogue, we joined father's family for a hot *cholent* (crock-pot oven dish), which brought contentment and lulled all to retreat for a nap. Life was good for me.

Although the elders were Orthodox in their beliefs and looked for answers from the Almighty, my father was a progressive thinker and had leftist ideals. They proclaimed that all were equal and that Jews had the same rights as all people.

The expression of anti-Semitism and learning about the beating of Jews by the hateful hooligans was a weekly occurrence. Somehow learning to live with these expressions of hate, the population attributed these acts to drunkenness, stupidity and ignorance of the assailants.

In the years before the German attack on Poland, many stories reached our area regarding abuse, arrests, and killings. Father, not wanting to become a prisoner, especially since he would be accused of being a Communist, left Piaseczno in August 1939 with reassurances that he would send a messenger to bring us to him as soon as he was settled. Mother was in her early months of pregnancy.

On Friday, September 1, 1939, the market was bustling with people when two German soldiers, one on the motorcycle and the other sitting in the side car, caused a stir of curiosity and apprehension. They asked directions to a beer hall. That midnight mother woke me in a panic and said that our building was on fire. Looking through the window, the sky was aglow with streaks of light from the tracer bullets. As we were getting out of the house, a German soldier, with a machine gun, shouted at us to get back in. We had no choice but to obey. The smoke was thick; it was difficult to breath. Again we tried to get out and this time a Polish soldier carrying a rifle said to us: "Why are you in this burning house?" Mother told him about the German soldier who threatened us with his gun to get back in. The Polish soldier instructed us to stay low and led us to a safe house. As he was opening the door to the courtyard, I heard a loud noise and saw our soldier fall to the ground; he was shot dead by the Germans. We hurriedly continued into one of the houses, went up the stairs, and found a safe corner in which to hide.

World War II began with bombs exploding and shooting all around us. Civilians were targeted on purpose in order to break morale and make the population submissive. The Germans dynamited some buildings that the bombers had not destroyed.

The next day all was quiet. The streets were littered with dead people and cavalry horses. We had to step over bodies. We could not avoid the carnage that was all around us. The Germans came in and controlled with directives and with threats to life.

Immediately, the Germans conscripted all Jewish men and had them dig mass graves to bury the dead. They had the men clean the streets of debris that had fallen from the damaged, bombed buildings. When they ran out of work, they had them transfer fallen leaves from one place and then back. They created work when no special work was available or needed. These acts, singling out the Jewish population, caused confusion, anxiety and fear. The oppression of the populace was immediate. They issued rations cards to control the population.

When we ventured outside, the Polish women accosted mother and me, stripping us of any valuables including outer jackets and shoes, to the approving looks of the Germans. My mother used her courageous attitude to stand her ground and not succumb to abuse. She retaliated, turning the tables against the Polish women. She told the German soldiers that they were speaking and cursing the soldiers and Germany. The soldiers chased the women away who yelled at mother "*Zhydowka* (Jewish) Witch," which fortunately the Germans did not understand.

We returned to our burned out leaky-roofed house and continued to live in one room trying to keep warm and dry as winter approached. We waited for the guide to come and take us away to meet up with father.

Mother struggled to keep us fed. The rations offered very little food so she resorted to barter for anything that she had, to keep us going. Most of the support came from my father's family who wanted us to move in with them, but mother would not hear of it; she was sure the guide was coming and wanted to be in the place where he would find us. We lived under the Germans for more than five months.

Finally in February, 1940, the promised guide appeared to take us away. Mother packed two suitcases for herself, a back pack and small suitcase for me, ready to follow the guide. We made the rounds to our family, saying goodbye. They tried to convince mother to remain, especially since she was far along in her pregnancy. Mother, in turn, begged them to come with us, but they refused and stated that they would be okay, that once the Germans establish their power things would not be bad. I knew that a great change was happening in my young life but could not possibly understand, just as no one could fathom the devastation that would happen to my dear family.

Our first journey with the guide was on a train that lasted about half a day. It was an adventure that I was afraid to explore or enjoy because mother warned me to remain quiet, unnoticed. We then continued on a horse-drawn wagon to a small village not far from Bialystok. The guide directed us to the border and said that he would not continue with us. He also told us that the only way to get in was to sneak in.

We listened to the guide's instructions and stood at a distance trying to figure out a strategy. We saw that most were turned away, beaten and some arrested. Mother saw our dilemma and could not arrive at a solution of how to succeed.

The village was overrun with refugees; we could not find anyone to take us in. For days we rattled about without any hope of crossing. We were hungry and without shelter. Following the example of others, mother dug us in a deep shelter in a large haystack, night after night. The Germans and collaborators patrolled the haystacks and poked them with sharp pitchforks to expose and even kill the refugees. Mother covered me with her body and said, "If I get hit, in the morning go to the border and cross by yourself. Your father will be there." We lived like this for two weeks, staying in the same clothes and not taking off our boots, which caused our legs to swell.

Two weeks is an eternity to live with hardly any food or shelter. Mother became desperate and came up with a plan. She said with determination. "Today we cross. Whatever I do you do and don't question me." We approached the border without being detected and then turned about and began to walk backwards to appear as if we were escaping into Poland. The guard stopped us, asking where we were going to which mother answered, "I don't want to be in Bialystok, I am going back to Poland." This ruse worked. He ordered us to return back to Bialystok to the Russian side. With nerve and the last effort, we walked into Russia. This success rejuvenated us, especially since we hoped to be reunited with father. And as we were walking deeper a few yards, there was father, just a short distance away, with a happy grin, holding a large loaf of bread for us. Our reunion was emotional and with great relief, hugging, crying. Father took me in his arms and carried me to his apartment. To be able to be in a dwelling, to take off the coats was a pleasure, but because our legs were swollen, father had to cut off the boots from our feet.

Life in Bialystok was a struggle. It was overflowing with refugees. We shared our meager quarters with our hometown acquaintances, which made our life feel more connected to our homes. Even though father's trade earned our subsistence, he thought it would be better to get away from the border with an offer of a better job in Magnitogorsk, where my brother was born in March 1940. The conditions there were appalling. We lived in a room of a barrack, sharing the primitive facilities with other workers. The winter was brutal and after a month my parents decided to go back to Bialystok, to our rooms where we left our Piaseczno friends.

After a few days, in the middle of the night, a knocking sent the two single young men hiding in the attic, as father answered the door. Without any ceremony or advising why, he was arrested and taken away. After days of searching for answers why father was taken and how to get him released, mother found out that he was inducted into the Soviet army. The Soviets questioned and asked her if she wanted to remain in Bialystok Russia [now in Poland], to which she replied that she wanted to go back to her family now that she was alone with two little children. They registered her and calmly assured her that she would be sent back as soon as there was transportation.

About June 1940, the police came to take us to the train to travel to Poland; instead we, including our apartment companions, became political prisoners and were sent off to Wak Wat –KOMI USSR, Siberia. Our group of 100 families and a number of children, all Jews, were deposited in two log barracks with big gaps to expose the weather, in the depth of a Siberian forest.

Finding ourselves in this foreign place with strangers, with only a couple of acquaintances from our hometown was a shock. The severe conditions, great hunger, without funds and very little left to barter, put us off balance. Mother was required to work in the forests, chopping down trees to match a quota, for which she received 100 grams of bread to feed herself without any consideration or provisions for me. My little brother, three months old, was held in a nursery school during the day, where he received meager food, while I remained in the barrack to fend for myself without anyone to look over me or provide for me.

Mother and her friend Herman found jobs after they finished their shift chopping down trees. They worked for the natives in the garden, cleaned houses, took care of farm animals, just to earn another piece of bread, a potato, a handful of grain, or an onion. The indigenous people were Tartars, most were Muslims. They are fair-skinned with Mongol features.

During these long hungry days, I ventured outside exploring and was befriended by an old Tartar woman who had no children of her own and took a liking to me. She sneaked some food to me, hiding me in her skirt folds so that her husband would not see.

We were imprisoned in this bitter land for 18 months without hearing a word from father. The newspapers applauded the victories but we knew that the Communists exaggerated and knew that the casualties were great. Mother lamented that father had been killed and was convinced that she was alone, a widow with two little children among strangers. The only security and trust that she had was in her hometown friend, who felt sorry for her and her plight and shared his occasional food packages that he received from his family in Kiev. These packages saved our lives. After two years, she married him and we became a family.

Around October 1942, the Soviets offered the Polish men to train for the Anders Polish Army that was being formed in exile. This event freed us from Siberia, (out of 100 families, only eight survived and only two children, my little brother and me) and we were able to resettle in Kyrgyzstan, Talman Kolchoz, at a communal farm. Many men volunteered, mostly single, without families, who trained to join the Anders army and marched away towards the East and Iran.

Even though the climate in this area was warm most of the year, life was difficult and we suffered severe hunger. Mother and my stepfather tried anything they could to maintain us. Thanks to a Polish priest who my stepfather befriended and helped him as a go-between, he provided us with a little food from time to time, which we were able to share with a number of the refugees.

After a few months at the farm, we moved to Bagish, Kyrgyzstan, where conditions did not improve, actually were even worse. The hunger was beyond endurance. For six months, the only food we had was grass, which mother boiled in water. The desperation to keep body and soul together drove me to walk around the town singing songs—begging for food—and on occasion I was given a piece of bread, which I carried back with a sense of triumph to my mother.

I did attend a Polish school with other Jewish children, walking 5 kilometers for two seasons, where we were given some food. I could not continue during the winter months because I had no shoes.

I remember hearing that the war was raging and many casualties were falling. Yet, I hoped that an end to this brutal existence may come, especially when on a few occasions we were doled out some American canned food. It seemed like another world was reaching out to us, the forgotten suffering displaced people. This meager, occasional gift was like opening a window, that something good is out there. We dreamed of not being hungry, of having a life that offered hope and a better tomorrow.

By 1944, the war front was moving further away from Russia. Conditions for the population began to improve and so it did for the displaced. Mother, with her dauntless dedication to save and sustain the family, began a little enterprise, to fry *pirogy*, thin dough buns filled with mashed potatoes. This was considered black marketeering and was really illegal under Communism, but she took these chances to keep the family fed and by enlisting me as the peddler at the train station. I was less likely to be arrested as compared to an adult.

When the war came to an end, the Polish citizens were given the opportunity to return back to Poland. We were a family of six now, two little sisters, my little brother, me and my parents. We boarded cattle cars on April 9, 1946, and began our slow journey back home, to Poland. There were many rumors that terrible things happened in Poland. We wondered and contemplated what we would find of our previous lives and families.

The journey of almost two months, being sidetracked often to give right-of-way to more important transport, again created problems in sustenance, how to maintain sanitary conditions, fresh water, no privacy even for personal needs. We were finally brought to Poland, where we were greeted with stones, jeers and shouts, "*Zhydo Do Palestiny*"—Jews to Palestine.

The train took us directly to Stettin where the remnant survivors were gathered. Those that arrived right after the war were able to get housing, but our late arrival gave us only shelter in a bombed-out building. Work was not available for Jews, even to sort bricks from bombed-out buildings. The only alternative was to stand in day-long lines for rations that were doled out to the masses by UNRA.

The tragic history of what happened to all our families struck us with disbelief. How could such premeditated atrocities happen, helped by collaborators, neighbors? Our entire extended family was wiped out. No trace is left, no grave marker. They are part of the ashes of Auschwitz, Treblinka, Majdanek. The only family that I discovered years later were a couple of cousins who escaped to Russia and one hid in the forests and fought the Nazis with the partisans.

Jews came to realize that Poland was not home anymore. People tried to get out by all means and so did we. After six months of struggling to keep the family fed and cared for, it was decided that we too must leave. The organized Jewish *Bricha* ("escape" in Hebrew) helped to arrange clandestine crossings by paying off a border patrol with some money, whiskey and/or sausages. We were taken in a canvas-covered truck, in the dark of night and brought to the displaced persons camp in the British Zone, Bergen-Belsen, Germany.

Bergen-Belsen was known for being a concentration camp, which killed people by sheer neglect, starvation, filth and disease in addition to being abused or beaten. The mass graves are a dimensional witness to the cruelty and murder that happened there. The Jewish DP camp leaders erected a monument to the victims of Bergen-Belsen, which remembers those who suffered and died with cruelty and were buried in mass graves.

The truck brought us to another section where the German army barracks now served as housing and a means of survival for about 11,000 Jews from all parts of Europe.

Bergen-Belsen, a tragic place for Jews, was also where the survivors renewed their lives and hopes for a future. Many young couples formed families, and the birth of children was extraordinary. The parade of young mothers with babies was a defiance that Hitler and his followers did not succeed.

My education really started here, in Bergen-Belsen. It first began in a Jewish Orthodox *cheder* (religious studies school) and then I transferred to the public school of the DP camp, where we learned Hebrew and other studies. I grew up taking on many responsibilities in helping our family succeed and provide our daily needs and concerns for the well being of my siblings.

In 1951, my family and I immigrated to the United States and settled in Chicago where we established roots and permanence without fear. I continued with my education while working to help the family. In 1954, I married Zelda Marbell. I served in the U.S. Army from 1958 to 1960 as a medic and was stationed in Ft. Devens, Massachusetts. After we returned to Chicago, we again had to rebuild our lives. I became an insurance agent and a father of two wonderful daughters who provided us with two granddaughters. They are our symbol of rebirth, not only of our families but also the Jewish people and remembering the six million.

In evaluating my life, my struggles and those of the murdered six million

Jews has left me with a message and lesson that we must live our lives by extending dignity and acceptance of all people. We must guard against an evil that would take away any rights of security, freedom of speech and religion. All people deserve their humanity and rights to a safe life!

Grandfather Moishe and Great Great Grandmother Bube Reshke

I Was a Child Alone

by Leon Ginsburg

I was born in 1932 in Maciejow, a small town in eastern Poland. My family consisted of my mother; an older sister, Blimele, and a brother, Hershel. My beautiful mother, Pesel, was an intelligent and concerned parent who became the sole provider for our family when my father, Kalman, died when I was just one year old. Although I have no memories of him, the affection and description of father by my mother has left an engraved picture of a man with black velvety hair. My mother's voice still reverberates in my mind as I hear her calling me Noikele, a name I cling to and which serves as a connection to my lost family.

My 80-year-old grandmother not only fulfilled the role of a grandparent, but also gave my mother the freedom to be the breadwinner for our family. She made us feel protected and lavished us with love and tasty treats. Mother ran her own fabric store, which attracted Jewish and Polish ladies for their sewing needs. The store also became a gathering place where the local ladies exchanged gossip and stories. My childhood was filled with laughter and fun—days were full of play with the children of the neighborhood and events that brought out much creativity and amusement. My paternal grandparents, who lived nearby in their own house and earned their livelihood in their own shoes business, enhanced our lives with a circle of love and safety.

September 1, 1939, was a date that shocked our world. Poland was attacked by Germany in the west, and Soviet Russia occupied eastern Poland, where our town was located. Soon, displaced Jews from cities under German occupation came to our area and seemed dazed and without direction. They spoke of an evil that befell Poland and the Jews. All heard but could not fathom such tales. We heard of their struggles and fears, but we felt safe under the Soviets. They stopped anti-Semitism by the locals and gave us hope. How could one not accept Soviet security and an end of anti-Semitism? Communism espoused freedom and opportunity for all. All one had to do was work hard and cooperate with the dogma. And so the town fell into step with a new normalcy that did not threaten or abuse. We lived in peace with all our neighbors and attended school under the Soviet tutorship.

In June 1941, when the Germans attacked the Russians and marched into Maciejow, I was just 10 years old and witnessed the first outpouring of hatred against Jews. A rabbi, with a display of bread and salt as a peaceful gesture of welcome, was shoved and told to get out of their sight. Suddenly, everything changed. Later that summer we learned that a mobile detachment of SS *Einsatzgruppen* had arrived in town. They quickly took control of our town. Persecution of the Jews started immediately. Jews were ordered to wear a white armband with a blue Star of David on it. We were restricted from leaving town and a 6 p.m. curfew was established and enforced. Then, an order was given that all men from the ages of 16 to 60 report to the center of town to validate their passports. I saw them lined up in rows and marched off, guarded by soldiers with machine guns, to the German headquarters, where they were shot. That was the beginning of organized and random killings.

At this time, they did not kill children. Our family was able to evade the roundups and the evil quieted down until 1942, when mass killings were carried out in nearby towns. The next time we heard of an SS group arriving in town, we went to my grandparents' house to hide. I faced German soldiers and their guns when they came to my grandfather Yakov's house, where most of the family was gathered. This incident is imprinted in my mind to this day. My grandmother, mother, sister and aunts were concealed in a corner of the attic, camouflaged by objects so that they would not be readily seen, while grandfather, my brother, and I stayed in the house. In those days, young children and the elderly were not taken away. We went to bed early and did not dare to use any lights in the house.

Outside I heard German voices from across the street, and young girls, our Ukrainian neighbor's daughters, were laughing happily as they socialized with the SS officers. None was concerned with the deadly measures taking place against the Jews. It got quiet for a while, and then I heard the sound of boots and the German voices coming closer to the house. I saw a flashlight shining on the ceiling through the window, as the footsteps were approaching our door. This was followed by a loud knocking. A command in German "*Yakob, Aufmachen*"—"Yakob, open up." It was apparent that someone had betrayed us because grandfather's name was used.

My brother Herschel was afraid to go to the door, so I went. When I opened the door, two big SS officers walked in carrying flashlights and started looking about. They asked me where my sisters were. I told them that they had been taken away, and with bravado I asked if they knew where they are. The officers continued their search, looking in the cellar and then asked about the attic. Not showing my anxiety, I pointed to the opening. They lowered the drop ladder and asked me if anyone was up there. I answered, "no" with an assured voice.

One of the SS officers took his revolver from his holster, put it to my forehead, cocked it, and again asked if anyone was up there; again, I said no without blinking an eye. "If someone is up there you are kaput," he said. The other officer climbed up to the attic and searched. I was transfixed, holding on to my innocent appearance even when I heard some noise as he stumbled over something in the dark. The officer continued to hold the gun to my head and asked his companion if he found anyone. He replied, "No." They then ordered me to lead them to the garden. I guided them to the back door to the garden, passing an area right under the attic, where my family was hidden. Any sound would have given them away. Finally, they walked away toward the road. Then my teeth starting chattering. I got back into bed. My brother held me tight to keep me from convulsive trembling.

Hiding became an art during those horrible days. Three of my aunts who were in the attic survived the war. By August 1942, the Germans unleashed an attempt at total genocide against the Jews. After the massacres in nearby communities, my town had to face the killings, carried out by the Germans and their collaborators, the Ukrainians. My mother, sensing that our turn for selection was coming, arranged for our family to hide in a secreted place. The entrance was under a moveable toilet, through a tunnel to a room underground. There were about 50 people with us, including a woman with five children and a little toddler who would not stop crying. Fearing that the child would be heard and give away our hiding place, the woman took the child upstairs, where she finally fell asleep. The mother left her there alone and returned to the hiding place. This occurred on the second day of Rosh Hashanah. All the houses were being searched for Jews and when they came into our house they discovered the child, who was asked to find her mother. She led them to the toilet and we were discovered. Mother, seeing a chance to hide me behind some boards that covered a window, told me to stay hidden while she hid between bedding and a mattress. Two Ukrainian policemen came down to the basement, looting valuables and stuffing them into their pockets. One was probing the bedding with a bayonet where mother was hiding and stabbed her. She screamed "No, no, I am coming out." The sound of her painful voice still rings in my ears. I didn't know how bad she was hurt. Those were the last words I heard from my mother.

I don't know where I got the strength or cunning to keep my composure and hold the boards in place. I stopped breathing and was not discovered. I stayed there, not knowing what to do. I had no one to advise me or help me. I was a child alone. After a few hours, I heard someone speaking in Yiddish. Recognizing a Jewish neighbor, I crept out from my hiding place. He came searching for rubber galoshes so he could hide in the woods. I followed him to his attic to stay out of sight. After a while, we heard Ukrainian militiaman in the house who spotted and arrested the neighbor; I escaped being discovered. Again alone, I was petrified, not knowing what to do and where to go. I knew I had to get away from the approaching soldiers, who were systematically looting Jewish houses and were getting nearer. I was panicked; I didn't know where to go. Remembering another hiding place in a nearby house, which mother had told me about, I stealthily made my way there, and as I was trying to squeeze through the tiny opening, feeling light headed, someone grabbed me and pulled me in and revived me with a drizzle of whisky on my lips.

There were a number of people hiding there, and it appeared that they had prepared for a long siege with a barrel of water and other supplies. Before long, we ran out of food and I ventured out to bring back some food. Along the way, I was recognized by a local youngster who knew me. I returned his glare with bluster, implying that I had a gun and would shoot him if he continued to pursue me. This stopped him and in those few minutes I realized that I was not a child any more, that I had to make life and death decisions for me; I had to save myself.

My hiding place was soon discovered. With a sense of survival, I made a decision to sneak out through a little window as the rest of the companions were taken away by the Ukrainian collaborators. Who is my friend? Where can I find shelter? These questions came to my mind as I remembered my grandfather's farmer friend who lived outside of town. I made my way there, but when he spotted me he cautioned me to remain in the nearby bushes. He said that he could not help me because the entire village was collaborating with the Germans. He advised me to continue to the ghetto in Luboml. And so I went, hoping to find my uncle Falik's house and safety.

The house was filled with people, including two of my aunts who had managed to get away from Maciejow. I was comforted that I was among my own family. I was still someone's child. I fell into a stupor-like sleep, relieved that I did not have to run anymore. After a few days, my brother Herschel also came to the ghetto, telling us of his own escape from death. He was wounded in the leg, but had escaped the searchers' notice. That night my brother promised me that he would never leave me again. But that was not to be. When selections started in the ghetto, my family and a number of people hid in a secluded room behind the fireplace where we waited for the selection to stop.

On the second day, our place was discovered. I woke up at four in the morning to the sound of gunfire. I knew what was going on: they were rounding up Jews, just as they had done in Maciejow. I ran to a second-floor window and saw Germans and Ukrainians with guns, bayonets, dogs, and large sticks, chasing people out of their homes in their nightshirts. Having experienced such events in Maciejow, I knew that we were trapped. I decided to sneak out, but was discovered by a Ukrainian who demanded gold for my safety. I crawled back and urged those hiding to give the jewelry to the policemen before more policemen arrived. As these policemen started to divide the loot, I motioned to my brother to follow me. He was so petrified that I had to pull him by his hair to get him out. As the policemen were absorbed and busy with the jewelry, I inched over to a window. Getting onto the window ledge I motioned to my brother to get up with me. A Ukrainian spotted us and ordered that we come down, but in that moment someone from the hiding place handed him more loot and his attention was diverted. Suddenly another policeman noticed what I was doing, pointed his rifle at me, clicked it, and yelled, "Get down or I will kill you like a dog!" I was sure that I was trapped. Sensing greed, I offered him a fountain pen that I had on me to let me go, but he refused. I visualized myself being marched to the pits to be shot. Not thinking of consequences any more, my brother and I ran to a bedroom up the stairs and hid under a bed. Miraculously, we were not discovered by our pursuers.

Herschel and I stayed concealed, changing hiding places. After a while we heard our companions from the hiding place being led away to their slaughter. A cousin's little daughter, eight years old, asked her mother, "Are they going to shoot us?" I could not hear nor bear to hear the answer. Our search to hide and keep body and soul together finally caught up with my brother. He was trapped in a hiding place, while I was away searching for food. My brother was discovered by the Germans and I never saw him again.

Alone again, I did not know what to do. Fortunately, I met up with my 19-year-old cousin, Esther, who was leading a group of six survivors into the woods, away from Luboml. Of course I followed. It was so dark I had to hold on to someone so I would not get lost. We had to cross a railroad track that was lit up with flares by the Germans in the area. When there was a short lull between flares, we ran fast, darting across the tracks.

The night was black as we trudged through the debris and thickets of the forest. Finally, we stopped for a rest near a Christian cemetery. I immediately fell into a deep sleep. When I awoke I found that I was alone; my companions were gone. My fright of ghosts and goblins was real, but my need to survive was stronger. Feeling my way in the darkness, I noticed a dark shadow and headed for it. It turned out to be a farmhouse with a barn, where I found shelter sleeping next to the warm breath of the cow. With the crack of dawn, fearing I would be discovered, I pulled myself up to the hayloft as the farmer's wife came to milk the cow. I coughed gently to get her attention, but it startled her. I reassured her that I meant no harm; I was lost and stopped to rest, I said, and I would leave right away. She said, "Don't leave now. Wait until the shepherd comes and takes the cows out." She brought me some of the fresh warm milk and a piece of bread. This feast almost made me feel secure that I had found a kind heart to help me. But as I lay hidden, I heard voices saying that there were Jews hidden in the graveyard who had gold and money. I knew that they must be talking about my cousin and companions and we were all in mortal danger. We were now in danger of the local peasants. Without bringing any attention to myself, I made my way to the cemetery and located my cousin and warned her about the impending attack. It was decided that it would be best to go to the next town, a couple of days away, to a ghetto that was still in existence. The weather was turning and the overnight stay in the outdoors froze the clothing on our bodies.

At one point, I volunteered to go into the woods to search for one of my cousins who had been separated from us. I wandered about, lost for most of the day. Without success, I returned to the group but I was exhausted and was lagging behind the others. Suddenly, I heard a noise behind me. It was a Ukrainian policeman on a bicycle armed with a rifle. He rode past me and then stopped, shooting his rifle in the air and yelling. I dropped to the ground and started to crawl away. I realized that he had not seen me. More Ukrainian militia were coming. I knew they were willing collaborators with the Germans. I started to run into a valley shielded by the dark evening. They must have heard my running and shot in my direction. Fortunately they did not injure me; the bullets just grazed my shoe.

Not wanting to be in the open, I crawled into a drainage pipe that went under the road. Luckily, the pipe curved so that when the police shined a flashlight into the pipe, it did not reach the curve where I was hiding. I was crouched in the pipe, afraid to get out. The sounds from above told me terrible things were happening. My cousins were caught and taken away. The stress and exertion of my wanderings made me collapse into sleep. When I awoke, I sensed that it was almost morning. I was afraid to get out of my hiding place. I stayed hidden in the drainage pipe for a long time. Finally, I did not hear any sounds from above. I dared to peek and found that it was safe to come out. With childish courage, I stuck out my head and saw that it was still dark and did not see anyone outside. I overcame my fear, got out, and started to walk. As I was passing a farm near a village, two large dogs began to bark. I was afraid they would wake up the farmer, so I stopped and crept past the farm.

It was still dark when I reached a fork in the road. Not knowing which way to go, I decided to take a chance and head for a farm I spotted a short distance from the road. I was exhausted and decided to find a place to rest in a hole in a haystack. I crawled in and immediately fell asleep. Suddenly I was torn from my sleep by a pitchfork and cursing as a woman from the farm was jabbing at my hiding place. She thought an animal was hiding in the haystack. Afraid that she would stab me, I stuck out my hand, which caused her to scream for her husband. He arrived in no time and demanded to know who I was. I decided to tell him the truth—that I was Falik Ginsburg's nephew from Luboml. The farmer nodded at me with astonishment and pity. He was well-acquainted with and respected my uncle and finally I received a friendly look from someone. He gave me milk and bread and directions to the village of another farmer named Sliva, who knew my mother and perhaps would provide my safe haven.

As I was walking on the road, a wagonful of Ukrainian police were traveling in my direction. It was Sunday, they seemed drunk, and were rowdy. I could not run without bringing attention to myself, so I walked indifferently, looking into the fields away from them. I figured that if they went after me, I was ready to run toward the field and be shot rather than be taken alive. To my relief, they passed me by, and didn't pay attention to me. They must have taken me for a Ukrainian. And so I continued walking. I walked the entire day. It started to get dark, when I noticed a small house near the woods. I approached silently and peered through the window. A woman and her young daughter were inside. They seemed safe to me, so I knocked on the door. I told them that I needed directions. The woman opened the door and gave me instruction to continue through the woods for about 5 kilometers, but since night was approaching and after consulting with her daughter, she offered to have me sleep in the attic. She warned me that her husband must not know of my presence. She said that he was away playing cards and would probably be drunk when he got back. She told me she would let me know when it was safe to come down from the attic, which she did. She gave me something to eat and I left for the Sliva farm, which was recommended by the first farmer.

When Mrs. Sliva saw me, she was shocked to see me alive and crossed herself uttering, "Oh my God." She told me to get to the attic because it is dangerous for both them and me. Mr. Sliva said that he was suspected of helping Jews and I could not remain with them. They would let me stay one night, but I understood that I could hang out longer when he told me that many farmers left the small door to the barn open at night. In this farming colony, most of the people were Seventh Day Adventists. They were more tolerant, and it was therefore safer for me to hide out in the area. I used to sneak into Mr. Sliva's barn at night and sleep in the hay and leave at the sound of the rooster's morning crow.

When Mr. Sliva told me he was going to Vlodzimer Volinsk, I asked him if I could come with him. I knew that the Jewish ghetto was still there and that was where my cousins were heading when they were captured. At four in the morning, Mr. Sliva dropped me near the ghetto and we made plans to meet a week later. At the gate a Ukrainian policeman with a rifle in hand asked me where I was going. I told him that my family was inside so he just let me walk in.

As soon as I entered I realized that I was trapped; the ghetto was encircled with barbed wire and was guarded by armed Ukrainian police. I began to wonder how I would get out. First, I searched for warm clothing. No one had anything left to give me. But in one of the abandoned houses I found a ripped sheepskin coat and some army shoes, both for the same foot. I was overjoyed to have found these treasures. A friendly woman mended the coat for me. To this day I think of her sad but kind eyes.

The people in the ghetto were helpless and hopeless. A month earlier, I was told, the German SS, with the help of the Ukrainian police, had liquidated a large part of the ghetto, killing 18,000 Jews. Only about 3,000 young people were left. I started planning how to get out. I noticed that in the morning, after the workers had their watery soup made from potato peels, they walked to the gate and lined up in rows.Two Ukrainian policemen counted them, opened the gate, marched them out and returned to lock the gate.

One morning, I put on the sheepskin coat and big shoes and when the policemen went to open the gate, I got into a line.They marched us out. When they turned their backs to close the gate, I got away from the prisoners and walked away. I went into a destroyed store to hide and expected them to shoot me. Once again I was lucky; the guards didn't see me.

I went to the meeting place with farmer Sliva, but he wasn't there. I waited a while but it was too dangerous to hang around very long so close to the ghetto. The important thing was to not draw attention to myself; Jews were still being killed everywhere. Finally, I started walking and eventually I met up with Mr. Sliva, who took me back to his farm. I then went to a farming family who agreed to let me stay. To my surprise this family already had other Jews hiding in their barn. I spent the entire winter there.

When spring came, I got a job pasturing cows. I worked for Mr. Huber. It was now almost a year since the Ukrainians helped the Germans murder the Jews in my town. Now they decided to get rid of the Polish families in the region. Organized groups of Ukrainians started attacking Polish villages. Some of the Seventh Day Adventists believed, as many Jews did, that God would protect them. Just like the Jews, these Poles were murdered. Forty thousand were killed there during that period. The family I was staying with knew the attack was to come against them. They sent me out on the road to watch for the attackers. When I heard shots, I ran back and joined the family. We all went with horse and wagon to my hometown for German protection. Mr. Huber registered me with a new name; I became Stanislaw Kwiatkowski, a Catholic.

We were all sent by train to western Poland. Mr. Huber and his family went to the city of Chelm, which once had a population of about 20,000 Jews. No Jews were left there now. Mr. Pyra, the mayor of a suburb, came to greet the unfortunate Poles who had been attacked by the Ukrainians. Mr. Huber told him that I worked for him and the Ukrainians had killed my entire Catholic family. Mr. Pyra took me to work on his farm, pasturing his cows.

During the summer of 1943, Hitler's SS Totenkopf Panzer division, which had suffered major losses on the Russian front, was withdrawn to be refitted, and was stationed near Mr. Pyra's farm. Several high-ranking officers took over a part of Mr. Pyra's house. Assuming I was Catholic, they tried to be friendly and offered me candy. When I got close and noticed the "skull and bone" on their uniform, I recognized that it was the same SS division that had killed the Jews in my town. I was frightened and worried that I might expose myself by showing my hatred for them. I was afraid to look in their eyes. They left several months later for the Russian front.

In the summer of 1944, I was liberated by the Russian army. I went to a DP camp in the American zone of Germany. In December 1946, I came to the United States with a group of orphans. I worked my way through college and became an electrical engineer. I married Betty Hellner, also a Holocaust survivor . We have three children and six grandchildren.

Although the United States has given me a chance to build a new life, nothing has allowed me to forget all that I witnessed as a young child.

Children's Journey to Stay Alive

by Regina (Rosa Feld) Glinzman

In 1933, my father, Abraham Feld, a twin and one of nine children, moved from Poland to Antwerp, Belgium, at the urging of his older brother, Zelig, who, seeking a better life, had moved earlier and established a grocery business. Father found that he, too, could sink roots here and build a better life. His grocery store on Langelemme Straas provided an acceptable livelihood, which gave him the means to marry his sister-in-law's best friend, Leni Schwimmer, who was from Munkacs, Czechoslovakia.

Father was a tall attractive man with soft blue eyes that exuded confidence and friendship. His integrity and honesty were admirable traits, and no doubt were the cause of his early deportation. Mother, of average height and darker complexion, presented an image of calm beauty and assurance. They were in their 20s when they married.

I was born on March 26, 1935, followed by my sister, Esther, just 20 months later. We were a welcome addition and were cherished and spoiled with love and a good life. While father was a pushover, mother was the disciplinarian. The family followed the customs of Orthodox Jews and I have pleasant memories of walking with my extended family to the synagogue every Saturday dressed in our holiday apparel, with expectations of a special meal with the family.

Because both of my parents worked in the store, we were well cared for by a German nanny in our apartment on the third floor. She exposed us to the German language, which became one of many languages I learned in my youth. My little sister became not only my playmate but served at times as my doll when I pushed her around in a doll pram down the street. Before the war reached our area, I attended kindergarten and looked forward with delight to the fun of learning even though the torturous taste of cod liver oil was a daily dose for each child.

On May 10, 1940, Germany invaded Belgium—which had a Jewish population of 100,000—and quickly occupied most of the country. After the first few terrifying days of shooting and explosion of bombs, life seemed to go back to normal and my parents were able to conduct business again. But this was the calm before the storm. Once entrenched, the Germans issued restrictions against the Jewish community.

Anti-Jewish actions began in the autumn of 1940. One of the first decrees was the banning of ritual (kosher) slaughter and other religious rites. Many actions followed, prohibiting Jews from various professions. By 1941, the Germans began to seize property, set up curfews, and confine Jews to cities. In early 1942, everyone over the age of five was required to wear the yellow Star of David outside of their homes. In September, the SS began rounding up the Jewish population and deporting them, mostly to Auschwitz.

> *In 1942 the Nazis had difficulty finding Belgian police officers who would help them put yellow badges on Jews. Initially, when the Germans had trouble identifying the Jews, most Belgians refused to assist and actually many helped Jews. Christian families hid Jewish children and usually honored their requests against baptism. After the war, almost all Jewish children were returned to their families.*

Like most Jews, my parents tried to find a way to escape Belgium, but to no avail. By 1942, my parents were no longer allowed to run their business, and, in the summer of 1942, father received a notice, delivered by a Belgian policeman, to report to the police station where he would be transported to a labor camp. Uncle Zelig urged him to take the family and run off to a remote region of Belgium. But father feared that if were caught there would be reprisals against the entire family. So he obeyed the summons and reported as notified. Of course, he did not realize that the labor camp was Auschwitz. He left in August 1942 and was killed in November 1942.

> *We did not know about his death until at least 40 years later when my son found my father's name in a book at Yad Vashem in Israel with the date of his arrival and death in Auschwitz. Many years later we also learned that my mother had been killed in Auschwitz.*

Not able to find hiding places for the three of us, mother decided that the only way to save my sister and me was to place us in a Catholic orphanage. One day, without telling us where we were going, she took us to a place in Antwerp. My most heart-wrenching recollection is the moment when we were led through a door that was shut behind us; mother remained on the outside and my sister and I on the inside. We clung to each other trying to find comfort. I was seven years old and Esther five. I could not understand why our loving mother would abandon us in this unfamiliar place to the care of strangers.

The nuns received us without exhibiting any emotions or comfort. They declared with firm voices that we were never to speak Yiddish or even mention that we were Jewish; our names were to be Regine and Estelle Felix. We held on to each other, finding little consolation; we had no one else who would reassure and protect us. We were in a state of fright much of the time.

The nuns hid us in a barn, in a nook surrounded by a haystack, during daylight hours. We sat there all day whispering in each other's ear so as not to be noticed, without food or water or even a pail for bodily needs. We were supplied with a change of clothes once a week. The conditions were spartan, but we survived.

This orphanage also served as a day school for the children of German officers. Only after school hours were we allowed out of the barn and only then were we allowed to speak to each other. When it became too dangerous to stay there we were shuttled from place to place, traveling at night, hidden in a car or a truck, always afraid but not knowing exactly what the danger was. Sometimes we were concealed in private houses, sometimes in other orphanages. Luckily, my sister and I always stayed together, which saved our sanity.

Years later we learned that a Christian women's organization was responsible for making all the arrangements in all these hiding places for us. The women did so at great risk to themselves. Because of such heroic people, a higher proportion of Jews was saved in Belgium than most other occupied countries.

Our living conditions, as a rule, were tolerable if at times severe. Not being able to keep clean, I developed a severe case of impetigo. My conscience was tested on many occasions when I was given ham, a forbidden non-kosher food. Even in those days of unbearable hunger, the idea of eating pork turned my stomach. My salvation was the pet dogs that learned to hang about near me. I sneaked the ham to the pets who became my companions, assured of a secret treat.

The deportation of Jews from Belgium began in the summer of 1942. Public protests on behalf of the Jews, along with the intervention of Belgium's queen mother, made the Nazis direct their efforts on the thousands of foreign Jews living in Belgium.

While many Belgian Jews went underground, many were deported to the gas chambers at Auschwitz. More than 16,000 were taken away between August and October 1942.

In 1944 we were sent to an orphanage in the Belgian village of Wesembeek-Oppem, where many Jewish refugee children were taken in. Again I had to face a new challenge of learning a new language. By this time I was able to speak Yiddish, German and Flemish; now I had to learn French.

In the winter of 1944, when Germany was sending V-2 rockets across

Belgium aimed at England, it became too dangerous to stay in Wesembeek. We were sent to another orphanage in a remote region of Belgium, which turned out to be in the area of one of the fiercest battles between the Germans and Allies, the Battle of the Bulge. The Jewish children were interspersed with the Catholic children; no one could distinguish the Jewish children from those who were Catholic.

The Germans occupied the orphanage and used the building as a fortress against the approaching Allies, while all the children were sent to a basement, bringing along whatever food we had in the kitchen. We slept on the ground on straw and had to use a barrel for our bathroom needs. We were forced to stay there for seven days without seeing daylight.

The American army captured the town. We were liberated by the Palestinian Brigade—who were part of the British army—sporting Jewish Stars on their sleeves. We were taken back to the orphanage in Wesembeek. It was spring 1945.

All the children in the home were in a state of limbo, not knowing if they still had a family who would claim them. Soon after liberation, survivors of the camps came looking for their children. The reunions were overwhelming. The tears, the love, the desperation that was in the air pierced my heart. Every time someone came to the home, I looked with a sense of expectation and hope. But I also was fearful that no one would come for us. And so it was: No one came for us.

In 1946, riding on a bicycle throughout Belgium for eight days, Uncle Zelig found us. He, his wife, and three children had survived hiding on a remote farm, as he wanted my father to do. When he saw us, he was frozen with both shock and happiness. It had been four years since we were separated from mother and the family. We had forgotten that we were part of a family, that we belonged somewhere and that we were loved. Estelle and I had to relearn that we deserved to be valued and cared for and to adjust with the horrific fact that our parents were not coming to us.

Uncle Zelig wrote to his older brother, Samuel Feld, who had come to America in 1913, to send for us. He was a widower without children and he agreed to adopt and bring us to America. We arrived on Aug. 19, 1946. Uncle Sam lived in Scranton, Pennsylvania, and that is where we settled. He restored our lives to ones of normalcy and of being cared for. Although my uncle was not accustomed to having children underfoot, with a little time we all learned to understand each other and we became a family.

Estelle and I were a great oddity in our town. We were the only Holocaust survivor children whose history led to Auschwitz. It was difficult at first, but I was determined that I had to recover myself and my identity as Regina—a good person, a good student, a devoted family member. I wanted to become a true American.

After high school graduation I moved to Brooklyn, near my Aunt Ethel, where I found a job and subsequently met my husband, Jack Glinzman, also a survivor from the forests of Poland. We married in 1954 and were blessed with three wonderful children, who we named after our parents.

When Estelle married, the two families bought a two-family house and we raised our children together. We became not only aunts and uncles to the children but also the extended family that we should have had. Between us we have five children and are the proud grandparents of thirteen grandchildren, all of whom are Orthodox Jews. Yet, the tragedy of losing my entire family in Belgium and Poland marks my history with a tremendous sense of loss. We lost our identities and the opportunity of growing up in the care of our loving parents.

Regina Glinzman passed away on August 22, 2008

I Was Meant to Die But Survived to Tell

By Judith Evan Goldstein

Vilna. Every time I say the name of this city, it gives me chills, and I become very nostalgic for the early years of my childhood. It fills me with many memories of my aunts and uncles, my cousins, my grandmother, my mother, and, most of all, my father, who did not survive the war. The last time I saw my father was at the liquidation of the ghetto, in September of 1943.

I was born in Vilna, Poland, now the capital of Lithuania, on October 11, 1932. To the Jews of the world Vilna, was known as the "Jerusalem of Lithuania," a Jewish cultural center of Eastern Europe. We lived in the heart of town, 21 Sadowa Street. It was a nice apartment, with a terrace filled with flowers and other plants. Gardening was my father Chaim's love and hobby in addition to his love of music. He was a mechanical engineer and provided a comfortable living for his family of four, including my mother, Yetta, who designed clothes, my brother, Meir, and me.

My father was a kind and caring man. He loved family gatherings, especially on holidays. My mother always referred to him as a good organizer. He was also very creative. He made toys, sleds, and later on, in the ghetto, he made a little ring for me out of a silver coin with the design of the Vilna Ghetto logo. The ring almost cost me my life in the concentration camp, as you were not allowed to have any possessions. I still have the ring today. One of my paintings, "Vilna Ghetto," is based on that ring.

One Sunday morning in June 1941, my father was taking my brother and me to the river for a boat ride. Before we even got there, we heard sirens all over the city. The bombs began to fall like hail, killing people and causing terrible destruction to the city. We were fortunate to get home safely.

A few days later, Nazi Germany occupied Vilna, and within a few months, my life changed completely. I ceased to be a child and grew old very quickly. I lost the precious carefree and playful years of childhood forever. I didn't even have a mother tongue yet. I had only a small vocabulary in the languages I spoke, with no linguistic advantage. I became a child and an adult at the same time. Is that possible? Yes, it is. One had to adjust to times of abnormality.

Soon after—even before the ghetto was created—mobs looted Jewish businesses, smashed windows, vandalized synagogues, and burned Torah scrolls. Jews were assaulted in the streets, particularly men and young boys. Many were beaten to death by the Polish collaborators, who assisted the Nazis.

In September 1941, my father, mother, brother, and I were forced into the newly formed ghetto, with only knapsacks on our backs. We became a tribe faced with murder and tragedy. We left all our possessions behind, which were immediately looted by our neighbors. The rest of our family—aunts, uncles, and cousins—never made it to the ghetto. They were taken from their homes to Ponary, where they were murdered upon arrival and thrown into pits. Ponary is a forest outside of Vilna. One hundred thousand people were murdered there, 70,000 of whom were Jews. The others were people against the Nazis.

In the ghetto, people were dying from hunger, disease, and extreme conditions. As many as 10 families shared one apartment. In each room, a family occupied a corner. One kitchen and one bathroom were shared by all.

Every few months, masses of people were taken away to Ponary, especially the elderly and children who could not do slave labor. Others were sent to unknown destinations and never returned. The population in the ghetto diminished in a short time. I remember once expressing my fear of dying to my father, he replied, "You will not die. I will." His dire prediction was correct.

Because of his profession, my father received a special certificate, naming him "*Wichtiger Jude*," meaning "Important Jew." Therefore, he was temporarily allowed to protect his wife and two children under the age of 15. Fortunately, we fit into this category.

One day, when the Germans were bombing the ghetto at random, we crawled into the sewers, into a particular bunker that my father and a few of his colleagues had built. At night, in the dark, I overheard my father say, "The only source of air in this chamber comes from the chimney; if we have to stay here more than two days, we will all suffocate." This fear of not having enough air has stayed with me throughout my life, especially when going through tunnels.

At the liquidation of the ghetto, near the end of 1943, everyone was ordered to gather at the ghetto gate. I will never forget the fatal blows some people received from the Nazi soldiers, and the traumatic separations of children from parents and the elderly. We were immediately separated from my father and brother. One SS commander fingered who would be shipped to concentration camps or who would be going to Ponary to be shot. My mother, anticipating what was coming, rolled my braids up to the top of my head so that I would look taller and older. I watched the tall Nazi approaching my row, my heart pounding like a metronome, I stood lifeless. He spoke to me in a resonant voice, "You little one, you must go with the children." As he was about to pull me out of the row, someone called his name and he glanced away and no longer saw me. From a short distance, only a few rows behind me, I watched my girlfriend, Itele, take off her knapsack and heard her cry to her mother, "Mommy, Mommy, they're taking me away! They will shoot me. Here are my clothes, please, please, don't forget that you had a little girl whose name was Itele." Those words and cries still ring in my ears and will forever. She was only seven years old.

My mother, aunt Frieda, and I were shipped by railway in boxcars to Kaiserwald, a camp in Riga, Latvia. It was an endless journey, without food, water, or toilet. The doors were not opened until our arrival. Before entering the camp, our heads were shaved, our clothes removed, and all our possessions taken away. We were each given a striped uniform with a number attached to it. We no longer had names, only numbers. We lived in barracks, with four people sleeping in one bunk bed, on a straw mattress infested with lice. Seven hundred people occupied one barrack; there were no showers and only two toilets.

Every morning, while it was still dark, we were driven out into the cold for an *Appell*, (roll call). Once, I received a blow to my head from a Kapo for not standing straight. I bled and started to have headaches. Many years later, after the war, it was discovered a plum-size tumor was growing in the same spot. Fortunately, it was benign. After many hours of surgery, it was successfully removed.

After many months at Kaiserwald, we were transported by boat to another concentration camp, Stutthof, Germany. The journey from Riga to Stutthof will always stay with me. All the women and children were placed at the bottom of the boat for days without food, water, or sanitation. Many died. I was very ill, burning with fever and thought that the end had come. My mother cried and pleaded with me to stay alive, so I listened and fought to hold on to life.

In Stutthof, I experienced many tunnels of death, but managed to survive by accidents of fate. One miracle in particular came one morning when all the children under 13 were asked to gather. Hundreds of children were taken away, when suddenly they stopped the process and left a handful of children. I was one of them. We all knew where the others went: the gas chambers.

After a short stay in Stutthof, we were sent to Torun, Poland, for slave labor.

It was winter and below zero outside; we lived in cold barracks, received one slice of bread and a plate of watery soup a day. I remember risking my life while looking in the garbage for food. If caught, I would have been beaten to death. After only a few months, with the threat of the Russian army approaching, the Nazis forced a death march in temperatures below freezing. The SS, seeing weakness in anyone, shot them, while many others froze to death. I was weak and could barely walk. My mother dragged me and once again saved my life.

We marched along and noticed that all the German soldiers disappeared, so most of us ran into courtyards of local residences and hid in little huts. A few hours later, we heard the Germans looking for the escapees. My mother and I crawled into a chimney while the others were near the door. The door was forced open and shooting began, hitting a young girl in the leg. Later on, we heard that her leg had to be amputated.

In the winter of 1945, my mother, aunt Frieda, and I were liberated by the Russians in Bydgoszcz, Poland, a little town near Torun. We heard that many other survivors were going to the city of Lodz, Poland. So after a few weeks of freedom, living in an abandoned cold building, we, too, decided to go to Lodz. I really don't remember how we got there, but we did.

We searched feverishly for my father and brother, only to hear rumors that my father had not survived. Unfortunately, it was true. We were also informed by some Buchenwald survivors that my brother, Meir, had been liberated somewhere and was hospitalized with typhus.

My mother went to the train station every day to look for my brother. She started to visit the central office in search of his name. One day, by chance, they actually found each other, and she brought him home. He told her later that while sitting in the train at the Lodz station, someone yelled his name and said, "Meir, Meir, get off the train! Your mother and sister are here and alive."

That day, I was at the playground with my friends. My curfew was 9 o'clock; I returned a few minutes late, mother opened the door and sounded angry. I thought she was about to spank me, but instead I saw my brother. We fell into an embrace, which lasted about 20 minutes. Then we looked at each other, and he told me that he could never accept the fact that his little sister might be dead, and how happy he was to see me. It was a very tearful reunion.

After a year of difficult existence in Poland, we crossed over to the American zone in Germany. Many times, the Poles, who were the leaders at the borders, betrayed the survivors by taking their money and killing them. One such transport, with children from a kibbutz in Lodz, was attacked. Many of my friends were in that group. They never made it to the other side. But once again, luck was with us.

In Germany, we settled temporarily in Kibbutz Ichud, a displaced persons camp in Zeilsheim, near Frankfurt am Main. For three years we waited for our

quota to immigrate to America. During this time, I had the opportunity to go to school and also attend the Offenbach Conservatory of Music in Frankfurt am Main. I studied the piano and developed a strong love for the arts.

I was no longer a child/adult. I became a teenager/adult. Neither stage was a fit. I searched for fulfillment through education, friendships, and family unity. The survivors of World War II and the Jews from all corners of the world hoped for the birth of a Jewish State. Eventually, in 1948, it came into being, and many survivors immigrated to Israel. In 1949, our quota opened, and my mother, brother and myself, emigrated from Germany to the USA.

From tragedy, weakness, and defeat, I grew strong and looked ahead to a brighter future. My mother, brother, and I tried very hard to resume a normal life. It wasn't easy, since we had no one to guide us or help us. My mother worked hard in a clothing factory for many years. She never remarried and after many years she died a lonely woman. I will never forget that she saved my life so many times.

I met a young, handsome, and wonderful fellow, Harry, also a survivor. His whole family, except for his sister, Magda, was gassed and cremated in Auschwitz. I was still a teenager, but we got married and raised a family. We have two children and three grandchildren. Our son, Leslie, now an attorney, has a son Liam. Our daughter Renée, an X-ray technician and an EMT, has two children, Matthew and Jillian. We are blessed with this beautiful family, along with health, happiness, and professional accomplishments.

While my children were growing up, it became clear to me that I needed to take a more serious approach to my musical career. I decided to become a music teacher. I attended college and received bachelor and master's degrees in music. After teaching music for several years, I realized that music could also be used as a tool for communication, and expression with the learning and developmentally disabled. I furthered my studies in music and art therapy and received certification from the American Association for Music Therapy.

By teaching college and also working with the neurologically impaired, I recaptured some of the missing parts of my own childhood. My very early childhood memories are vague. I often have to rely on chaotic memories and feelings. With great determination, I will hold on to what happened during World War II and will not betray my history for the convenience of others. It is a historical fact, not an interpretation. My past is a contribution to education.

As time passed, my mind became an archive of times, and I remember being robbed of dignity by an evil society. I was a person, but no one knew it.

98

During the war, so many Jewish people were degraded to the status and conditions of vermin and eradicated by poison gas.

Wars bring people into a sea of tragedies, but the Holocaust was a massacre so willfully orchestrated and so brutally executed by the Nazis. It left a scar on every survivor, including me.

Because I was personally touched by the Holocaust, I am still a great source of intellectual and historical inquiry. I have learned never to be silent about my past. As the past recedes, I need to make sure that the secrets of history are not passively or actively forgotten, distorted, or denied. Over the years, I have found my own artistic language that helps me paint and create essential truths about the Holocaust and my childhood. I paint the canvases of my childhood and sing the images I see. Many of my paintings appear in my book, *"Images of My Childhood: From Sorrows to Joys."* In addition to Holocaust art, I have composed music and lyrics to numerous songs, several classical vocalises (music for instruments or voice without lyrics), cello and piano, and a major classical piece in four movements for piano and orchestra. My music has been performed in many important places, and was performed for the first time by the chamber orchestra of Westchester, NY on November 22, 2009. Recently, I appeared in the documentary film, *"As Seen Through These Eyes,"* which shows the Holocaust through art.

As my pendulum swings and swings, I will speak for those who cannot speak, sing for those who cannot sing, and live for those who could not live.

Comfort at the End of the Path

by Rosette Goldstein

My mother, Bronia Baum, was born in Lodz, Poland; she was the eighth of nine children. When just a child, she and two of the younger siblings were placed in an orphanage after their father died and left her mother destitute. Very early in life Bronia learned how to look after herself and grew mature beyond her years. When she was 16, her older brother withdrew her from the orphanage and brought her with him to Berlin, Germany, where she learned the trade of dressmaking. While in Berlin, she became reacquainted with one of her orphanage friends; he eventually became her husband and my father, David Adler.

In 1934, my father relocated to France, where he joined up with his older sister, her husband, and two nephews. He learned hat making from his brother-in-law, and in order to establish himself speedily as a French citizen, he joined the French army in 1936. In 1937, when he felt that he could provide for a wife, he had my mother come to France, where they married. I was born the following year.

We lived in a one-room apartment in a fifth-floor walkup. It was located in an historic building in the Third District, where we were the only Jews. Our neighbors extended a friendly pat or small treat to me and I felt secure among all their warm smiling faces. My world, on the fifth floor, in the cozy room, and in the courtyard, were my safe places, being surrounded by my loving parents and a sanctuary of kindness. Mother worked at home at her sewing machine, positioned under the one window in the apartment. The whirling sound of the sewing machine lulled me to sleep nightly.

The law of October 3, 1940, known as the Jewish Statute, declared Jews to be different from other French citizens, and according to the law, foreign Jews were subject to internment at the mere whim of the prefects. Jews were dismissed from all jobs because they were of foreign descent. After the defeat of France by the Germans, the Vichy government applied this anti-Semitic legislation. This comprehensive statute excluded Jews from public life, required their dismissal from positions in the civil service, the army, commerce, and industry, and barred them from participation in the professions, including medicine, law, and teaching. They were forced to sell off their businesses in anticipation of "Aryanization" measures.

The Vichy regime, enjoying popular support, used anti-Semitic policies to make the Jews scapegoats for the defeat of 1940. The Vichy regime linked national revival with anti-Semitism; Jews were officially blamed for all ills of society, from high prices to food shortages. The Vichy government volunteered to round up and hand over to the Germans all the foreign Jews from the unoccupied zone of France. The anti-Semitic policies of the Vichy government, the identification of the Jews, stamping of ID and the ration cards with the word "Juif"—Jew—the internment of Jews, the extensive use of French police in roundups, helped the Nazis in the "Final Solution."

Foreign Jews were particularly vulnerable. Thousands of Jews were sent to internment camps, such as Gurs near the Spanish border, where many died. The German authorities also deported 4,000 Jews from Gurs to Auschwitz. There were other major camps in which (mostly foreign) Jews were interned, included Saint-Cyprien, Rivesaltes, Le Vernet, and Les Milles and many smaller camps as well.

To protect us from being interned, father enlisted to work in a labor camp, Beauregard Clefs, a small town labor camp. He worked as a lumberjack with 70 other Jewish young men, cutting trees in the forest for the combined French and German war effort. Their group worked hard under primitive and difficult conditions.

Meanwhile, mother and I were in Paris. Life in Paris became a daily ordeal to keep safe and provide nourishment for us; everything was rationed. Because mother was determined to supply our meager needs and knowing that arriving late in line would result in having no rations; she got up 5 o'clock in the morning to stand in line to get a little milk and bread. In July 1941, Vichy inaugurated an extensive program of "Aryanization," confiscating Jewish-owned property for the French state. Many Jews were left destitute. Jews were not allowed to go to theaters anymore; they were not allowed to take their money out of the bank. On June 7, 1942, all Jews over the age of six were ordered to have a Jewish star with the word *Juif* sewn on their clothing; it had to be worn in a clearly visible position on the left side of the chest. Jews were not safe anywhere. Things were getting dire.

The first deportation train left Compiegne on March 27, 1942. Father's sister, brother-in-law and two sons were deported to Auschwitz on Convoy No. 8.

After a hard day's work in the forest, father managed to sneak away from the guarded compound to search among the locals for any means to help us. He befriended a farmer, Monsieur Albert Martin, and his family who lived nearby. My father offered to help with any chores that were needed. To cut his traveling time, Monsieur Martin supplied him with a bicycle. Thus he earned and bought some food, which he was still able to send to us in Paris.

Realizing what was happening and not trusting the "protection paper" that he was issued by the authorities, father asked Monsieur Martin if he would hide his little girl—me. Monsieur Martin told him he would discuss it with his wife, Juliette, and would get back to him the next day. The next day Monsieur Martin said, "We have three daughters, we will have four, bring little Rosette to us."

Mother and father made arrangements for me to be brought to the farm by our next-door neighbor who wasn't Jewish but who nevertheless undertook this courageous act. I still remember this day although I was only three-and-a-half years old. Wherever we went, we saw the Nazis goose-stepping with their rifles. I was going on an adventure, on a train with Monsieur Raffa. I was told not to speak to anyone and if there were any questions, I was to say that Monsieur Raffa was my father. The warning really wasn't necessary. At this tender age I was very frightened being away from mother and didn't want to speak to anyone. We arrived at the farm without any problems.

Father was waiting for us. His strong arms cuddled me gently and reassured me that I would be safe among strangers. We ate together. The generous spread of food and even wine and cider overwhelmed me. Exhausted from the trip, I slept peacefully that night, sharing the bed with the two younger girls. The next morning I woke up and was distressed and frightened when I did not see father. Monsieur Raffa had returned to Paris and mother was far away. I felt I had been abandoned with strangers. The Martins soothed my fears and distracted me with many farm animals and explorations.

The Martins were tenant farmers, living in a small two-room house with outhouse and water pump outside. The attached granary storage building where they kept the animal feed and adjoining animal barn were part of this property; this was my new world where my only toys were the drying pumpkin seeds spread out in the silo attic. Monsieur and Madame Martin were very good to me and the three girls, Denise, Simone, and Odile, ranging in age from

14 to 22, were my protectors. I soon learned to adjust and was comforted when father came to see me every night. I waited for him at the end of the path of the farm. He came riding on the bicycle, whistling. Our daily meetings were a loving reunion. Father held me on his lap hugging and kissing me. My little body clung in his arms with a warmth and passion which made me feel protected and which I cherish till this day. My love for him and our tender meetings have given me comfort throughout my life.

One day mother appeared at the farm. That night our family was reunited; father remained at the farm overnight. How I remember and enjoyed that evening! The scene of being with my good-looking parents who lavished me with affection has rooted memories of belonging to a loving family.

The next morning father went directly to the forest rather than to the camp. Without warning, men and soldiers brandishing guns burst into the house; with angry voices they demanded to know the whereabouts of father and why he had not been at roll call that morning. My mother tried to placate the intruders, explaining that he was working in the forest. They warned that if he wasn't back in camp within the hour, they would come back for my mother and me. Monsieur Martin saddled his horse and rode into the forest to tell father of the threats and that he needed to return to camp, which he did. After this warning, mother went back to Paris. I did not see her until after the war.

Meanwhile, life on the farm continued. The soldiers did not return; it seemed that they forgot about my being on the farm. The Martin girls took me wherever they went, to tend the cows and sheep, feed the chickens and geese, pick apples and dig up the potato crops. Whatever they had they shared with me.

One day I was waiting for my dad at the end of the path. I waited and waited and he didn't come. He had been taken. I never saw him again. I never said goodbye. I never sat on his lap again and hugged him.

They took the 70 men to Drancy, from where they conveyed them to Auschwitz then to Buchenwald, and then to a camp called Langenstein/Zwieberg, where father was murdered by the Nazis five days before the camp was liberated by the American army.

One day while playing near the path, I saw a truck with soldiers dismounting, rifles in their hands. I knew they were Nazis. I ran into the house to tell Madame Martin what I had seen. She grabbed me and pushed me into the other room; she lifted the mattress and hid me between the spring and mattress, and then covered and smoothed out the bed. I was cautioned to stay there no matter what happened. The soldiers came into the farmhouse, looked around and commandeered all the food they could take and left. On another occasion, a convoy of Nazis came. This time Odile, the youngest daughter, and I climbed up to the storehouse, on top of the barn, where the grain was stored and hid there.

I stayed with the Martin family for three-and-a-half years. After father was taken away, I became lonely and sad. I was just a little girl who could not understand why she was different and why she had to hide when the soldiers came, why she no longer had her mother or her father.

Finally, the American army invaded. Every night the bombs were bursting and lighting up the sky. The farmhouse trembled from the distant explosions. On cool nights, I was bundled up and we all stayed outside to watch the American planes streak across the sky. The spectacle was both frightening and joyful because we knew that the Allies were winning and the war would be over.

Soon American soldiers reached the countryside of our farm. They were everywhere. We gave them fresh vegetables and fruit and they gave us C-rations and chocolate in return. I was enchanted with these friendly faces who just gave away chocolate. I had never tasted it before, and it was a pleasurable delight for me.

With the war over, mother felt safe to come for me. Somehow, she hitchhiked her way to the Martin farm. Our reunion was halting on my part. It was over three years since I had seen her. I had to convince myself that my mother was my friend and that it was safe for me to trust her and feel affection for her. She stayed a few days to have me feel comfortable with her and then we began our journey back to Paris, hitchhiking with American GIs and another family. My ride in a Jeep, squeezed in with the other family, was an experience that stands out in my child's mind. At the front on the hood of the Jeep rode a black American soldier with a rifle at ready, protecting us against snipers. I was mesmerized by him; I had never seen a black person before and thought that he was the bravest man.

Life in Paris was not normal. Mother found out that father had not survived. She worked day and night to provide for our needs. To provide a better life for me and have me start my schooling, she placed me in a Jewish orphanage with children who were gathered from all over. The difference was that they did not have any parents. After six months of the happiest memories of my childhood, all the children were sent to Israel, except for children like me, who had a parent.

My situation changed drastically. I was placed into a number of foster homes where I was ill treated. My misery was evident to mother, which made her decide to return me to the Martins for one year. I attended school in the village and enjoyed life with my hero-family. Not able to stabilize her life, in 1949 mother sent me to live with her older sister, my aunt Zofia Baum, in New York. I crossed the ocean on the Queen Elizabeth. I was ten and a half years old. Mother followed a year later.

America saved me from the upheaval that was my life. I did not want to go back to France. I worked to be the best American that I could be, including losing any accent, which might be a sign of my tumultuous young life. The United States is my country; I honor and love it with all my heart.

In 2000, I had the Martin family honored as "Righteous Among Nations" by Yad Vashem.

I revisited the places of my young life and was able to validate my memories of suffering and love. Telling my life story and what happened to one Jewish family is my memorial for my father, David Adler. I have to make my father matter, to give him a life.

I married Gil Goldstein and have raised a loving family, a daughter and son who have enriched our lives and added wonderful life partners and five adorable, accomplished grandchildren.

I have cheated the evil plan of the Nazis. I live and prosper and contribute to good causes and teach my family that we are a people who have learned to survive and teach kindness and goodness as was demonstrated in deeds by my wonderful Martins.

To Find My Family

by Rosalyn Haber

I was born on March 15, 1931 in the village of Varpalanka/Polanka, Czechoslovakia. I was the youngest and the only girl among six brothers, which was like being a princess. On Saturday nights, sounds of merriment and enjoyment reverberated through the house and courtyard. Some of my brothers played instruments or sang and I was handed from brother to brother as a dancing partner. As I look back on my childhood, I remember it as an ideal life.

The Polanka Castle, situated in the hills above the village, was originally erected in the 9th Century as a small fortress and was rebuilt and modernized into one of the most impenetrable castles through the ensuing years. It seemed to hover like a halo and protector over the community. The population was

Schwab Germans, Czechs, Jews and some Gypsies, who were not a rooted group in town.

Our main building, which fronted the one street, housed some of the family and served as a customer reception area for measuring clients for father's tailoring business. The interior courtyard had a number of small dwellings, which accommodated my siblings and the six employee tailors who were part of the labor force that helped father produce men's clothing.

Our basic comforts were primitive—we had no indoor plumbing, running water or electricity—but I cannot recall that we lacked anything or were covetous of the modern facilities of the big city. This was our home, which was filled with love, and we appreciated being among the many aunts, uncles, cousins, and friends. Our home was always full of merriment, laughter, and welcome.

My father, Chaim/Hugo, always dressed impeccably in a suit, vest and tie. He demanded cleanliness of his children and required inspection of our hands and nails before meals. He was a tall handsome man, with dark looks and gentle hazel eyes whose piercing gaze would immediately bring a fast halt to any behavior that he did not approve of. Nevertheless, he did not have to use his authoritative looks often, because none of us would consider bringing any displeasure to this kind and honorable man.

My mother, Etta/Etuko (Lebowitz), was a gentle, caring woman whose reputation of good deeds, industrious homemaking for her family and the employees preceded her. She was an expert homemaker whose breads, challa and especially pastries were a great draw for drop-in guests at our table. Her smiling blue eyes exuded a love for her children and she was slow to anger. After six boys, her desire for a girl was unwavering and she said that even if it would take a dozen more children she must have a daughter. I came along two-and-a-half years after Yankele, my youngest brother, who became my guardian and almost a shadow to protect and entertain me. Our walks with our parents on Sabbath were a delight to me because I had my parents' attention pretty much to myself.

When our area was turned over to Hungary in 1938, life changed overnight. People we thought were good friends and neighbors suddenly became hateful and shunned us. Our walks to and from school became an ordeal, as we tried to avoid the flying stones or abuse.

One Friday night, in mid November, a frightening banging on the door with shouts of "In the name of the Hungarian army—open the door!" startled all in the house. The terror was shocking as the soldiers used their bayonets to smash the bedroom windows, where mother was cooling the chicken soup on the windowsill for the Sabbath. I still can see the scene in my memory, like a slow motion movie, the overturned pot spilling its contents in a stream down the wall.

The militia forced its way into the house and demanded that father go with them. With terror and hysterical crying, I held on to my father, not letting go. The soldiers somehow had pity on my out of control howling and screaming: "No one will take my 'Tatika' away." They left, promising to return the next day, but they never came back. I am sure that my hysterics saved my father from being killed by the thugs.

Our life continued with many hardships, shortages and the need to adjust to the anti-Jewish edicts. Father insisted that we continue to live as normally as we could and enrolled me into the Hebrew Polgary-Preparatory School to continue in the "Munkacs Gymnasium." The daily 3-kilometer walk to and from school was an ordeal for a child of 11. My brother Yankele met me at the crossing bridge to protect me from the gauntlet of jeers and rocks. But these obstacles did not halt me or the determination of my father for me to continue my education.

Young men, including my father and three older brothers, were taken away to Obinka labor camp. The Jewish young boys were taken to dig ditches, while their gentile friends were trained to be soldiers. After six months of hard labor, father was released because he had three sons in the force.

The family lost its passion and gaiety after the boys were taken away. We lived with hope that things would get better and we would be reunited. But conditions became harder and harder. In 1944, the day after Passover, all the Jews were rounded up and taken to the Munkacs Ghetto. My father, mother, three brothers and I were among the gathered. We were the last transport to be sent to Auschwitz. The boxcars were filled with people and one couldn't move. The sanitary conditions were non-existent. As the train was stopped a couple of times, dead bodies were taken out of the cars. The shock of these conditions and seeing my parents' suffering made me wish that I, too, were among the dead taken off.

Three days later, we arrived at Auschwitz and were ordered to leave all of our possessions. The heartless treatment of children and the elderly made me shiver and wonder, "What was this place where all humanity was obliterated?"

Men and women were separated and lined up in columns. My mother and I were lined up in a column of selected women. I learned after a short time that my father was taken to the gas chambers right from the train.

Mother and I were together for two weeks in barracks with horrible conditions. She made me promise that I would do all I could to survive and that some day we would be together. We suffered hunger, were deprived of sanitation, and were in a state of terror. After two weeks, Josef Mengele came to an *Appell* (roll call) and pulled mother. Seeing my mother being selected, I told Mengele that "I want to go with my mother." He replied, "Your time will come." The shock of being separated from my mother, alone at age 13, without a friend, traumatized me. I never have been the same.

I survived the months in Auschwitz by being like another person. I was numb to all emotions and moved as ordered following the other women. In the fall, we were to be shipped to a different camp. I was pulled out from the lines and placed in a holding section, behind a fence. When the SS soldiers left, the girls shouted and urged me to dig my way out from under the fence. When we were counted again, the SS said that all would be shot if the extra person didn't come forward. But before this threat could be executed, the train whistle blew and we all jumped into the waiting cars which brought us to a camp in Unterlusse.

Here we dug ditches for bunkers for the SS and then had to continue working the night shift to put powder into bomb shells at an ammunition factory. Our daily march to the factory was debilitating. The winter was bitter cold. We had no warm clothes—just thin striped uniforms and clogs. We were given a slice of black bread and some warm coffee twice a day, which was supposed to sustain us. I deduced that they really were starving us to death.

As the fighting was coming to end, we were herded on to trucks that were open to the bitter winter condition. On the way we were told to dismount and were lined up to be shot, but the British planes overhead stopped the killers. We were herded back on the trucks and were taken to Bergen-Belsen.

A few weeks later, on April 15, 1945, we were liberated by the British. We were more dead than alive. People were dying like flies from typhoid, which was never treated by the Germans; they just left us to die.

With the guards gone, people roamed about searching and looking into faces, hoping that someone would recognize them or find someone. I, too, searched and was recognized—I don't know how—by my half-brother, Itzig, who I had not seen since I was seven. He insisted that I take off my striped uniform, and from a pile of clothes I took a dress that came down to the floor. He said, "Tomorrow I will have a potato for us to bake." The next day I was at the appointed spot; but Itzig did not come. I learned that he had died the night before.

I soon became sick with typhoid fever and do not remember much of anything. When I recovered, I succeeded in getting a job working for the Jewish Agency, distributing news from what was then Palestine. Moshe Dayan, Abba Eban, and David Ben-Gurion were frequent visitors to our office. In 1948, when Israel declared and was acknowledged as an independent, Jewish state, I had the honor to dance a hora with Ben-Gurion.

In November 1948, I came to the United States when uncles Adolph, Benim and Eugene Lebowitz from Ellwood City, Pennsylvania, my mother's brothers, arranged for visas for all of us. We were so fortunate to have such a great family. Finally, in 1949, my brothers Phillip, Ben, Bernie, Bill, Sam and Alex came from Czechoslovakia. We were finally all together.

No matter how many stories one reads or hears about the Holocaust, it can never be described as we lived it. To murder six million people just because they are Jewish is as incomprehensible as it is unforgivable. Where did this kind of madness come from—this cruel murder done with such precision?

After losing my dear parents and large extended family, I find that my humanity has not been lost—not been taken away. We must accept all people, show compassion for the suffering, and speak up and act upon it when we see acts of injustice.

Commitment to Remember

by Magda Hammer

I was born in Beregszasz, Czechoslovakia, in 1925. My father, Markus—a tall handsome man with piercing intelligent blue eyes—and mother, Poula (Ruth) Grunfeld, tiny of stature and with hazel eyes that glistened and appeared to know all, enjoyed all the privileges that their financial freedom and status provided, including summers at the spa in Carlsbad for my mother.

They raised four children among our closely knit extended family, which surrounded and enveloped our lives with warmth, love and sharing. My oldest brother, Naftali, only two years older than me, had his hands full trying to keep his position as the eldest. My special treatment by father who doted over me with love, compliments of being the smartest and prettiest, apparently went to my head because I became headstrong and willful and stood my ground. My younger brothers, Albert and Kalman, made up a full house. Our house was always abuzz with activity.

The Sabbath always transposed our home into a palace glowing with a special festive mood and aromas of delectable dishes permeating the air. These were times that became indelible in my soul, where father's entry into the house always was accompanied by a guest or needy person to share our plentiful bounty at our table. These were the scenes that enhanced our growing years.

Father and mother followed Orthodox values. Mother wore a *sheitel* (wig), which was customary for Orthodox married women, while father was clean-shaven since his business required him to travel and deal with non-Jews. My father's business included vineyards, wineries, and selling wine products throughout Europe. We lived in our own comfortable home, surrounded by fine furniture and a couple of rooms that served only for show and very special guests.

I attended public school, and as I look back I don't recall being abused because I was Jewish. I do recall that when I was about four years old, a gentile girl approached me and said, "You are a Jew, you killed Jesus." The shock of being accosted with such a violent accusation brought me to tears. I could not understand such blame and ran home to mother for comforting. I have forgotten many things and blocked many horrific memories, but this scene is vivid in my mind.

In 1938, our part of Czechoslovakia was taken over by Hungary and we immediately felt a different treatment. The democratic government, as we knew it, was gone. Many edicts and laws placed a burden on our lives. I had to stop my education since only one child per family was allowed to attend gymnasium, which was a prep school for university entry and studies. Life became more serious, more cautious, and we were fearful of the future. Most youngsters joined Jewish Zionist organizations, which filled an educational gap with studies in Hebrew, in awakening of a return to the Promised Land, and of cultivating the land as training to relocate and settle in Israel.

On March 19, 1944, the German army occupied Beregszasz, followed by the Gestapo 10 days later. They quickly recruited the Jewish elders to be the intermediaries to the Jewish population, bringing down all the statutes and restrictions that were decreed by the Nuremberg Laws. Looting of businesses and raids of Jewish homes became a normal state of our community. The synagogues were looted and desecrated. We were stripped of all valuables, including radios; we could not continue with our business, could not employ non-Jewish maids; we had to live within the curfew hours to be able to buy anything. We were ordered to apply the yellow Jewish star to our clothes and were forbidden to leave town. We were imprisoned in this restricting existence. The separation from my eldest brother, Naftali, who was conscripted to work with other young man in a labor camp, stripped my mother and father of their usual confidence and strength.

Until May 1944, we managed to survive all the difficulties that had become our lot. Then we were ordered to leave our home, bringing with us only a small valise with immediate needs and were marched into a makeshift ghetto on the outskirts in a brick factory. As we walked, our neighbors cheered and jeered at our plight. The memory of those faces makes me realize that we did not live among countrymen, but among people who wanted to destroy us. We stayed in the ghetto for about two weeks, in tents, with meager food and in primitive unsanitary conditions. I know we were there, but my memory has blocked out our first experiences on the road to our suffering and demise.

On May 14, 1944, we were ordered to line up and were marched to the railroad, where we were packed into cattle cars, 100 to a car. No one could sit;

it was standing room only. The doors were slid shut and locked. The devastation of being put in these conditions resulted in people crying and screaming, shoving without hope of finding a comfortable position. The mayhem in the cars was hopeless; no one could find comfort for even a minute.

The train moved slowly and made many stops. At one point the train stopped and an unusual-smelling smoke started to filter in through the small windows, which brought the captives into panic that this was our end, that we were being gassed.

We continued this torturous journey for two days, finally arriving at Auschwitz. The doors slid open to a rush of fresh, yet unusual-smelling air, and to shouts of the German soldiers and the Kapos. At first I was relieved to be in the air; we all thought we were brought here to work. Physically drained and emotions dazed, incoherent, stripped of even our little possessions, we reacted like robots. I was in a state of shock and at the same time relieved, not realizing that our lives were in the hands of the devil.

We were lined up five abreast and prodded to go forward. Mother and father each held the hands of my little brothers, while I helped carry my little cousin while my aunt marched along clutching her large brood of nine children. A Kapo, seeing me holding this little girl, snatched her from my arms and made her walk on her own. She waddled along haltingly and none of us could challenge or oppose this act. I still don't know if I should thank the Kapo or detest him: was it an act of kindness on his part to save me or just plain cruelty?

Upon arrival, we were presented to a tall German soldier, who we learned was Josef Mengele. He, along with his underlings, divided the column to the right and left. My parents and little brothers were sent to the left, while I was pointed to the right. Of course, at the time, I had no idea what was awaiting them. All adults holding on to children were sent to the gas chambers as soon as we were separated. I never had the opportunity to say goodbye to my family.

We then were separated from the men and were marched to showers, where our heads were shaved, we were powdered with a disinfectant, and herded along the line where we were handed only a striped dress. Fortunately, we were allowed to keep our own shoes. Next we were brought to the barracks, which housed 800 women. The three-tiered sleeping shelves, which were just boards divided into sections, were assigned to 10 women; we had to turn in unison to change a position.

Every morning and evening we were lined up for hours for a count, no matter how bad the weather or how ill one felt. A slice of dark mud-like bread with a little slab of margarine was our morning meal, and a cup of watery, horrid smelling soup was our dinner. We were led to the latrine once a day, where the experience was torturous and degrading. At one point, I was selected to be sent to the gas chambers, which by now we learned was the final road for our families. I managed to slip back into the *Appell* (roll call) line and mingle among the women, and so escaped being one of the victims of the gas chambers.

I connected to a young girl, who I called my *Lager* (camp) sister. We helped each other by using our daydreams and reminiscences to keep up our spirits and will to continue. Even though a Kapo shocked us with the idea that the smoke from the chimneys were our families, we did not want to accept such a truth. We dreamed of a future, of going to Hollywood because her uncle was the famous movie-maker Joseph Pasternack. I don't know if it was true, but I wanted to believe it to be so and so we dreamed.

After about three months at Auschwitz, I was selected and taken in cattle cars to work in the country at Gelsenkirchen to rebuild a destroyed Krupp factory. Some 300 women were housed in tents with straw as bedding. The back-breaking work at the Krupp factory—sorting bricks and clearing rubble was grueling—but the conditions were an improvement from that of Auschwitz. We worked day and night to get the factory ready to open, when one day we heard sirens blaring. American planes were flying overhead, motors roaring. The Germans ran into their bunkers, while all the prisoners were left to the severe bombardment. The bombing raid killed many of the prisoners, while many more were badly wounded. Fortunately, I escaped without injury, but seeing the devastation left me anesthetized. I was not prepared to experience such evil. My life had never prepared me for this road of survival.

Again the Germans transported us on a train, which was bombed, but somehow we managed to escape unharmed. We were deposited in a town in Scamerda, in Bavaria, Germany, where we worked in underground factories, producing ammunition. Our day and night shifts were long, hard and dangerous, working with explosive materials and heavy machinery. When prisoners deteriorated physically, they were sent back to Auschwitz.

The Allies were getting closer. Again we were taken away, and when the train was damaged in bombings, we were marched through forests. We had no food. We ate the wild vegetation that we could scrape from under the snow. Each of us had a blanket, so we organized five to sleep together using one blanket as a protection from the ground and use four blankets to cover us, as we cuddled together for warmth. My Lager sister and I realized that we were heading east and to an extermination camp, so we made a break in the middle of the night, hiding in a haystack. We managed to steal some clothes drying on a clothesline and also stole a couple of bicycles. We took on the identities of Hungarian refugees. We reported to the Burgermeister, the mayor of the village who believed us, and let us stay and work for the locals in their homes and farm.

One day, not long after our arrival at this town, the woman who I worked for cried hysterically after hearing on the radio that Germany had lost the war. I joined her, and for the first time in a long time I shed tears. But I cried because I was finally free. All the residents of the village hung white sheets in their windows as signs of surrender. Soon, American soldiers appeared and among them was a Jewish soldier, We told him that we too were Jews. He was overwhelmed and almost danced for joy that he was able to free Jewish captives. He immediately saw the mayor and advised him that we were to be well treated and cared for and not to be placed in any danger.

It was a time of extremely mixed emotions. Two Jewish girls among Germans, liberated, yet captive in our own memories and hopes of connecting with our families. We decided to go back to our homes. We biked to a rail station and were able to get on a train heading for Prague and managed to bring along our bikes. In Prague we found survivors who were housed and supported by UNRA in a hotel where I was able to finally satisfy my hunger. The rich and abundant food landed me in a hospital for three weeks.

When I was released from the hospital, I discovered that my brother Naftali had survived Mauthausen, and I headed to our home. Arriving there, I went straight to our house with heart pounding, hoping that I would find my family, my house, and return to the loving arms of what used to be. Instead, I found our house looted. A Hungarian couple was living there. I looked about and could not remain. I knew that nothing would ever be the same again. I found my brother staying with friends and our emotional embraces and tears overflowed for all the years of suffering that I had not cried.

As we walked about, we felt that the non-Jewish neighbors were staring at us as if we were ghosts. The undercurrent of anti-Semitism was evident. We could not remain. Moreover, rumors were rampant that the Soviets were close and would occupy and bring in another form of oppression. I had enough of being ruled by dictators; I wanted to be free. We got away and arrived at Budapest. We were received and housed by a Zionist organization, where we learned Hebrew and worked on Moshavs—cooperative farming communities—for immigration to Palestine. Here my brother met his future wife and together they were part of the illegal Aliya (immigration to Israel) crossing the Mediterranean trying to break through the British blockade into Palestine. Unfortunately their ship was stopped and they were all sent to Cyprus.

I still don't quite understand why I decided to go to America. Perhaps I did not want to impose on my brother's happiness. I don't know. I made contact with an uncle and aunt who immigrated in the 1920s who offered to send me the required papers and money for the crossing. While waiting for an affidavit and ticket; I attended high school, and among other subjects, learned to sew.

Finally, in 1947, all the papers came through and I sailed for New York. Seeing at a distance the colossal Statue of Liberty and the skyscrapers, I became overwhelmed with emotions of both hope and fear. I was so alone. I was a stranger among strangers. What would I find in this new land? How would I survive? Would my family accept and love me?

As I disembarked from the ship, I was overcome with the tumult and saw people greeting each other with gladness. My desire of being united with a family who might replace my dear lost parents was a burning hope. My aunt and uncle spotted me and we did have a reunion that brought us to tears, but my welcome was short lived. I found that I needed to learn to stand on my own two feet—and quickly. After a short stay with my aunt, I found a job at a sewing factory, and boarded with a good lady where I established my personal corner of safety. I worked diligently, joined the union, and attended night school in order to fit into the American way and pace of life. It was not easy, but I guess my honed survival skills were a good training ground for me to be self-sufficient, resist defeat and build a future.

In 1949 I met my husband, Aaron, who took me in hand and who taught me about culture, appreciation of the theatre, music, and all the fine arts. We married after a two-year courtship and enjoyed a happy and adventurous life for fifty-two years. I lost my dear mate and friend in 1996, but his teachings and love of life are carried on by our wonderful son, daughter and grandsons.

I am compelled to share my Holocaust life story because I hope that it may serve to carry a message which the world can use as an example of what hate, discrimination, racism, and anti-Semitism create. We are still in great danger today. My life, my story, is my "Commitment to Remember."

Totally Intolerant of Intolerance

by Andy Hartmann

The Austro-Hungarian Empire was where my father, Julius' (Yechiel's), family lived. He was one of 12 siblings—seven brothers and five sisters. The family earned a good living in farming, which attracted three brothers to follow in their father's footsteps.

Father and his brother, Bela, ran a farm in the village Roskoviany [now in Slovakia], a population of 600. He was well regarded and appreciated as an upright employer and earned the respect of the community.

Our village did not have electricity, indoor water or sanitary facilities. But our home site provided excellent living conditions for the two families. Our property consisted of a comfortable home, leased lands for growing wheat and other grains, a barn for our many animals, cows, sheep, chickens, geese, and a bountiful fruit orchard. We employed many local peasants—residents of the village—whose children were my schoolmates in the two-room school when I reached the age for education.

My birth on August 11, 1934, was a celebrated occasion for my parents. I was the apple of their eye. Their long wait for a son, a *Kaddish*—the family namesake and carrying on the tradition of remembering the parents after passing—was a blessing and fulfilled the desire for a boy who now joined three sisters, Bianca, Olga and Valika.

Our family was Orthodox in traditions and actions. We had a kosher home but dressed in modern clothes, and my father was clean-shaven. My memories of my father are of a disciplinarian but a caring parent and companion. He took me along on all his farm duties and was attentive to my questions. Because of his deep religious convictions, his duty to God of praying three times a day would occur even in the fields. During stormy weather, father prayed for safety and taught me the blessing for thunder and lightning. On his market-day trips

117

to the city, he always brought back a toy or some unusual souvenir for me.

My mother, Tereza (Rifka) Gelb, was one of seven children. Her family lived in Hungary. She was well schooled in prayer and in Hebrew. Her kind, sweet demeanor always offered a protective shelter from father's rebukes, which were seldom but usually well deserved. Mother spent many hours in her kitchen, cooking and baking. She appeared like a ghostly vision, dusted with snow from the flour that she sieved and kneaded into delicious bread and cakes.

My sisters, although much older than me, were my companions and let me accompany them into the woods for mushrooms and berry picking. Valika, only six years older, was my home playmate since the older two were away at school in the city. My childhood, until the threat against the Jews reached our little village, was a happy one. My days were spent in exploration of nature, school, learning Hebrew at home, farm projects, and winter sledding off the hills. It was an exhilarating time.

Czechoslovakia was splintered by the demands of Hitler and the appeasement of the European countries. On March 14, 1939, Slovakia declared its independence, calling itself the Slovak Republic. Slovak radicals were organized into the paramilitary Hlinka Guards, who cooperated closely with the Nazi-oriented German minority led by Franz Karmasin. On March 15, 1939, German troops began to be stationed in Slovakia.

The Hlinka Guard began to attack Jews, and the "Jewish Code" was passed in September 1941. Resembling the Nuremberg Laws, the code required Jews to wear a yellow armband. A drummer/town crier marched through villages and proclaimed the edicts. We became an identifiable population by wearing these armbands, which brought about a change of attitudes by my gentile school mates. Soon after the armbands, a new edict decreed that all Jews wear a Star of David pinned to the front of their jackets, followed by a larger star that had to be sewn on.

I continued to attend the two-room school. At the age of seven I was isolated from any participation with the children. A derogatory remark by the teacher or a slur shouted in my direction by some kids "*Zid idz do Palestiny*"— "Jew go to Palestine"—left me stunned. What had I done to deserve this hostility?

The first shock that left our family numb was when the edict of March 1942 reached our home. My 17-year-old sister, Olga, and 16-year-old cousin, Magda, were to report to the railroad to be transported to a labor camp. Gloom and tears streaked our faces. Mother helped Olga pack things that would be helpful in a labor camp: canteen, cooking utensils, some food and water for the journey. The next day we learned that farming families were excluded from this selection, but it was too late to get the girls off the train.

By this time we already knew that some trains were being sent to

Auschwitz. And it wasn't long before we learned that this was the destination of the train with the young girls. They were taken directly to Auschwitz and the gas chambers.

Our house was overcome with grief and weeping. Father ripped the lapel on his and my jacket as a sign of our loss. We sat *Shiva*, seven days of mourning, for Olga, covering all mirrors and observing all the customs of mourning. The veil of tragedy hung heavy. I was seven and half years old but my mind could not absorb or find comfort. My eyes were constantly searching the faces of my parents and sisters hoping to find an answer and comfort. I could not accept the permanence of our loss; my eyes fixed on the door, hoping that Olga would walk through at any minute.

After our own personal experience of oppression and loss, things were not the same. Deportations continued. Until May 1944, Jewish farmers were safe, but then our exemption was cancelled and father was tipped off that we would have to report for deportation. The family got busy, bundled up the necessities on a horse-drawn wagon, and in the middle of the night we left our home hoping to elude the roundup and escape to safety.

After a few hours of traveling we were arrested and the family spent one night in jail while I was taken in by a Lutheran priest. The next day we were placed on a train and were taken to a tobacco plantation in Zemanska Kert (now Zemianske Sady), where all adults worked in every aspect of farming. At the age of nine-and-a-half, I was leading a life of freedom along with the other Jewish children, playing in the fields, and after many years again had a care-free feeling.

On September 9, 1944, one month after my tenth birthday, German SS, assisted by the Slovak Guard, appeared with trucks and gathered members of the village—including my parents, sister Valika, and other members of my extended family—and took them away. My sister Bianca, who was 11 years older; her boyfriend, Fred, and I happened to be outside the perimeter of this roundup. I felt someone grabbing my hand and pulling me along into the near-by forest, escaping the roundup, where we met up with an aunt and uncle, their teen daughter, and a Polish-Jew escapee. We were a group of seven, moving from place to place, keeping out of the grasp of the SS and Slovak *Garda* Police who were sweeping the forests for Jews.

We wandered about under cover of night in the woods, without either warm clothes or food. Our emotions were numb, knowing that our family was headed for annihilation. We found some nourishment by stealing tomatoes and grapes from the fields. After a couple of weeks of struggling, with the weather getting harsher and without shelter, the adults decided to seek a better way to hide and survive. Fred and Lacko, familiar with the area, left us in the safety of the forest and ventured into the village, approaching a house that was situated a distance away from the other houses.

They knocked on the door with great trepidation not knowing what to expect. *Pan* (Mr.) Pavel Cuvala opened the door, with a surprised expression. He peered at the desperate faces as they asked him for help; they told him they were Jews searching for help. *Pan* Cuvala hesitated briefly and said that he had to consult with his wife, who without delay agreed to help; both knew the consequences of hiding Jews.

Pan Cuvala gave the men tools, plywood, and tarpaper to help them dig a shelter-bunker in the forest. The bunker was dug with great exertion; then the dirt was carried in sacks and dispersed to distant places in order not to give away its location or existence. When it was finished, it was camouflaged flush with the ground with the saved turf. This dugout provided space for the seven of us to lie down. We had a bucket as a toilet, which was emptied at different spots at night. Once a week, two men went to the Cuvalas, who provided them with water, bread and *slonina* (pork fatback). I found myself unable to eat the pork. My struggle to follow in my father's teachings could not change, even at this drastic time. All I survived on was bread and water.

We lived like this until it became evident that the winter snow footprints would give us away. My sister's boyfriend, Fred, appealed to Pan Cuvala to help again, to build a shelter under their barn because our location in the forest was no longer safe. The Cuvelas agreed to have us dig this shelter and helped us dig it at night.

My legs became atrophied; I could not walk. Fred carried me to our new bunker in the barn under cover of night, where Bianca made me understand that father would approve of eating any food in order to save life. Our existence, although always filled with fear of discovery, was better than it had been in the forest bunker. Mrs. Cuvala brought us cooked food. We continued our underground life until April 1, 1945, when the Russians liberated our area. We had spent a total of seven months in hiding.

Once liberated, we said heartfelt good-byes to the Cuvalas, then traveled by all means—walking, carts, trains, flatcar trains—through Hungary to East Slovakia and returned to my uncle's village, where we tried to establish an order of life.

That summer I was admitted to the gymnasium at 11 years of age. I remained with my uncle's family, while Bianca lived with a Hungarian noblewoman from whom we had leased our land in Roskoviany. Bianca and Fred soon were married and established their own home life.

After a year, it was decided that I would be sent to America along with my cousin, Alfred, who was 22, had lived in Palestine and had volunteered to serve in the Jewish Brigade of the British army. (His family was taken away in the roundup of September 9, 1944.) In September 1946, as I began the second year of gymnasium, a visa was approved and affidavits arrived for Alfred and me. Arriving in the United States, I was received with great warmth by my Aunt

Sari and Uncle Alex Fuchs, who resided in Brooklyn. I quickly shed my sorrow of the war years. This was made easy because I was received by my aunt and uncle as their child and found comfort and love from them as a son.

I integrated myself into the American life and did not want to be identified as a Jew. This resolve, however, did not last too long; my aunt and uncle provided a tutor and I became a Bar Mitzvah. I also became busy becoming an American. Everything American was dear and I wanted to meld in and be like my schoolmates. I embraced the Brooklyn Dodgers, big band music, the crooner stars, westerns, and hot dogs. My proudest moment was when I was assigned to be the flag bearer in the ninth grade. I made lifelong friends and carried my pre-American life as only a distant link.

I continued with my education, built a career in pharmaceutical sales, married Sandy Chandross and built a lovely family of two daughters and four grandchildren.

Thirty-eight years after the war, when the Holocaust revisionists tried to rewrite the history of the evil perpetrated against the Jews, I became enraged. I had to confront my own losses and my own survival. For the first time since I came to the United States, I had to deal with my own painful history and come face to face with the Holocaust.

When the Spielberg project asked for volunteers to interview survivors and collect personal testimonials, I decided to participate in the project. I had an obligation to my lost family. I had to speak out; I had no choice. My position is that brick and mortar are not good enough memorials for the lost 6 million. Speaking to students is a living memorial; they carry our voices, our histories, our losses.

I joined the Child Survivors/Hidden Children Palm Beach County. I discovered a need and obligation to my lost family and became more focused on remembrance. When I learned that a Conference of Child Survivors was to be held in Prague in 1999, I decided to return to where I had been saved by the Cuvala family. My sister and brother-in-law jumped at the opportunity and joined me in returning to our places of survival.

Arriving in Prague, we traveled to Bratislava and continued by car for an hour and a half, arriving in Zemianske Sady. An old man by the road pointed us to the house of one of the Cuvala daughters. Anicka and Bozena met us, looking intently, trying to recognize the strangers. As we identified ourselves, the emotional outpouring from all was a scene that brought forth all the suffering, sacrifice, and remembrance of our past.

The Cuvala parents had passed away, and we were saddened by the fact that we never had them acknowledged during their lifetime for their unselfish sacrifice. Bozena and Anicka never knew that seven people were hidden under their barn. The barn was off limits to them.

Since the time of our visit, we have exchanged mail and sent gifts, but nothing can ever repay the goodness that was exhibited by the elder Cuvalas. We became determined to have this family acknowledged by Yad Vashem. We had to meet all criteria for them to be honored, and we did so. A couple of years later, the Israeli Consul requested that the Cuvala family, all 17 members, attend a formal ceremony along with 10 other Righteous Gentile families to be honored in the Parliament building. The Slovak and Israeli flags were flown together. This gathering was attended by the president of Slovakia, the mayor of Bratislava, the American ambassador and the Israeli ambassador, who awarded medals and Righteous Among Nations Certificate to the Cuvala family and the nine other saviors, which are registered at Yad Vashem in Jerusalem. We had a warm festive reunion with Anicka, Bozena, their children and grandchildren, and I communicate with them to this day. The Holocaust is the ultimate result of what bigotry and intolerance can lead to. Each one of us has to do everything we can to be totally intolerant of intolerance.

An Invisible Child

by Frieda (Fredzia Gelcman) Jaffe

Piotrkow, located approximately 26 miles southeast of Lodz in central Poland, was an important Jewish cultural, religious, and Hebrew publishing center, with three weekly Yiddish newspapers and numerous Jewish organizations and institutions.

On the eve of the Holocaust, there were 18,000 Jews in the city, which comprised one-third of the total population. In October 1939, the Germans established a ghetto in Piotrkow. It was the first in Poland. The Jewish population of the ghetto swelled to approximately 25,000 because many were brought in from the surrounding villages.

I was two years old when Germany invaded. I was born in Piotrkow, where my family, a large, close family, as well as many other relatives, had lived for many years. In 1939, however, I lived with my mother and father, and later on, my baby brother, in a small town not far from Piotrkow. My father, Josef Gelcman, was a chemist who, I was told, had developed a process for making fine leather from rough animal hides, a formula that the Germans very much wanted. My father would not give them the formula and refused to work for them.

One day, due to illness, he did not report for work. An armed detail came to our house and marched my father, my mother, me and my baby brother to the town square. Here my father was thrown to the ground and made to crawl on his knees over very sharp pointed stones; blood was all over the path which led to the gallows erected in the square. Father passed out from the pain and loss of blood, but this punishment was only the beginning. He was dragged along with two other men to be hanged in front of the gathered crowd. My mother, carrying my baby brother in her arms, tried to cover my eyes so that I would not witness this horror, but a soldier knocked her hand away and forced me to look at the horrible scene. I remember him saying, "She has to watch, she has to learn a lesson". And I learned the lesson well. This picture is burned in my memory and taught me to hide from evil wherever possible and to try to be invisible.

After my father's murder, my mother, little brother, Szimek, and I were forced out of our home in the country and taken to Piotrkow, into the ghetto, where our family lived as best as we could. The sudden change and shock of daily hardship, cruelty, overcrowding, and food shortages was a rude awakening for my family.

Life in the ghetto, especially without father, was a continuous struggle. My little brother's cherub face was drawn and his large sunken eyes scrutinized everything with only occasional whimpers. It is as if he knew that crying would not produce any food to comfort his hunger.

On October 22, 1942, some 22,000 Jews of the Piotrkow Ghetto were deported to the death camp at Treblinka. Among them were my mother, little brother and extended family of over 80 people.

I remember that day. The Jews from the ghetto were assembled at the railway. Cattle cars were waiting. Soldiers were herding people onto them. I wandered away from my mother and remember hearing my name called and I ran toward the sound of mother's voice, but someone grabbed me and literally stuffed a hand over my mouth and shoved me down to the ground. It was my aunt Gittel, one of my mother's sisters. My mother, holding my baby brother, boarded the train as I watched. I never saw them again.

At first, I asked my aunt when mother was coming back. After a while I stopped asking. I understood she was not going to come back. Years later I learned that they had been among the more than 850,000 who died in the gas chambers at Treblinka.

For two years after mother's leaving, I survived mostly on my own by blending in—hiding in the ghetto, staying with people who were still doing slave labor. By November 1944, with the Russian army advancing from the East, the Nazis rounded up Piotrkow's surviving Jews for the Final Solution. I was among them; I was all of seven years old and all alone.

The women, already sick from desperate conditions in the ghetto, were crammed into cattle cars with no food or water and sent off to the German death camps. Here, barbaric medical experiments on twins were conducted and newborn children were deprived of their mothers' breasts to see how long they could live without food; here, Jewish women were routinely sterilized and malarial parasites were injected into human guinea pigs.

Arriving at Ravensbruk, my curly locks were completely shaved off by a female guard. I remember that some of the most vicious acts were committed by the female guards. After six weeks in Ravensbruk, I was sent to Bergen-Belsen, where I was imprisoned for three and a half months. Thirty-five thousand Jews died—or, rather, were killed by starvation, disease, beatings and shooting. Among the victims was the young woman who moved the world with her diary, Anne Frank.

Bergen-Belsen: Words cannot describe those gathered who were hardly living, skeletons dying, surrounded by mountains of unburied corpses, piled high. I was brought to this Hell on earth without anyone even acknowledging my presence. I was left all alone in the world. Nobody took care of anybody here.

Raging typhus, vermin, filth, lack of sanitary conditions, muddy polluted water, the gagging wild beet soup and a chunk of bread was our daily scene. Death was constant.

The filthy earth floors of the barracks—without windows or roof, where hundreds were squeezed in together—were our shelter. There were no bunk shelves, no blankets, nothing to protect us from the bitter cold. I remember that a little friend and I dug a hole at the roots of a stripped-bare tree and covered ourselves with debris up to the neck just to keep covered and warm.

Each morning, the dead were pulled out of the barracks and piled onto the heaps. Corpses were burned in open pits. The stench of burning flesh hung in the air. Death occurred faster than we were able to dispose of the bodies. The mountain of corpses just lay in the open, decaying. All I saw was death, destruction, and disease.

So how did I manage to survive, alone and seven years old at the end of the war? I often ask myself this question. I learned and instinctively knew that I had to blend in to my surroundings. I was resourceful enough to use my surroundings to my advantage. Looking back, I was like a wild dog—uncivilized.

In April 1945, British troops liberated Bergen-Belsen. Frightened, I continued to hide in my hole under the tree. When I did come out and the soldiers told me that I was free, I was confused. Free? All I had ever known was the ghetto and corpses. They said, 'The war is over." I thought, "What war?"

A small number of starving children, under the age of 10, were among the Belsen survivors. I was one of them. The handful of children was scheduled to be sent to Sweden for adoption. I was extremely willful and refused to go. I burst out, "My uncle is coming for me!" The officer just looked at me and asked, "What uncle?" I had remembered my mother's brother, one of the last of my family to be sent to Buchenwald. I had convinced myself that he was coming for me, because anything else was unacceptable. I didn't know if he was dead or alive, but I really believed that he was coming back and I would be living with him. I told this to everyone in the displaced persons' camp. They humored me, but told me to get ready for the bus to Sweden. Again I managed to hide so they had to keep the bus waiting for three hours while they searched for me. When they couldn't wait any longer, they left without me.

And indeed, as if my words and wishes created a reality, my uncle Bernard, my mother's brother, came searching for any family and found me. Soon I was reunited with my aunt Gittel. We transferred to Paris and then to Brussels, where we lived until 1951.

The family remembered a great aunt who had immigrated to Texas in 1913. We contacted her and she sent us visas. Aunt Anna Weisblatt adopted me, but the lack of understanding of my memories and losses created a wedge in our relationship. They provided me with a roof over my head, but the nurturing, comfort, and recognition of the pain that was lodged in my heart taught me again that I had to rely only on my own strength and be self sufficient.

Hungry for education, I excelled in all studies and whizzed through classes to catch up with my own age group. I attended the University of Texas and Texas Christian University, where I majored in French literature and minored in Spanish and German. I graduated with honors.

I met my husband, Harold, on a blind date while in my junior year of college. We were married in 1959. I continued and finished my college education, and we made a home of our own. We rejoiced at the births of our two wonderful sons who have enhanced our life and helped establish a family that I can love and embrace as our treasures and with recognition of their being a continuation of my lost family. And my greatest joys now are my three fantastic grandchildren.

My life in the Holocaust has left me with an obligation to bear witness to my experience and as an advocate for fighting anti-Semitism and/or any discrimination. I hope that my life story will pass on to future generations and the voices of the millions who speak through me will be loud and clear, that yes, evil exists and has always existed, but we, Jewish children, survived and will teach goodness and humanity for as long as we live. And perhaps the world will learn something from our pain, from our tears. It has to, or there is no hope for peace and acceptance in the world in which we live.

Remembering Painful Memories

by Michel Jeifa

My father's family had their roots in the Ukraine town of Zhytomyr. Because of the Czar's army draft and pogroms against the Jews, my father, Bernard, ran away to Paris in 1905. He was 17 years old. In Paris, he established a men's custom tailoring and haberdashery store, with an apartment at the rear, on Rue Claude Bernard, in the Latin Quarter.

My father was a self-educated man who valued formal education and provided this opportunity for his children. He was a moral, cultivated man, as well as a meticulous dresser who was always well groomed. Although he loved his family dearly, he did not display emotions, playfulness, or endearment. His family knew that his austere bearing was only a facade and humored him.

By 1907, my father's father, Moishe, and three of his siblings were already in America, while his mother, Ida, and three of the remaining siblings were fortunate to get visas to America and stopped in Paris to celebrate father's wedding to Adele Tarder in 1907. My mother, Adele, was born in France to David and Rachel Tarder, who immigrated to France in 1870 from Warsaw and became naturalized citizens. My mother was a sweet person, who saw only good in people. Even if one was criticized, she always defended and made excuses for the person. Her light brown hair, tinged with early gray, framed her blue eyes and always-smiling face, which exuded warmth and kindness. Although we lived an assimilated life, not following any of the Jewish rituals, father stated emphatically that he would rather give up his life then give up being a Jew.

Mother and father worked together at their fine tailoring store. She was a clerk, supervising the haberdashery end, while father created fine suits and garments for an upscale clientele, which even included a Minister of the Interior.

A year after their marriage, my sister Marguerite was born. I was born 19 years later, in 1927. When I was four, my sister got married, so all the attention was on me as an only child. A housekeeper cared for me, so mother was free

127

to help run the shop. My life was tranquil and full of love and security. When I reached school age, I attended a public school where I was one of only a few Jews. I was never abused nor felt any anti-Semitism and had a happy experience throughout my school years. As I was approaching Bar Mitzvah age, father insisted that I learn Hebrew and be prepared to become a Bar Mitzvah, which I did in 1940.

When World War II erupted, father was drafted into the Home Security forces, which guarded the neighborhood to make sure that the blackout was observed and no lights filtered through from houses and apartments. He dressed in his uniform and marched out proudly to serve his country.

In June 1940, when the Germans entered Paris, people stayed off the streets and out of sight in case of violence or trouble. The takeover seemed peaceful, so we cautiously returned to following our usual life. By the end of 1940, an edict was issued that all Jews must register at the police station. My father, being an obedient citizen and proud to be a Jew, reported as ordered.

In 1941, my sister's husband, Solomon Karczmer, who was a Russian immigrant, was arrested and sent to a concentration camp until 1942. After the war, we learned that he had been deported to Auschwitz. When the Russian army began to approach the camp he was among those sent on the death march to Buchenwald, where he perished. After his arrest, my sister Marguerite and her two little boys, Jacques and Claude, were befriended and looked after by a social worker, Madeleine Jaquet, of the small town where they lived. It appeared that this woman also had contacts in the resistance.

During all this time, I continued my schooling. My non-Jewish friends did not change their attitude nor did they treat me any differently. Indeed, when, in June 1942, all Jews had to wear a yellow star, my friends came in the morning to walk with me to school as protectors in case of any mischief against me.

A couple of weeks later, a neighbor police inspector came to warn my father to hide because an order was out to arrest Jews. It turned out that 20,000 non-citizen Polish Jews were gathered and sent off to the concentration camp, followed by the arrest of Rumanian Jews a few months later and then other non-citizens. The arrest of French Jews occurred sporadically as they were picked up for any excuse. At this time, my parents agreed to care for a little seven-year-old boy, Emile, whose parents were arrested in July 1942 and had no one to look after him.

A list of restrictions against Jews was enforced. Jews had to obey a curfew; they could not attend movies, theaters and parks; they could ride only in the last car of the subway train and the back of the bus; shopping was restricted to 11 a.m. to 12 p.m., which left empty shelves by that time. Jews also had to turn in their radios, bicycles, and automobiles. Father gave his radio to a neighbor and thus every evening we were able to listen to the London broadcasts and keep abreast of the war events.

On December 20, 1943, the police came to arrest my entire family. I was at school and father was at the synagogue reciting the mourner's prayer for his own father's yahrzeit (anniversary of death). My mother was at home alone with Emile. She instructed Emile to go speedily to stay with a neighbor and proceeded to comply quickly with the police in order that they should not meet up with father returning from the synagogue.

As father was walking home, a neighbor stopped him and told him about the arrest. He hastened to the school, picked me up, and proceeded to Marguerite's house outside of Paris. Marguerite immediately got in touch with the social worker, who was able to secure false papers for me and father. Madeleine advised us that we should not stay together; to separate was the only chance we had. By this time we knew through the London radio broadcasts of the dire conditions for Jews and the massacres that were happening in Poland. We had to follow the advice and hide as directed, even though we could not believe that such inhuman atrocities could be happening.

Because father spoke with an accent, Madeleine sent him back to Paris, where he would be less conspicuous among many. In Paris he worked for a French tailor in his quarters and was advised to keep out of sight. But since mother's arrest, father was in a distraught state of mind; he roamed the streets of Paris hoping to find out anything about mother. During one of his excursions he was stopped and it was discovered that he had falsified papers. He was convicted and sent to a French jail from March 1944 to July 1944. When he was released, he was turned over to the Germans. Father was deported on the last train out of Paris on July 31, 1944, together with many Jewish children from the orphanages.

I was placed with a Protestant family in the south of France in Basses Alpes, where I worked with them as a forester and helped in the production of charcoal. My life was hard. Being separated from my family and not knowing of their whereabouts or safety was psychologically difficult. The host family were avid Christians and their zeal and goal was to convert me. I finally told them to stop or I would return to Paris. They relinquished their quest, but informed me that they would pray for me. At the same time, Marguerite was also hidden with her boys till the liberation.

When Paris was liberated in September 1944, I returned to our apartment, broke the seal, and entered the bleak surroundings. A cup filled with coffee was standing on the table, as if mother was about to return from another room. It made me shiver with pain as the tears rolled down my face. My distraught state drove me out of the flat and I sought shelter with friends. Shortly after, my sister came with the children and that is when we moved back to our apartment, believing that any day, any moment, our parents and my brother-in-law, Solomon, would walk through the door.

In January 1945, the French Auschwitz survivors were returned to France, where they were housed in the Hotel Lutetia. Every day a list of survivors was posted there. I ran daily to see the new list and returned home disappointed. In May 1945, when the truth of the Holocaust became public knowledge, it brought shivers to one's core, but we still hoped that our parents would return. After Paris was liberated on August 15, 1944, one of the orphan girls from that train, who survived Auschwitz, returned. She told me that my father was sent directly to the gas chambers on arrival. My mother's whereabouts or how she died were never discovered and to this day I am in pain when I think or speak of my mother.

When all hope was gone to reunite with my parents, and after I received a letter from my grandmother and family from New York inviting me to America, I insisted that my sister and her children accompany me. We left France in 1947. I had to leave France; I could not live in a cemetery.

In New York, I continued my education, earned a bachelor's degree while I taught French at Berlitz. In 1951 I was drafted and served two years in the army. When I was discharged I continued school and received a master's degree in accounting. Although I developed a loving, stable and productive life, I still live with nightmares, fear, and distrust. My memories and survival trials are with me every day. I always wonder: "Why did I survive?"

In 1955 I married Blanche Greenwald, a wonderful wife and partner. We raised two children: a son, Bernard, who has his own title-insurance business, and a daughter, Gisele, who is the director of Financial Aid Services for the state of New Jersey. Blanche and I have five grandchildren: Jordan 12, Erica 10, Jacob 8, Alexa 7, and Gabrielle 5, who are the sunshine of our lives and are the answer and the reason why I survived.

After the war, Mademoiselle Jacquet (married name—Madame Boisseille) gave me this tragic yet treasured letter from my father. His words break my heart, but they also serve as a tangible message and good-bye, since I never said good-bye to either of my parents.

A Letter from Bernard Jeifa from the French Jail

July 6th, 1944

Dear Mademoiselle,

> *I received your letter of June 30th on Tuesday and it is always with a renewed pleasure that I read yours. I am always so happy to get news from my dear children whose separation is so painful to me. I regret so much not being able to correspond directly with each one. I have to accept your good judgment and in spite of the suffering I do accept this need to assure their safety.*

Today I am very downhearted and once again I must impose on your charitable devotion.

Yesterday I appeared in front of the Court of Appeals to obtain an increase in sentencing which would allow me to witness the coming events which hopefully will soon put an end to our martyrdom. Unfortunately I was unable to obtain what I was looking for.

I am therefore, to be released from here in the morning of July 21st. This is when my worries will start or rather increase. I am sure that you do understand that for me it means nothing else than "Concentration Camps" with all the horrible consequences for us Jews. This I wanted to avoid at all cost.

Since I have not been able to prevent my release please, I would want you to get in touch immediately with my attorney Mr. Hector Rivierez, 18 Ave de LaBourdonnais telephone Inv 7756 and to consult with him on the possibilities to save me from this horrible future reserved for me and which terrifies me.

Since I will have served my sentence there is no way to appeal. I will be released on that date.

A different way to act would be to try to build up a new case against me that would force my staying here during the investigation. Please review these possibilities.

Please allow me to point out to you the extreme urgency needed for action since on the 21st—less than weeks from now—I will be turned over to the Prefecture and what will follow. There is not a minute to waste. I apologize to you but to me it is a question of life, and this is why I appeal to you, the only one who can act usefully, the only one I can confide in and the only one that can understand the situation. I trust my life to you.

Please let me know as soon as possible what my attorney says and what course of action he advises.

If you find it advisable, talk to my friends Rue Claude Bernard so that they may be part of the plan to help me.

I will be awaiting anxiously to hear from you and I want to thank you for all you are doing for me. Please believe dear Miss Jacquet in my deepest respect and friendship.

Jeifa
If you find it useful—please keep this letter.

In the Grip of the Devil

by Helen Sternlicht Jonas

My father, Szymon Sternlicht, was a man of integrity and kindness. His attention to his family was with devotion and good humor. My two sisters and I would cling to him, eager to hear his many stories and learn from him. He served in WW I in the Polish army and shared accounts of the trials and successes during his service. He earned a comfortable living running a small metal shop in ironwork and lock-smithy and treated his few employees with fairness and generosity.

My mother, Lola, was a beautiful woman who filled our apartment with good cheer, playfulness, and songs of the day. She was a good cook and regularly contributed meals for sick people in a sanitarium. She carried them a long distance, with me as her companion. Mother was a passionate person whose commitment to justice was unquestionable. When my mother found out that our Polish helper did not go to church on Sundays thinking that my parents would not approve, my mother forced her to go or she would lose her position with us. My memories of my mother bring to mind her ability to laugh and enjoy being child-like, dressing up for the Purim holiday as Charlie Chaplin.

I was born in April 1925 and was the youngest of my sisters. Sydell was the oldest, followed two years later by my sister Betty, and I was three years younger than she. Our residence on the outskirts of Krakow is where our family found security and did not experience discrimination or anti-Semitic expressions. When we moved into the city of Krakow, my parents were uneasy letting my sister Sydell go out in the evenings because of the hooligans who were attacking Jews.

Our family was modern in our daily life; but we were observant, following all traditions of Judaism. My maternal grandparents, who lived nearby, conversed in Yiddish and I learned to understand the language, even though Polish was spoken both in and out of our home.

Just before World War II, about 68,000 Jews lived in Krakow and the surrounding villages. It was one of the largest Jewish communities in Poland, making up a quarter of the Krakow residents. The city was an influential cultural center and became the center of Jewish political and social life in Poland.

After finishing my public-school studies, my plan was to continue my education at a vocational school. But this never materialized because the Germans occupied Krakow on September 6, 1939. Krakow became the capital of Nazi-occupied Poland under *Generalgouveneur* (general governor) Hans Frank.

Persecution of the Jewish population began almost immediately with the establishment of a *Judenrat* (Jewish Council). SS-*Oberscharführer* (staff sergeant or senior squad leader) Paul Siebert, who appointed the members of the *Judenrat*, ordered them to execute the German commands with unconditional obedience and accuracy.

Throughout Krakow, synagogues were ordered closed and all their relics and valuables turned over to the Nazi authorities. Jews were enlisted into forced labor. In November 1939 restrictive edicts were issued. As of December 1, 1939, all Jews 12 years and older had to wear identifying armbands with the Star of David. Jewish children could not attend schools; Jews could not walk on sidewalks. Businesses were taken away. Meager ration cards were issued and curfews enforced. Religious Jews were accosted in the streets and their beards and side-locks were cut off with laughter and abuse.

The more important Jewish enterprises were handed over to Germans; the smaller and less significant ones to Ukrainians and Poles. Father was still allowed to keep his shop, working for the Gestapo, which gave him a sense of security of being a needed worker.

Life was in a constant state of fear and expectations of trouble; unexpected maltreatment would appear out of nowhere and for no reason. Houses and apartments were stormed into by German officers with kicks, shouts, and beatings; they looted anything of value that appealed to them, often confiscating various articles and food for their own personal use or just creating havoc to frighten and subdue a beaten Jewish populace.

I was taken to work for the Germans, cleaning their quarters, cleaning streets, and, in the winter, shoveling snow. Everyone lived in fear and with a sense that any minute things could become drastic. No one could plan or find safety.

On March 3, 1941, the Krakow Ghetto was formally established. It was situated in Podgorze, on the right bank of the Vistula River—the town's poorest quarters—separated from the rest of the town by the river and limestone quarry. The ghetto consisted of less than one square mile with about 350 squalid houses and some two-story structures. The ghetto was encircled with tombstone-shaped walls, which was prophetic of what was to happen to the Jews. All windows and doors facing the "Aryan" side were ordered bricked up. Only four guarded entrances allowed traffic to pass through and only with approval. The gates were guarded by German and Polish police, assisted by the Jewish police, the *Ordnungsdienst* (order keepers), who were selected by the *Judenrat*.

The Jews who had not evacuated Krakow, as directed earlier, were ordered to move to Podgorze by March 20, 1941. We were told to pack only what we could carry and relocate there within two days. How one decides what is important to bring became a problem; we did not know what we would have to face and what would be a necessity. We walked across a bridge to the ghetto, searching for a place in a house already filled to capacity. Eventually, the ghetto housed 20,000 Jews, not just from Krakow, but also from neighboring communities, crammed into an area previously inhabited by 3,000 people.

Life in the ghetto was one of hunger, disease, and overcrowding. Many died trying to get food or medicine from outside the ghetto; the usual punishment for those being caught was to be shot. Conditions were unbearable, but we found strength in the fact that as long as we were together, we could endure. Even under these conditions there was a spirit of community, as the Jewish Council leaders established a hospital and educational programs for the children.

From May 30, 1942, onward, the Nazis implemented systematic deportations from the ghetto to surrounding concentration camps. The SS marched into the ghetto, ordering all to line up for an *Appell* (roll call). Selections began, and two SS soldiers took my father to join a selected group. Father, believing his own message, said, "Don't worry—nothing will happen to me. They need my skills." The gathered were kept in the square for a few days and then were taken to the waiting cattle cars. Our hope was that they would be working somewhere, but they were taken to an extermination camp. Thousands of Jews were transported in the succeeding months. The first transport consisted of 7,000 and the second numbered 4,000, and all were deported to the Belzec extermination camp. My beloved father was among those taken away.

During these selections, the Germans massacred hundreds of people; the ghetto streets were awash with the blood of their victims. They executed hospital patients, the old, as well as children from the ghetto orphanage. These sudden searches and liquidation of the orphanage and children's homes were a shocking sight as children were thrown into trucks. Mothers, running after the trucks in shock and screaming frantically, were shot. Everyone walked around with big unfocused eyes, shocked faces. I thought that we were living in a nightmare, but it was reality.

My sister Sydell worked outside and sought help from our Polish friend to hide mother, but he refused with a look of disdain and without caring. She then  appealed to another Polish family, which agreed to shelter mother for only one night, and so she escaped the deportation that took place in the ghetto. Those deemed unfit, about 2,000 Jews, were killed in the streets. The ones that survived and not selected for Plaszow (forced-labor camp) were sent to Auschwitz.

In December, 1942, the ghetto was divided into two parts: Ghetto A for "workers" and Ghetto B for "non-workers." At this time, the construction of the camp at Plaszow was already underway. The camp was on the site of a Jewish cemetery and near a quarry. SS *Untersturm-fuhrer* (lieutenant) Amon Goeth took command in February, 1943.

On March 13 and 14, 1943, the Nazis carried out the final "liquidation" of the ghetto. Eight thousand Jews were taken to the Plaszow labor camp. Most workers in the ghetto camp, who initially went back and forth from the ghetto, were now housed in barracks in the Plaszow camp. Most were employed by German industrialists, among them Oscar Schindler and Julius Madritsch, who came to make their fortune and make use of the cheap labor force.

Camp Plaszow was encircled by double barbed wire tall fencing with a ditch of water in between. It was guarded from three guard towers, situated close together and equipped with machine guns, telephones and revolving searchlights. The camp guards consisted of Ukrainians until it was restructured into a concentration camp and then was under SS men. The prisoners were starved and treated with cruelty.

Shortly after my arrival in Plaszow, I was washing the barracks windows when a very tall SS man stopped in front of me and said, "If a Jewish girl is smart enough to clean the windows on a sunny day, she is good enough for me." The next day an orderly came for me and took me to the SS man's house. I did not know who this man was but soon learned that it was the commandant, Goeth. He asked me, "What is your name?" I answered, "Helena." He said, "I already have a maid named Helena; I don't need two Helenas. Your name from now on is to be Susanna." And so my life as a maid for Goeth began. At first I thought that being a maid was better than being a laborer in the camp; but the reality of the precarious tightrope of my life soon became very evident. Was I to have it better than all the other women, including my mother and sisters, or was I now in the eye of the storm?

The first incident to make clear what my new reality would be like occurred when I was ironing his shirts. As Goeth was passing by he slapped me on my face with full force and declared with anger that in Austria girls iron better. I went reeling and crying. He demanded that in his residence there not be any sadness or tears. I held back my emotions and tears and answered "*Jawohl, Herr Commandant*"(Yes sir, commandant.) I learned that I had to grow up fast and had to be strong. My one relief was when I was able to return to my barrack at night. And so my life of terror began, serving the devil himself. I reported to Goeth's house every day. Goeth ruled the camp with a reign of terror—beatings and shootings were everyday occurrences.

At first Goeth lived in a small house where Helena Hirsch and I took turns to remain overnight until his villa was built for him. It was called the "*Rotes Haus*," (Red House). Shortly, Goeth's mistress, Ruth Kalder, an actress, arrived, cuddling a little black dog. The nightly parties, drinking, and orgies began, attended by many officers, women and various men, among them Schindler and Madritsch. I was in total amazement to see such decadence; it was beyond my understanding. Helena and I tried to do everything we could to provide them with food and drink and stay out of their sight so as not to become a target of Goeth's explosive tirades and abuse.

With the mistress now residing in the villa, Helena and I had to remain in the villa at all times and had a room in the cellar. We were not allowed to go to the barracks. I was in a constant state of terror; the sound of Goeth's heavy steps on the upper floors sent shivers of fear through my body. The name calling, the beatings with his huge hands, or shoving me down the stairs became a normal condition and were not a surprise to me anymore. I held back my pain, my anger, because I could not be sad. The sound of his bellowing voice calling my name or the ringing of a bell sent me into panic; but somehow, as I appeared in front of Goeth, I had the sense to hide my fear. The added stress of not knowing what was happening to my family made me daring on a few occasions to sneak away to see my mother and bring her a little food, which she always shared with some of the inmates.

We had another servant working for Goeth, a young boy, Lisiek, who ran errands and polished Goeth's boots. One day, one of the guests asked Lisiek to get the horse and carriage ready to take him home, which he did. After the guest left, Goeth confronted Lisiek, asking him who gave him permission to obey the guest. Without waiting for an explanation, Goeth pulled out his revolver and shot him. Another truly evil occasion was when Goeth told some of his workers to hit each other, but when the fighting was not vicious enough, he demonstrated how it should be done to make them bloody one another, which they did. This finally satisfied this evil Satan.

The brutality and just plain cold-blooded killings went on in front of our eyes. On one occasion I saw him on the balcony, his fury rising as he spotted

136

some men not working hard enough or moving slowly. I snuck out of the villa, and slid down an embankment to warn the men that they should get out of his eyesight or be shot. When I think back to my audacity, I am in awe of the child that I was, but perhaps because I was so young I felt immortal at times or just stopped caring if I lived or died.

I knew that my time would come when he would kill me too, but I prayed that my mother and sisters would survive. And yet I felt a power, an obstinate belief in God, that I would endure and be released from this hell. I believe that my strength and a determination to be a Jew came from my home and the teachings of our history and people. I lived with a belief that whatever I would encounter, it was God's will.

During my time under Goeth's roof, I met Schindler. I could not understand how this gentle-appearing man could be friends with Goeth. He always looked at me with kind eyes, and never called me names. I remember on one occasion he came to our basement room, which at first alarmed me. His gentle demeanour and words, calling me "kindchen" (little child), almost made me scream for help, but I kept my composure; I could not trust anyone. He asked me if he could help me with anything. I told him about my sick mother. On his next visit he brought medicine for her. He said not to worry, it will be okay. He walked me to the window and said in a subdued voice, "You will be saved." But my mother never survived. She died from complications of pneumonia. Her biggest wish was not to be part of the mass graves. My boyfriend, Adam Sztab, buried her at night and placed a bottle with her name as a marker. I never discovered her burial place.

I met Adam during my excursion to the barracks. He was the leader of the Jewish resistance organization ZOB (*Zydowska Organizacja Bojowa*), the Jewish underground organization. He became my boyfriend. Of course, our meetings were innocent, but it helped me to feel that I still was a girl who could be admired by a boy, and especially Adam, who was of strong character and trying to make a difference. He told me that he was working with the underground resistance, who were readying for an escape. Adam gave me a small camera and asked me to get the plans for the sewer system of the area and other documents, which I did. I still don't know where I got the courage to get the documents for him. Adam's plans never materialized; he was denounced by a Ukrainian man who was supposed to have sold him some arms. Adam was beaten without pity, shot, and then his body was hung with a sign warning the inmates of Plaszow: "This is the end of all who hide weapons."

The Polish book, "Zaglada Zydow W Krakowie" (Destruction of Jews in Krakow), by Aleksander Bieberstein, tells about Helen's participation in getting important information to the underground:

"... a small group of prisoners decided to organize a resistance against the Germans. To this group belonged the maid of Goeth, Helen Sternlicht, who found certain secret documents in the desk of Goeth, which she copied and gave to the members of PPR outside of the Camp. She gave stamped documents to a small group led by Adam Sztab. Taking advantage of the documents, they succeeded to enter the barrack of the armor, telling the guards that they came to fix the plumbing. The plan called for getting the Ukrainian guards drunk and take arms out of the store-house. Unfortunately, one of the Ukrainian guards recognized Sztab and notified Goeth about the plan and undertaking. Goeth killed Sztab and ordered the body to hang on the gallows. This took place on the same day that they shot Chilowicz and his accomplices. On the gallows that Sztab was hanging, they had a sign with the inscription: This is the end of all who hide weapons."

After Goeth was reprimanded by the SS for having Jews living in his house, Helena and I had to live in the SS women's building next to the villa, in the cellar, taking turns to stay nights at the Goeth villa.

The days of the Jewish prisoners usefulness in Plaszow was coming to an end because the Russian front was getting closer. One day, the women from the barracks were gathered and lined up in fives. The camp was being liquidated. I saw them being marched for deportation, from the villa window, and ran frantically towards them, hoping that I could have my sisters taken out of the lines. I was ready to join them in case they could not be saved. An SS man who knew me, mumbled to me that I should tell my sisters to slowly walk backwards. He said there were not enough cattle cars for the assembled. At the same time, Helena awoke the mistress, Ruth, and begged her to intercede for me and my sisters and tell the Jewish police to pull them out from the line. My sisters were among those that were returned to the barracks. My sisters were safe. I could not believe our good luck. When I returned to the villa, Helena and I pleaded with Ruth not to tell Goeth about our appeal and her intervention, but Ruth did tell him. A few nights later, Goeth came looking for me; instead, he confronted Helena and beat her severely. I imagine that he got the full measure of hate out and did not continue on me.

As the Russians were coming closer, Goeth ordered that all the buried bodies be dug up and burned. The frantic energy of covering up the deeds of the killers was urgent. During this time of covering up the murderous deeds, two civilian Germans came to the villa asking for Goeth. They confronted him with some papers and took him away. They found out that he was stealing the wealth which was being confiscated from the Jews and sending it to his Austrian home. Right after the war, the Russians turned him over to the Poles. He was tried for his crimes and hung.

So now Helena and I were left alone in the villa. It felt unreal that we had such freedom. One day I heard the doorbell ring. I struggled to keep up my courage, not knowing what was waiting on the other side. Schindler was standing at the door. He said, "I built a factory in Czechoslovakia and you and Helena are coming with me." He asked me if I had any family, and I gave him the names of my sisters. Three hundred women, including my sisters, and 700 men were on a list to go to his factory. We were loaded into cattle cars and started our journey full of hope that we had escaped the killers. But the 300 women were taken to Auschwitz. It appeared that Schindler was arrested for some infraction and could not get us freed.

Auschwitz: the red sky, the smoke, the smell, greeted us. We had to go through a shower and I thought that we were destined to add to the smoke. I was grateful that our sick mother did not have to endure the evil that was here.

We were in Auschwitz for three weeks when at a roll call our names were called from a list to go to Schindler's factory. When we arrived in Brinnlitz, Czechoslovakia, Oskar greeted us with a huge smile and said, "Finally you are here."

We worked in his factory for seven months, but nothing was produced there; it was a façade. When the Americans and the Russian cavalry liberated us, Schindler gave each of his saved Jews a piece of cloth and leather for shoes so that we could have clothing made for us when we got back to Krakow. Out of gratitude for his selfless acts and for saving us, those who had gold fillings or gold crowns pulled them out of their mouths and fashioned a ring for Schindler with an inscription inside, "Thank You."

Schindler's Jews knew that as a Nazi the Russians would arrest him, so the survivors helped to sneak him away into the American Zone, where he was safe. I can never forget the evil that befell my family and the Jewish people, but I also will never forget Oskcar Schindler and his sacrifices and his saving over 1,100 Jews.

When we returned to Krakow, my sisters and I found no family left in Poland. Like the thousands of survivors who could not find a safe home in Poland, we crossed the borders and arrived in a DP camp in Austria where I met my husband, Joseph Jonas, who also was saved by Schindler.

In 1947, we were able to come to America and settled in the Bronx, New York, and rebuilt our lives and family. My blessings—my three children, son Steven and twin daughters Shelley and Vivian and four beautiful and accomplished grandchildren—are my reward for surviving.

My dear husband Joseph struggled for many years with guilt for having survived while his family was murdered. He was only 16 years old when he offered to replace his father in the selection and was refused. His father's name became his constant doodling on every paper, even the borders of the daily newspaper. The trauma of this separation was a pain that he could not bear. At age 57, my husband decided to end his life.

The tragedy to me and to my children was beyond description. Our children don't want to carry any anger or hurt against their father, but they want the world to know of the scars and the pain that survivors endure.

We cannot forget and we cannot forgive.

My own life story is not only that of a survivor, but of a witness. I saw the evils of the Holocaust: I lost my parents, my extended family, six million Jewish people. I witnessed the evil of Amon Goeth personally. But, just as importantly, I was blessed to have been saved by a good man, Oscar Schindler, who saved the lives of Jews because he found his humanity and it was the right thing to do. On his grave stone it is written: "Righteous Among the Nations." As the Bible tells us, when you save one person, you save the world.

Recently I took part in the documentary film, *"Inheritance."* In the film, Goeth's daughter, Monika Hertwig, now 60 years old, tries to understand and find the truth about the atrocities her father executed during the Holocaust. At first, I did not want to participate in the film, but with the encouragement of Steven Spielberg I agreed to take part. It was difficult to return to the villa where I had suffered so greatly. But I did so in the hope that it would serve as a memorial to my lost family and the six million, and would inspire students to try to comprehend how such horrors could happen. This film finally allowed me to face my own history and has become my stepping stone in sharing my Holocaust experiences.

Amon Goeth Villa Balcony
Plaszow Concentration Camp

A Conspiracy of Kindness

by John (Josef) Koenigsberg

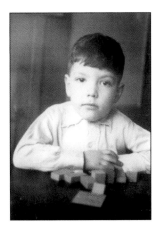

My father, Bernard, experiencing anti-Semitism and the hardship of life in Poland, came to Amsterdam, Holland, in 1918, after serving in the Polish army. He left his family, parents, and siblings behind and struggled to survive in his new life. His position at a hospital as a porter was only the first step in his rise to more prestigious and rewarding work. He eventually earned his living on the administrative staff of the hospital. In time his life was enhanced by a lovely young woman, ten years younger, my mother, Sally (Scheindel) Starkman, who also emigrated from Poland with a couple of her siblings. She found a way to educate herself as a nurse and began her working career at the same hospital. They established a good life and possibilities of a good and safe future and consequently encouraged her eight siblings and parents to join them. And so our family grew including my arrival, in August 1937.

Father always presented himself in a suit and tie, standing tall, with an air of sophistication and assurance. His outward demeanor appeared stiff and important, but in reality he was a thoughtful, moral man who was ultra-Orthodox in his belief and guided me in this direction too. My parents were strict in their expectations, which was not unusual for those times and culture.

Our apartment was in a large u-shaped apartment complex, where I played in the courtyard sandbox and was taken care of by my extended family—who also lived in the building—while my parents worked. I remember the special days—the Sabbath and holidays—when our apartment was transformed by a festive mood and the aromas of special foods and fresh challa.

On May 10, 1940, when I was less than three years old, Holland was overrun by Germany. Because the country was geographically situated on the North Sea and across from Britain, it was of strategic importance to the Germans, and we became an early victim of their war machine.

Hitler's propaganda of hate against the Jews awakened the NSB, the Dutch pro-Nazi party. The persecution and control of Jews became their prime concern. First they had all Jews register, including their properties and assets. By April 1941, they followed through on the Nuremberg Laws with zeal. Jews had to live only in designated areas in the city; they were not allowed to walk on sidewalks, play in park playgrounds or even sit on park benches. Jews were forbidden to enter hotels, restaurants, theaters, public meeting halls and movie theaters. Jews in Amsterdam could no longer move out of the city to live anywhere else in Holland. Jewish professionals could only work for other Jews. The Gestapo, who were assisted by the administration and police, gathered Jews right off the streets and from their homes. People simply disappeared.

In April 1942, all Jews had to wear a yellow star with the word "*Jood*"—Jew—printed with Hebrew letters in the center. That summer Jews had to form a *Joodse Raad* (Jewish Council) to assist the Germans in fulfilling their demands. A curfew from 8 a.m. to 6 p.m. was imposed and shopping for food and necessities was limited to between 3 and 5 p.m., by which time there was just about nothing left to buy.

July 6, 1942 has become an important date. That is when Anne Frank's sister Margot was to report for deportation forcing the family and their companions to enter their famous hiding place. In August 1942, the Nazis arrested Jews, who were easy targets, since they were living in a concentrated area of Amsterdam. They conducted nightly raids, blocking off areas and arresting Jewish families, apartment by apartment.

Early 1943 brought the Gestapo to our doors. Pounding loudly, they arrested my widower grandfather, who lived with us, while mother and I hid in a back bedroom. Mother became wordless; it was as if she was in a stupor. I knew that something bad was happening, but as a child of not yet five, I could not understand the harshness of our life. I knew enough to maintain a low profile and be a good little boy.

Holland's geographical locality offered no possibility to escape. It was virtually surrounded by Germany, German-occupied Belgium, and the North Sea, which was under tight and strong control. The country was flat and heavily populated. There were no great forests or isolated areas where Jews could possibly find shelter and escape.

It was not long before my father and I were picked up off the street and incarcerated in the Dutch Theatre—*Hollandse Schouwberg*. The theatre was the staging area of the arrested people to be sent to Westerbork concentration camp, which was a three-hour drive east of Amsterdam on the German-Dutch border. (From Westerbork, people were loaded onto cattle cars. Ninety-three trains left Westerbork. The first one departed on July 15, 1942; the last on September 6, 1944. About two-thirds of the trains were sent to Auschwitz; most of the remaining ones went to another camp, Sobibor. Only about 5,000 Jews survived to return. Thirty-five thousand Jews of Holland survived the war; 105,000 did not.)

Because my father had an ID as an important worker, he was released from the theater while I remained among those arrested. Before leaving, my fast-thinking father, acting distressed, placed me with the nurse, stating that I was having an appendix attack. I was released and allowed to be taken to the Jewish hospital. The charade of my attack continued by my actually being anesthetized. When I awoke I was in pain. My appendix had not been removed, but an incision had been made to fool the authorities.

My parents placed me with a gentile family for my recuperation. It turned out that they were Dutch pro-Nazis. To save me from being exposed, father's contacts with the underground came to my rescue and took me to the tiny village of Vaesrade' to live with a Catholic family, the Snijckers. I was welcomed by this loving family of a mother and father, three daughters, Fientje, Mia and Tonny, and a son, Jan, with whom I shared a bed and was clothed in his altered outgrown clothes. I was introduced to the community as Johnny Snijckers, a sickly relative from Rotterdam. During this time, these good people hid many transient hiders—little children and adults—as an interim safe house to continue to more permanent hiding places.

The location of this village was in the forefront of the possible invasion of the Allies, so it was well guarded by the Germans, and as a result the area was a target for frequent bombings. The recurrent night air raids of impending bombings drove us running into the bomb shelter dug into a nearby hill or lying flat in a trench near the house, cupping our ears to muffle the noise of the planes and exploding bombs. It was a miracle that none hit us directly.

I attended the church school and was given a number of Christian amulets and a cross to wear. I don't recall how this masquerade affected me. During my two-and-a-half-year stay with the Snijckers, my parents did not know where I was.

At the same time, my entire extended family was dispersed; most were arrested, deported and murdered in the killing camps. Only Aunt Frieda survived Auschwitz and Bergen-Belsen, and her daughter, Liesje, survived because she, too, was hidden.

No one knew where to find shelter or if it was safe. Mother, with the help of the underground, was hidden with a Christian family in their basement for over two years. Here, her nursing skills came in handy by assisting the lady with birthing two children during that time. No one knew that she was hidden with them. Father shifted about from safe house to safe house, working for the underground, facilitating in procuring safe houses to hide fellow Jews.

By 1943, the Germans had deported nearly 110,000 Jews from Holland. The remaining 30,000 went into hiding. Most were hidden as individuals; very few families as a whole went into hiding and many did not want to abandon their families who did not have a place to hide. Of the 30,000 Jews who went into hiding, two-thirds were Jews who had come from Germany. About half of the Jews who were hiding were captured.

Most of Holland was liberated by the Canadians, but a little-known fact is that the southern tip of Holland, where I was hidden, was liberated by the Americans in the fall of 1944 . These friendly, rough and tumble American soldiers were not frightening at all. They showered me with chocolates and cookies and brought packages of food that we had not tasted in years. The rest of Holland was finally liberated in March and April of 1945 to exuberant welcomes of many grateful Hollanders.

My parents searched for me without success. Appealing to the International Red Cross, they finally were able to find me. Father came to the Snijckers' house. As he walked on the path, I examined this tall man, afraid to be wrong, afraid of having to be someone else again. This did not look like my father as I remembered him. There was a resemblance, but this man was thin and his black hair was completely white.

He waved at me, holding out his arms into which I ran hoping that I would be met with gladness and love. The feeling of being myself, Josef, again was tumultuous. I was only eight years old and was overwhelmed with all emotions. I knew that I would have to say good-bye to my Snijckers family and to my safe life as a Catholic boy. Our good-byes were sad and we promised that we would soon see each one another again.

When I was reunited with my mother, she was a complete stranger. She did not look the same and her beautiful dark hair was red. Again I had to concentrate hard to recover my mother from this image.

Our family was together, but all our extended family, over 40 members, was killed. We were alone in Amsterdam and had to learn to be a small family of three. My parents rented another flat in the same u-shaped apartment complex and returned to their previous jobs. My life and identity had to be rebuilt. I was a Jewish boy and regardless of the horrors that befell our people, my father returned to his Orthodox roots and we continued life with this family heritage. I was enrolled into an Orthodox Jewish school and attended first, second and third grades in the first year. I did adjust and advanced with my education

144

and rooted in my Jewish identity. We lived a comfortable life, and in 1949 my brother David was born. I was 12 at the time and acted as a parent to him.

We were able to immigrate to the United States in 1953 and settled in Cincinnati, joining an American part of our family who had come to the States in the 1920s and 30s. It did not take long for me to integrate into the American way of life. My parents also found comfort living in America. They saw their children and grandchildren live in safety and peace and build their own families.

I married my wonderful partner and best friend, Beverly Rosenstein, and we built our own family of two daughters, a son, and five grandchildren. I never spoke about my Holocaust experience and survival, but after giving testimony to the Spielberg Shoah Project, I became inspired to share my experiences and speak in schools and organizations.

In November 2007, I visited the Snijckers family. The parents had passed away, but one of the daughters, Tonny, shared with me a poem and drawing that I had put in their diary. I am now filling out the papers necessary to have this family remembered and honored by Yad Vashem as "Righteous Among Nations."

*Snijckers family, 1945 (after the war). This is the family
that hid John from fall 1942 until the end of the war.*

On September 3, 2009, my very special family was honored by Yad Vashem in a ceremony held in Maastricht Holland, about 20 kilometers south of the little village where I was hidden. Certificate and medals were presented by the Israeli ambassador and witnessed by dignitaries, the mayor of Maastricht and the consul general of the Israeli Embassy. My wife, Beverly, her sister and husband, and all my children attended the ceremony.

A Survivor's Challenge

by Benno Lindenberg

"Ven das Juden blut fun messer shpritzed, den geit es unz noch mal zo gut."
["When Jewish blood will drip from our knives, then our life will be so much better."]

This statement was openly proclaimed throughout Dortmund and Germany in January 1933 as Hitler came to power.

I was born to Polish immigrants who came to Germany in 1918. My father, Chil-Mayer, came to escape the hardships of life in Poland with the expectation of filling a shortage of needed laborers to work in the Dortmund coal mines after the First World War. Instead, he established a business in textiles, selling fabrics for the production of suits. My mother, Toba Kryger, joined him a year later. Both came from observant families and followed the laws of Judaism. Their house was always full of guests and hospitality was boundless. They blended well into society, both Jewish and German, and gave and received warm friendship.

I was born on May 14, 1920. Even though there were two synagogues in town, there was no mohel (circumcision rabbi) and so a surgeon performed the sacred obligatory surgery. After 18 months, a second child, my brother Leo, was born. The family grew, prospered, and enjoyed life.

Because mother was needed to help run the business, her mother, Rifka, came from Poland to live with us and help supervise her grandsons. She made sure that her grandsons excelled in their education, especially in their study of Hebrew and prayer, which was provided by a rabbi/teacher who came daily to instruct us.

My father was elated with his sons and treated us like little princes, dressing us in the finest clothes, and introduced us to the world at large by attending a variety of sport events and excursions in the mountains and on the river.

At age six, I was sent to an elite private school and after four years continued in the Hindenberg Real Gymansium, where I chose Modern Studies. I was the only Jewish boy in a class of 40 and was integrated in all activities without difficulty.

In January 1933, Hitler came to power, and suddenly life changed for many Jews. Overnight, 39 of my classmates joined the Hitler Youth and the bullying and contempt began. My teacher strongly urged that I not return to class because he could not guarantee my safety.

At that time, in the middle town square of the nicest neighborhood, the brown-shirt muscle-boys built a huge bonfire and burned every Jewish book  and Torah they could find. People who were good neighbors and social friends avoided the Jews like lepers. Even relatives who intermarried with Jewish cousins became distant and disassociated themselves.

Prior to Hitler's rise to power, word of his evil leadership reached an incredulous Jewish population. They knew that a great danger was rising, yet they did not want to accept such a conclusion. After all, they were good, productive, hard-working, contributing members of the society. But matters were soon made clear to the Lindenbergs when the employees of the family business openly and brazenly announced that they were now running the business and no Jew would be their boss.

Having come from Poland with basically nothing and knowing what anti-Semitism felt like, my father sent away any salvageable possessions and valuables to Belgium. After the threat to our safety by our own employees of so many years, my mother and father left for Liege, Belgium, in May of 1933, while my brother and I were sent for the summer to our aunt and uncle in Hamburg. Here we had to take on a role of being Hitler boys in order to remain safe and continued this charade as we traveled to Liege to rejoin our parents, who arrived at the end of August. We remained in Liege for one year, establishing some normalcy of life. I returned to school, where I became fluent in French.

During this time, my uncle Shmil Brot, who was living in the United States, sent us an affidavit to immigrate to America, guaranteeing financial responsibility of the family. But the quota was closed until 1942, so we were stuck living in Belgium under "In Transit" papers, which had to be updated every six months.

At the end of 1934, the family moved to Antwerp for better opportunities. We again established roots, not knowing that here, too, we would not be long-term residents. I started school and learned Flemish and Dutch. Father's business success with a Belgian citizen partner allowed the family to thrive and live a lavish life. I joined Jewish organizations, excelled in school, and enjoyed a life of a student teenager. It was full of escapades and tested my charm on many girls enamored of me.

That all came to an end when, on May 10, 1940, Germany attacked Holland and Belgium with brutal bombardments. By this time, I was 20 and had learned much about being independent. So while my parents escaped to Paris, my brother and I went by car to be reunited. We were caught up in many strafings and bombardments against the retreating British and all borders between the countries were closed. Not being able to get through, we returned to our apartment in Antwerp and found it almost completely looted. Soon our parents also returned, only to face the edicts against the Jews. We were not allowed to remain in Antwerp and had to move to Brussels. We continued to live with the oppressive decrees until May 1942, when my parents went into quasi-hiding under gentile identities. In the meantime, I smuggled my way to Nice, France, with false papers in order to join the French Free Armed Forces in Africa. I was arrested and placed into the Rivesaltes concentration camp, from which I managed to escape.

I returned to Belgium to get my family out and managed to get them into France with forged non-Jewish papers. Each night the Germans ordered all IDs to be inspected; I was caught and sent to a camp where Spanish refugees were detained. A cousin on the outside, a veteran of the French army, who had the same name as me, managed to smuggle duplicate papers to me to replace mine. With these in hand, I hid in an empty latrine barrel and was carried out from camp.

With this new identity, I was able to get father, mother and their 16-year-old foster child, Friedel, united and safely situated from immediate danger. Learning of a Gestapo visit, I escaped to Nice, where two French girls sheltered me. In December 1942, I was stopped for an ID check by the Vichy Police, who arrested me. When I was searched, they found that I carried two sets of ID papers, although they did not discover that I was a Jew. They beat me without mercy. The court sentenced me to two years of hard labor and the appeal court held up this sentence. I was transported in irons and chains to an old prison dating back to Napoleon's time. The conditions were brutal.

When a delegation of SS and other examiners arrived to look for Jews among the political prisoners, they lined us up and ordered us to drop our pants. Jews could be identified by their circumcision. Because the surgeon who circumcised me was not as skilled as a mohel, I was not identified as a Jew. I escaped the selection and the gas chamber, but my 24 Jewish companions were recognized by these means. (Only two of the 24 survived.) I spent 15 months there.

In March 1944, the French "*Maquis*" underground attacked the prison and pulled out the political prisoners and I ran with them. I was dropped off at La Camarque near Marselles, a labor camp for foreigners. Here I worked as a conscripted worker in the production of salt and other byproducts from the evaporating salt beds. It was in Vichy-controlled France, but the camp was guarded by the feared Ukrainian SS forces under the German command.

In August 1944, all the officers ran away, taking the labor force with them. I decided to jump into the nearby water. Remembering a Paul Muni movie in which he breathed under water through a reed, I did the same and stayed submerged for hours. When I felt safe, I searched for help and found a refugee Spanish family who gave me fresh clothes and advised me to go to the town of St. Gilles Du Gad to make contact with the French Resistance.

The Resistance, shorthanded and lacking talent, was glad to have me join, especially since I was fluent in six languages. I was put in charge of the captured SS Ukrainians. The first statement that I proclaimed to them was: "As of this moment you will be commanded by a Jew." They cowered with fear. Soon the Russian army demanded that they be handed over to them, and, as it is well known, they were dealt with as treacherous enemies and collaborators.

On November 11, Armistice Day, I and my French fighters walked down the Champs de Elysee and were greeted as victors. I was a lieutenant and was promoted to captain by the time I was discharged. The following year I was reunited with my father and mother and we returned to Brussels, where we learned that the Lindenberg family was blessed. Not a single member of the large family had perished. But we soon were to learn that my mother's family in Poland had been murdered; no one remained.

I met my wife, Selma Koltanowsky, in Paris on November 9, 1944, and we were married in 1946. Our first son was born in 1947 and in 1950 we immigrated to New York City. Within a couple of years I established a men's clothing manufacturing business. We soon were blessed with two more sons. Our firstborn son, Daniel, works for the U.S. government customs. Louis, an attorney, is married to Dawn, and they have two children, Andrew and Olivia. Marcel, a CPA, is married to Lisa, and they have two children, Alexa and Jillian. My wife and I retired to Boca Raton in 1993.

When I look back on our painful past, it is with sadness, but we are able at this stage in our lives to find satisfaction in using our knowledge and experiences by sharing. We are pleased to be part of the Child Survivors/Hidden Children of Palm Beach County and I participate through the speakers bureau in talking about the challenges I faced in Europe. The miracle of my family is that our entire immediate family, the Lindenbergs, survived, some by being protected by kind, righteous gentiles.

In 1993, Dortmund invited Selma and me to visit my birth town, where I was received as a lost treasure. It was a melancholy experience, hard to enjoy, hard to remember with kindheartedness. There are Jews again living in Dortmund—Russian Jews. I went to attend their synagogue. The experience of being inspected through a peephole in the door before being allowed entry filled me with a sense of past fears, of danger and the unknown. Who is at the door and is it safe?

To Live Again—To Smile Again

by Max Markovitz

My father, Aron Markovitz, was an observant Jew. He was a kind, well-respected man and a good provider to his wife and five children: Arya, Henry, Leah, Zita, and me. Our mother, Ida (Kleinman), was overjoyed with the blessings of all the little ones and ran a household full of plenty, with a tender touch and caring.

My father was an entrepreneur and had a successful business and warehouse, dealing in retail and wholesale leather goods. The Markovitzes lived among my mother's extended family and had an enjoyable involvement with many aunts, uncles, and cousins in the city of Svalyava, Czechoslovakia. The town was composed of a large population of non-Jews and about 800 Jewish families. Svalyava was 25 kilometers from Mukacheva, a well-known university and yeshiva town. [Both now are in Ukraine.]

I attended *cheder* (Jewish religious school) and the city public school. Since I was next to the youngest, I had a special standing with my siblings as protector and protected. My little brother, Henry, offered me the opportunity to express both superiority and nurturing.

When our part of Czechoslovakia was annexed by Hungary at the end of 1940, the Jewish population started to feel an undercurrent of anti-Semitism. But life was manageable and all hoped that this phase would pass and things would return to normal. But that became just a wishful idea when, in 1943, the oppressions and vile discriminations started to be acted out. It was decreed that all Jewish businesses were to be appropriated by the new order, and that Jewish owners had to work and manage their own businesses for the benefit of the oppressive regime. The exploitation of Jews was everywhere, and all rights afforded to the gentiles were taken away from the Jews.

Everyone had to learn a new language, Hungarian. Food was rationed. Friendly neighbors turned away from even noticing the Jews. Acts of anti-Semitism became commonplace. Once-friendly schoolmates became adversaries who confronted Jewish kids with violence. The Jewish youths were forced to work details at a variety of menial labors on farms, cleaning the rivers, maintaining sanitation or sweeping the town streets.

In 1943, my brother, Arya, was mobilized into a civilian labor camp. The family was devastated to be separated from the eldest child, but we were not alone. All families were stripped of their children. My parents at least had the younger four safe. These changes were accepted with a helpless resignation and heavy heart and with hope that the war would soon end.

In March 1944, suddenly and without warning, all Jews were commanded to pack a small suitcase with personal belongings and were taken to the railroad station, where we were packed into cattle cars and transported to Munkach ghetto. The living conditions there were deplorable. People traded or sold whatever they could just to get some food to survive. We were kept in the ghetto for about three weeks, after which we were transported on a journey of several days in cattle cars and in shocking condition to Poland.

We arrived at Birkenau in the late afternoon and were kept in the cars until night. All at once, the doors were swung open, blinding bright lights flashed at the arrivals, while a multitude of armed guards—SS men with German shepherd dogs—shouted and produced a din that shocked and confused the senses. We were brutally pushed and prodded into lines.

My mother and little brother Henry, age 11, were sent to the right and were never heard from again. My sisters, Leah and Zita, were in another line and assigned to what was known as the "Canada" section of Auschwitz; father and I, along with other men and boys who appeared strong and hardy, were sent to the left.

Although by this time we knew about the killing of Jews, we still could not reason that we were facing the killing machine. The shocking stench permeating the air was evidence of a horror that was real, but somehow we became numb and followed the lines to our own possible demise.

After 10 days at Auschwitz, my father and I and selected others were transported to Mauthausen concentration camp, where we were kept for a few days and finally relocated at the sub-camp Gusen 2. The backbreaking work that we were taken to every morning, in cattle cars, was for digging the St. Georgen Tunnels (where the Messerschmidt manufacturing was occurring) and loading the debris onto coal-mine type of cars.

Within a few weeks, I was separated from my only protector, my father. We were sent to different barracks and I never saw him again. When I recall being separated from my father, my soul trembles and weeps.

I continued to work at the tunnels and eventually about a half-dozen younger boys and I were chosen to remain in camp to clean the barracks and grounds. Every morning at *Appell* (roll call)—bodies upon bodies of those who had died from starvation, illness or brutal strangulation by the Kapos were stacked up. Anyone who appeared frail and was not able to report for work was found strangled in the morning. The ruthless brutality of the Polish Kapos surpassed the ire of the German Kapos. Every time an inmate was within reach of a Kapo, the result was a blow with a *shlauch*—a rubber hose—accompanied by vile curses. This became a sport to show off to their fellow Kapos. Prisoners who lost all hope and ran for the electrified wire fences to kill themselves were shot. The dead were gathered and displayed at the morning *Appell* to a warning announcement: "That's what happens when you run away." Even running towards death was prohibited. My experiences hardened me to these sights. My memories and attachments were put aside. I don't know how I survived.

In March 1945, the entire camp of 2,000 was taken on a death march. We marched for five days under barbaric conditions, without food or shelter from the weather and no overcoats to shield us from the cold. One-third of the original marchers never reached the final destination.

Camp Dunskurchen was the gathering place of death-march arrivals from many camps. To my unbelievable joy and relief, I discovered that my oldest brother, Arya, was also in this camp. Our embraces and reunion was as if in a fairy tale. I finally had someone to smile at and care about.

On May 6, 1945, the American army liberated the camp, which became a scene of confusion, greed and not knowing how to recapture one's humanity. I became very sick and was nurtured back to health by the American GI-supported hospital. After I recovered, my brother and I decided to return to Svalyava hoping to reunite with any of our surviving family. The chaos of the transportation system and the robberies by the Russian soldiers were a constant threat. We traveled sitting on top of the rail cars for many days and finally arrived in our hometown.

The joy of discovering our sisters Leah and Zita alive rekindled our will to live and rebuild.

We, the four siblings, were the largest surviving group of one family from the entire Jewish population of the town. We searched out our home and found it completely ransacked and looted. Everything was gone except the four walls. Besides the survivors not having anyone to welcome them from their own families, the residents of the town turned their heads as if to ignore the fact that they we were alive. We became non-entities to the looters and neighbors.

My siblings and I tried to see if it were possible to live in Svalyava, but found that there was nothing left with which to connect. The town had been stripped of all Jewish life and it was useless to live among a population that was unhappy to see the survivors return. We moved to Burna and resided there for a few months. My brother managed to earn some money through his interior decorating skills, while my sister's fiancée also provided subsistence through his trading and bartering with anything of value that he could get ahold of.

Finally, in 1946, we moved to Cheska Kaminitche, where I attended school and enrolled in a trade school training to become a radio mechanic. I learned about a Jewish Refugee Committee program being organized to take some youngsters to England. I went to Prague and placed my name and Zita's on the list. We were transported together with 100 youngsters in an RAF bomber to a village near Edinburgh in Scotland.

The Polton Manor House was established in 1939 to shelter the *Kindertransport* children from Germany. Here is where we truly began to face a new future by working on an organized farm; we learned a trade, gained a general education, and learned the English language. The British government provided teachers at the Manor House to educate the young people. On many occasions, the local village kids were brought by to socialize with us.

Zita and I remained at the Manor House for close to a year. Then we moved to London, where I attended the ORT School, learned electric engineering, worked to help subsidize my needs for food, and rented a room from a Jewish family. Finally, in 1951, Zita and I received our quota visa permitting entry to the USA.

At first, I lived in Pittsburgh, but soon I moved to Detroit. There, I worked as a technician for RCA, and after some time developed my own business—a video service. I married Sharron Gould and my children and grandchildren have become the symbol of my survival and my future.

154

Simply Because We Were Jewish

by Georges Miliband

My prolific family originated in Warsaw. Between the years 1918 and 1920, ten of my grandparents' 12 children left Poland in search of more hospitable surroundings. Seven landed in Belgium, two in France, and one, my father, in Germany.

My father had been drafted into the Tsar's army at a very young age and spent 10 years of his life in Russian uniform. At the end of World War I, he found himself in Germany as a civilian and he remained there for a few years. He died in Paris in 1938 at the age of 49. (Six family members who sought refuge in Belgium and France, and most of their close families who were by then already Belgian or French citizens, were forcefully taken back to Poland and were massacred in Auschwitz during the dark years of World War II.)

I was eight years old when my father passed away; the oldest of four children and the only boy. My mother was left completely destitute, in charge of four young children. I don't know how she managed, but I do not remember ever being hungry.

I do not have any nice memories of my childhood. As a matter of fact, the few memories I have are rather sordid. Still, my mother, with the financial assistance of Jewish welfare organizations, managed to twice send me on short vacations in the countryside, to some farmers' families where I had a good time enjoying rich food, the discovery of farm animals and very different surroundings. The rest of the time, I used to play in the street after school with boys my age.

What has always haunted me—and still does—is that I have no memory whatsoever of having ever been seated around a table, having a meal with my sisters and my mother. I don't remember ever playing with my sisters, or teasing them. Since the day in July 1942 when I saw what happened to my destroyed and plundered home, every semblance of the past has been completely erased.

My mother was 39 and my sisters were ten, eight and four when they reached Auschwitz to be annihilated upon arrival. I think if my former playmate hadn't handed over to me the few pictures he had picked up at the apartment, I wouldn't even remember my mother's face or that of my three sisters. All I know is that they existed and were brutally snatched away from me.

I do not remember having ever had a celebration at home, a birthday, a seder—nothing. I know I was considered a very good pupil in school, but I don't remember any teacher or school-mate—except the one who pointed at my yellow star and asked "what's that?" What I sensed at a very tender age was that it was not desirable to be Jewish in the time and place that I lived. As a matter of fact, it did occur to me that it was actually a calamity and an attribute that was definitely to be hidden, preferably not to be talked about. Although I had never been in a synagogue, nor had ever taken part in any Jewish group activities, I knew I was Jewish. I knew it because I heard of the horrors that could happen to me. Of course, I was thoroughly confused and had nobody to turn to for any comfort or explanation. Mme. Vallon, although a devout Catholic, never tried to influence me even though at one time she made me understand that she would be willing to adopt me.

During my summer vacation of 1942, my mother managed to find some money to send one child on a two-week vacation outside of Paris. I will never know why she chose me instead of one of my sisters. On the afternoon of July 15, my mother, holding my youngest sister by the hand, took me to a private school in the neighborhood, whose principal, Madame Denise Vallon, was organizing a summer camp for city children in her country house in the suburbs of Paris. All I remember is that the departure was nearly canceled as Madame Vallon was not feeling well. What I do not remember is having said farewell to my mother and little Liliane, whom I was never to see again. The next day, at dawn, all the Jews residing in my building were arrested by the French gendarmes and shoved *en masse* into a sports complex under horrendous health conditions. In the meantime, I was on vacation, completely unaware of the tragedy. I later learned that on the 16th and 17th the Paris police rounded-up some 13,000 Jews of Paris, old and young, without discrimination.

A few days later, Madame Vallon, who may have realized that she had a Jewish child in her group of vacationers, called me over and suggested that I go back to my apartment in Paris "to see how my mother and sisters were doing." So, I did what she asked me to do. Of course, I did not have any trouble finding the house I had lived in for quite a while, and, after running up the stairs as usual, I found myself in front of the familiar door. However, the door

156

was ajar and there was a broken seal on the lock. I pushed it open and my head started spinning: The usual spotless rooms looked as if a tornado had gone through them. The apartment had been ransacked, plundered. We didn't have much, but whatever was left was broken, devastated and … there was no trace of my mother or my sisters. I felt totally bewildered. In a daze, I started to leave when a boy my age, with whom I used to play after school, came up to me and told me that the police had taken my mother and sisters away with all the other Jews living in that building. My friend had entered the apartment to see if he could salvage anything. He then gave me a few kitchen towels and the most precious gift ever: half a dozen precious family pictures! Like a zombie, I went back to Madame Vallon's; there was no other place I could go. Everyone I could think of was in hiding. So, I went back and told Madame Vallon that my family was nowhere to be found and the apartment had been destroyed. She didn't show any reaction and didn't say anything. However, a few days later she had me put on my jacket, to which she had sewn the yellow star, and took me to the local police station. I didn't understand what was going on but I knew enough to be absolutely petrified.

I was taken to a room where an impressive police inspector was sitting behind a big desk. He looked at me, a skinny, shaking 12-year old in a rather shabby outfit with the Jewish star in place, asked me for my identity card, and questioned me about my parents' whereabouts. I told him that my father had died four years ago and that I did not know where my mother and sisters were. I did not realize at that time that I had in front of me a decent human being and not a Nazi sympathizer. He did not stamp "Juif" on my identity card; he just said, "Go, go". From that day on, I gather, Madame Vallon was able to legally get ration coupons for food for me. I hope this was the reason she made me go through that ordeal. I like to think that she personally knew the inspector and felt sure that he wasn't going to send me to my death which, of course, he had the power to do.

Madame Vallon was a very kind lady. She had accepted me in her vacation house for two weeks and kept me with her for over five years. When, in September 1942, the new school-year started she took me with her to Paris, to her apartment, and I started to attend the private school of which she was the principal. She was a married woman and had no children. I do not remember having ever had a conversation with her husband, but at no time did she make me feel that I was a burden to her. She never even suggested that I attend church services with her, although she was clearly a devout Catholic. Somehow, the Jewish resistance found out that she was sheltering a Jewish child and contacted her with the desperate request to save more youngsters. In 1943, another boy my age joined me at her apartment. We shared the same bed and Robert still is my best friend. Moreover, the summer-camp in 1943 and 1944 turned into a safe hideout for Jewish children. During the summer holidays Madame

Vallon was at times giving temporary refuge to at least a dozen Jewish kids. (Years later, Robert and I would declare her as a Righteous Gentile at Yad Vashem.)

For me, life did not brighten after the war. Of my father's 12 siblings, three survived the war: a brother in London, a brother in Paris, and a sister in Belgium. They discovered me by accident since they all were convinced that I had been taken together with my mother and sisters. One of my surviving aunts recognized me in an open market while I was grocery shopping for Madame Vallon. My relatives decided that I had to be brought back to a Jewish atmosphere and they chose a childless brother of my mother to be my guardian. I was 14 years old when France was liberated; I was 17 by the time my family succeeded in imposing their point of view on Madame Vallon. All she could do was to insist that I remain in school till the end of the school year. I was not consulted, and at that time I was in no condition to make a decision for myself. I was completely ignoring reality and living in sort of a daze since the day I had gone to my apartment and realized that I had no mother, no sisters, and no shelter anywhere on earth. I did not fight my relatives' decision.

Madame Vallon had sheltered me, fed me, and protected me after my family was decimated, but she always remained "Madame" Vallon for me. She was very reserved and I cannot claim to ever having had a kiss or hug from her. A few days after I was moved into my uncle's household, I was put to work. I was never given a choice; there was no question of staying in school. My uncle was teaching me to work with leather. I hated it. I realize now that 1945 was a very difficult year for most of my relatives. They were survivors, but had a hard time to integrate into normal routine—with work, with their relationship with their own children, with just simply joining normal living again. It took some of them months, even years, to find a decent dwelling. Their furniture and belongings had simply disappeared, confiscated by the occupation forces. In any case, my uncle's wife disliked me and made my life miserable, so that when the time came to join the French army it was a most welcome relief for me. I never went back to my uncle's place. In the meantime, my father's only surviving sister invited me to Brussels for the 1948 New Year's festivities. It was in her house that I met Gutki, whose father had been murdered in Auschwitz and whose mother and young sister were preparing to leave Belgium for the United States. We felt that we had a lot in common and liked each other very much. We corresponded, saw each other in Brussels or in Paris at every possible opportunity, and soon married.

My mother-in-law had immigrated to the United States with her younger daughter a few years earlier. She had a large family in the United States: two brothers and four sisters. All were married and had children who were more or less my age. They all accepted me wholeheartedly and I immersed myself in their affection and devotion. Moreover, the American-born new generation became substitute children for Gutki and me. They still are. A new family life was very soon created and we were a well-integrated part of it. My new family was extremely Jewish with strong Zionistic feelings. Here, I participated in the first seder of my life, with an uncle, the patriarch of the family, an authentic rabbi from the old country, presiding, and his son, an active Brooklyn rabbi, officiating to a large reunion of outgoing, loud and happy-go-lucky relatives. I was impressed, but I never could develop any religious fervor.

In the meantime, I was frantically trying to master the English language and registered for courses at the United Nations. There, I had the good fortune to meet a French woman who introduced me to the French Consul-General in New York and I was hired for a temporary summer job at the Consulate. It was ironic that I, who was eager to leave France behind, found myself in a totally French atmosphere and learned to appreciate French humor, friendship, and food while I was far away from the country and with colleagues who were more or less in exile. However, for a long time I hid my past. I did not mention that I was Jewish and was relieved that nobody asked. Of course, the fear disappeared with the arrival, at a much later date, of other Jewish employees. I had a very kind boss with whom I worked in the archives. Then I was put in charge of the diplomatic pouch, and little by little my summer job turned into a permanent one and I stayed at the consulate for 35 years before I decided to retire. I had become familiar with the work of all branches of the Consulate and I felt useful and very confident in the job I was doing, dealing both with French and American citizens.

After close to 40 years on the East Coast, we moved to Florida, where a friend introduced me to a group of Hidden Children of the Holocaust. Shortly thereafter, a law was passed that mandated that all schools in Florida teach the history of the Holocaust. So, I started talking to schoolchildren, as well as to teachers who felt they needed to be better informed. I will continue to do so as long as there is a request for it and in order to contradict the despicable deniers. I tell the students what happened to my mother and my three little sisters who were put to a horrible death, together with six million other innocent people, simply because they were born Jewish.

From Hope to Despair to a New Beginning

by Alex Moskovic

My family—father Josef, mother Gizi, older brother Zoltan, and younger brother Erwin—lived in Szobranc, a small town in Hungary, together with our widowed grandmother (*Buba*), uncles, and their families. A complex of three houses was our own little enclave, where I spent a happy childhood amongst a loving family and many cousins who were also my playmates and protectors. Grandmother, who spoke only Yiddish, had her own apartment in one of the houses. She took care of my siblings and me during the day, while mother and father worked in the family business, a general store on the main street of town.

A magical time still lingers in my memory as I see mother light the Sabbath candles, cover her face, and tenderly whisper the prayer. Saturdays and holidays were especially joyful days as the whole family gathered to celebrated together. In those times the duties of Judaism were happy occasion and fun for the children.

I did not encounter much anti-Semitism, and if someone picked on me I bravely stood my ground. The bullies knew they would have to deal with my numerous cousins if they harassed me.

Our life was uneventful till the end of 1943. In the winter of 1943-1944, the Jewish people were hopeful that the war raging all around would soon be over. The Soviet armies were just across the Carpathian Mountains and the feeling was that by the spring of 1944, they would cross and the war would end. Instead, Szobranc and the rest of Hungary were occupied by the German armies. A few days later Adolf Eichmann was dispatched to Hungary to take care of what by then were the last remnants of the Jewish problem.

It started with wearing a yellow Star of David on our outer clothing, followed by edicts of oppression and hardship. A few weeks later we were notified of a resettlement and, shortly after, the police (*czendors*), came to our homes, ordered each of us to take only one bag of belongings, and escorted us to our synagogue, where we were registered and loaded into trucks. The Jewish population of our town was taken to Ungvar, a town about 10 kilometers away, to the brick factory, which was converted into a ghetto where we lived in hardship for the next six weeks.

Towards the end of this period, we were told that in a few days we would be resettled to a permanent place. And true to their word, a few days later the Hungarian police took everyone to the railroad station. Cattle cars, guarded by German SS, were waiting on one of the tracks. We were separated into groups of 80 to 100 people and were loaded into the cars. Luckily, the families were able to stay together at this time. The cattle cars were bare except for two buckets, one with water and one that was empty. When all the cars were loaded, the doors were locked from the outside and within a few minutes the train started to move.

In the afternoon, someone placed the empty bucket in a corner, which was intended to be a toilet for the trip and was shielded by a blanket to create some privacy. The train continued to roll at a very slow pace till that evening, when it stopped. It was dark in the car, but we were able to somehow settle in for the night. Exhausted from the day's stress, I found a place to sit down, leaned against the side of the car and fell asleep. As the train started to roll again at daylight, the sudden jolt and noise woke me. The crying of small children, voices praying and an unbearable stench brought me to reality. During the night the human waste overflowed the bucket onto the floor. Fortunately the wooden planks were spaced with openings in between which allowed most of the overflow to seep through onto the tracks, but the stench clung in the air without relief.

The second day we again proceeded very slowly and again stopped for the night. The German troops were transported during the night on all available tracks from the Soviet front to Germany in order to keep them safe from Allied bombings. The suffering in these confined cars, amidst the anguish around us and seeing my own family in distress, was overwhelming for a youngster who had had no concerns but safety and comfort all his life.

On the third evening, the train stopped again. After a few hours, we started to move ahead. The train went through a large gate in a brick building and continued till we stopped at a platform. The doors were opened and the stench started to dissipate as a strange-smelling air replaced it. We had arrived in Birkenau!

Shouting and shoving pierced the night as a swarm of Kapos, speaking German and other languages, ordered everyone to get off the train and leave all belongings in the cars. Dazed with exhaustion, sudden shock, and yet with relief and hopefulness, the searching eyes peered through the harsh lights and dark scene to try to discern what was happening.

On the platform we were told to line up in separate groups, one for men, the second for women, and the third for the elderly and children. As soon as the third group was formed, which included my grandmother and 11-year-old brother; they were surrounded by SS guards with dogs and were marched down the platform. As they came to the end of the platform they seemed to disappear into blackness as they walked down the steps.

> *I learned later that they were led to a yard where they were told they would be deloused and showered because of the unsanitary conditions in the cattle cars. They were guided into a large room where everyone undressed and was then herded into the showers. Once the shower room was full, the doors with a small peephole were locked by the SS guards. The guards went up to the flat roof of the building, opened the covered metal cylinders that were connected to the false showerheads inside the room and dropped pellets of Zyklon B into the openings. As the pellets mixed with the air, they started to dissolve into fumes, which filled the room with the deadly gas. Within 20 to 25 minutes, everyone in the room had died a slow, torturous death as the SS watched through the peepholes to see if anyone was moving. After the fans cleared the fumes, the men of the Sondercommando came into the room, cut off the hair, searched the bodies for any hidden valuables, pulled the gold teeth from the mouths, and dragged the bodies to the crematorium.*

My father, 19-year-old brother Zoltan, and I were separated into the men's group. A few minutes later a German army car pulled up to the platform and three officers in SS uniforms stepped out. One approached the front of the men's group and with a calm, expressionless manner started the selection. As each one of us stepped in front of him, he motioned to go left or right. I was picked along with father and brother to join the group that was to work.

Our group was marched down to the middle of the platform where we were directed to turn right and we walked down an alley between Camp C, the women's camp, and D, the men's camp. After a short march we turned left to the gate of Camp D. We were taken to a barrack where we were permitted to climb into bunks and collapsed in sleep.

Early the next morning we were jolted awake with shouts and prodding and ordered to line up outside in front of the barrack for a roll call, *Appell* (roll call), then taken to the real showers, and received striped clothing to wear, after which we were allowed to return to the barrack. Three days later, during the day, we had another roll call, but this time the SS officer from the platform returned and separated all the boys from this barrack. We were then marched to barrack No. 11 in the same camp. This was the day I learned that the officer was Josef Mengele.

Barrack 11 had 200 boys around my age, 13 years old, and within a week it was filled with 1,500 boys and so was the adjacent Barrack 13. These barracks were isolated from the rest of the camp. The only time we were able to leave the barracks was when the rest of the population was at work, which was during the day, and only at this time were we able to use the latrines and wash up with the undrinkable, polluted running water.

We heard a rumor that the reason for our isolation was that Mengele was getting ready to do some type of experiments. We never found out what the experiments were because their schedule was disrupted by an outbreak of typhus, the result of the unsanitary conditions, the foul water, and the infestation of lice that afflicted everyone. A few days later the sick boys were taken away. The following day we were inoculated against the disease.

About a week later more boys got sick, and they too were taken away. A few nights later we were awakened around midnight at which time Mengele arrived and another selection took place. One thousand boys were taken away in trucks and were never seen again. One week later another selection occurred and again 1,000 boys were taken away. We had learned quickly what the selections meant and many of us sought out places to hide, including the holes of the latrines. Even there we found no safety. The Kapos, with their bribing methods, found traitors among the prisoners to disclose even this hiding place.

The last selection came 10 days after. Mengele arrived with a group of SS men and the selection began. Naked, holding our clothes in our arms, we presented ourselves in front of Mengele. He stood there in his crisp uniform without an emotion, directing each to the left or right. When my turn came he motioned me to go to the right, to the smaller group. As I started to go in that direction, an SS man stopped me and told me to go to the other group but I refused to obey and argued with him. This act was very dangerous because one did not dispute any orders unless you wanted to be dead. I felt that at this point that it did not matter anymore. As we argued, Mengele turned towards us; he did not say a word—he just looked right through us. With this, the SS man walked away from me and let me join the group to which I was selected. After the groups were separated, the larger group was herded outside and into trucks. Fifty-one boys were left in the barracks after the new roll call. Since then I have been asking myself: Was I the fifty-first?

The following day we were transferred to Camp A, to the children's barrack, where we met some other boys. I was tattooed on my left arm, B-14662, and so I became part of the work force. In the evenings all during this time we were given our food rations, which consisted of a two-inch slice of bread and a small bowl of potato-skin soup. This added up to about 600 calories. If one was prudent and disciplined, you ate the soup in the evening and saved the bread for the morning, but one had to be watchful so that no one would steal the bread while you were asleep.

I was picked with 13 other boys to work in the *Schiesekommando*—the garbage detail. Our job was to clean out the waste from the latrines, collect the garbage from the kitchens and dump it in the area where Section Mexico of Birkenau was going to be built. Each morning we met at a large wagon equipped with 14 harnesses, which was standing next to the barrack. It had three openings at the top, where the garbage was deposited. The bottom and sides had removable wooden planks to release the garbage. It had a secret compartment that was built under the wagon. We learned about this compartment from the Kapo on our command, who was one of the carpenters who had built the wagon in Bikenau.

Each morning we harnessed ourselves to the wagon and pulled it to different camps to collect the garbage. When the wagon was full, the garbage was dumped. This job gave me access to all camps in Birkenau. At the women's Camp C, I tried to find out what happened to my mother. Here I met Frieda, who had worked for my Aunt Giza in Szobranc and was the head (block *altester*) of a barrack. She told me that my mother had been in Camp C for about a month or so and then she disappeared. This information numbed me. My still unyielding hope was that my mother had been sent to a work camp. I kept in touch with Frieda each time I was in the camp for any information about the women of our town.

A few weeks later Frieda asked me for a favor. Apparently one of the women in her barrack was pregnant and they were hiding her condition from the SS, who would kill both mother and baby. The favor was to help dispose of the body after the baby's birth. After this meeting, I conferred with our Kapo to help take the body out of the camp. He agreed to do it even though it meant danger to everyone in the *kommando*. A few weeks later, when I visited Frieda, she gave me a package wrapped in old rags. I took the package to the wagon and we placed it in the secret compartment. That evening, as we were disposing of the garbage, we buried the baby in the garbage dump and said Kaddish for the unknown human being. This was possible because the SS guards, who were following us, usually stopped before we reached the dump; they did not like the foul smell at the dump.

Weeks passed. Working on the Scheisekommando probably saved my life because I was able to pick up scraps of food in the kitchens and smuggle it back to my barrack

In the middle of January of 1945 we were beginning to hear cannon fire. The Soviet army was getting closer to Birkenau. One morning we were awakened earlier than usual, and were lined up outside our barrack. We were handed two rations of bread and luckily I was able to save some food from my kitchen encounters, which enabled me to trade for other goods, such as a backpack and even tins of meat to take along.

The morning was extremely cold with blowing snow and piercing wind. The SS guards, fingers on the triggers of their submachine guns and dogs ready to pounce, marched alongside this tattered humanity and forced us to stay in line and keep up the pace. People unable to stay in line due to this grueling march and extreme weather fell back or collapsed. They were immediately dragged to the side of the road and shot.

Determined to survive, my only thought was to stay as close as possible to the front of the column and be able to mingle in the middle if I should get tired; I did not want to become a straggler. We marched all day, into the night; the only time the column stopped was to allow us to relieve ourselves. We grabbed some of the fresh fallen snow to quench the thirst and ate the bread to keep up our strength.

We arrived at our destination, Gleiwitz *KL* (concentration camp), the following morning. I was able to get into one of the barracks, found a space on the floor, and slept most of the day with my backpack as a pillow. The next day I decided to walk around the camp to see if I could find anyone from our town. I knew that people from other camps around Auschwitz-Birkenau also had been marched to Gleiwitz. I did not recognize anyone in my search but I could not stop and kept looking. After a while I came across a group that caught my attention. I circled around and it seemed that a silhouette of one man looked familiar from the back. As I got closer he did look familiar but I was not sure. I stood there staring. After a while our eyes met and kept looking as we walked towards each other. With excitement and great relief, I recognized my older brother Zoltan. We hugged and the only thing we could say was our names. As we separated, I glanced to the side and recognized my father. With tears flowing, we hugged and kissed, and could not let go of each other. This encounter was an unbelievable miracle. To this day I am tortured by the memory, my eyes teary. Our joy of being together both gladdened and broke our hearts.

After a while we were able to settle down and make plans on how to survive; we decided that if at all possible, we were going to stay together from now on. We knew that the war was going to end soon.

A few days later when the Buna Camp people, including father and Zoltan, were called to be relocated, I joined them and went to the train station where we were loaded into open coal cars for this trip. It was extremely cold and the only way we could stay somewhat warm was to huddle together. In the beginning it was not a problem because each car was full, but as the days went by many people died and we ended up standing and sleeping on dead bodies. Once a day the train stopped in a non-populated area where we got off the train and took care of our bodily needs.

Luckily the three of us had enough bread and some margarine, which was the food that I gathered during my excursions to the kitchens to last us for this trip. After about a week, the train ended up in Buchenwald, where a roll call was made; of the 10,000 people that had left Gleiwitz, only 4,000 were alive. The worn out, emaciated survivors had to unload the dead from the coal cars.

For a while, father, Zoltan, and I stayed in the same barrack and looked out for each other. In March 1945, father got very ill and could not walk. Zoltan and I were desperate and were unable to help him in any way. I appealed to the block altester to help father, and the next day two men came with a stretcher and took him to the hospital. That was the last time we saw him alive. Without father, my brother and I were moved to the children's barrack in the *Kleine* Lager (childrens camp). We stayed there till the beginning of April 1945.

On April 6, 1945, we had a big *Appell*. The SS picked people to go on another death march and my brother was among them. The rest of us were told to go back to our barrack and wait for the next transport. The next transport never left Buchenwald. On April 11, 1945, I was liberated by the U.S. Army.

After the war I found out from friends that on April 7, 1945, on the way to Theresienstadt, my brother was shot to death when he could not keep up with the punishing march.

Two months after my liberation, when I had recuperated, I returned to Szobranc. I found two older cousins who survived while in a forced labor battalion on the Soviet front. I was the sole survivor from my immediate family—grandmother, aunts, uncles and cousins, a total of 41 people who had been taken to Birkenau.

On July 3, 1946, I immigrated to New York with the help of my uncles, and continued my education. After years of studying and working, I met and married Jo Roppolo. With perseverance, I landed a job with ABC Television, where working for ABC News and ABC Sports for 30 years (Wide World of Sports, Summer and Winter Olympics) I was recognized for my work with 10 Emmys. During this period we had two sons and three grandchildren.

After my retirement in 1993, we moved to Florida, where I volunteer my time speaking to students and adult groups of my experience in the Holocaust and the importance of tolerance and acceptance. I have served as president of the Child Survivors/Hidden Children for a number of years and am involved in many Holocaust issues as an advocate.

Out of the Darkness into Light

by Cecilia Jaget Pearlstein

A Thousand Faces

Aching is the heart of one who remembers
A thousand faces looking up from the past
Questioning eyes and silent voices
"Why us? Why us?"
Ages went by since I saw you last
Traveled far and many things did I
Beloved new faces came into my life
But nothing shall erase your questioning eyes
"Why us? Why us?"
My deepest thoughts are with you still
My eyes see the beauty you might have seen
I touch the objects you might have touched
And hear the music you might have heard
I sing the song you might have sung
And all the things you might have been
And all the deeds you might have done
And all the children you might have borne
They are also with me now
A thousand faces are in my eyes questioning softly
"Why us? Why us?"

Prior to the outbreak of World War II, I lived with my parents and younger twin brothers in our hometown, Bobrka. It was situated in the southeastern part of Poland, near the city of Lvov. [Now Lviv, Ukraine.] The town's population of 6,000 included 3,000 Jews. After the German killing machine went into high gear, only 22 Jews survived, among them only five children, my twin brothers, and me.

My father was successful in his restaurant-tavern business and everyone liked him. He inherited the business, building, and property from his father.

Our living quarters were above the restaurant, and my mother—a pretty, intelligent, and talented woman—helped in the restaurant whenever possible.

I was born in 1929. I attended public school in the morning and Hebrew school in the afternoon. At the age of seven, I began violin lessons and later on performed in orchestras. I had many friends: Jewish, Polish, and Ukrainian. One day, a Polish friend, Kristine, said to me: "I like you, too bad you are Jewish." I felt an immediate pain, and I remember running home and telling mother about it. She told me that there are Polish people who do not consider us to be countrymen: "Jewish people are not well liked." She went on trying to comfort me, "So one day we shall go to Jerusalem."

For several years, my mom, our hired helper, the boys, and I spent our summer months in various resort places. Our last such trip was in 1939, and for the first time my father was able to join us for a weekend. It was then that I heard my parents and their friends discuss Hitler and the possibility of war. At home, my parents and neighbors listened to Hitler's speeches on the radio. He shouted a great deal and I understood the seriousness of the situation. We were preparing for war. Windows were taped to protect them from being shattered by the bombs, while the sirens would cause us to run to the cellar. Two days of constant bombings suddenly ceased. The silence that followed was shocking. We expected an invasion by the Germans invasion; instead Soviet tanks and soldiers occupied us. They took over our restaurant, but were allowed to stay in our home. I attended a Jewish school where Yiddish was the spoken language. My teachers were wonderful. We had poetry recitation and many singing and dancing performances. I was a happy participant.

In June 1941, war between Germany and Russia erupted. As the Soviets retreated, the German army moved in. It was known that whenever they entered a town the first thing that they did was to round up young Jewish men for labor camps. My father, along with many other men, left town to stay in the forest for the first days of the invasion.

My mother, brothers, and I went next door to my father's uncle's house. After several hours, we heard terrible noises from the outside. The gates to the property were forced open and we found ourselves facing a dangerous local mob. My aunt was killed, and my cousin injured and disfigured. My mother was also injured, but she managed to run away from the mob as she called our names to follow her. She led us to a house of gentiles who knew us and gave us shelter.

After a few days, we learned that our house had been broken into and robbed. My mother was still bedridden, nursing her injuries. I was very upset. I decided on my own to return to our home and see if I could retrieve some clothes and shoes for the twins. Upon entering, I found personal belongings strewn all over, and was frightened by a German soldier who was stuffing my parents' valise with my father's silver goblet. He recognized me from my portrait on the wall and shouted in German as he kicked me with his boots, "What are you doing here, you cursed Jewish beast?" I ran away as fast as I could, and fortunately he did not follow me.

My father soon came back from the forest and we returned to our home. We settled into a life filled with apprehension and anxiety. The edicts against the Jews were enacted immediately. We were not allowed to go to school. We had to wear a white band with a blue Star of David. Some of our Yiddish-school teachers attempted to teach us secretly in one of our synagogues, but that did not last very long.

In the early summer of 1942, the first *Aktion* (roundup for deportation) occurred. There was no place to hide in our own building because the Germans occupied our restaurant and cellar. Twelve people squeezed into a neighbor's attic. After surviving the *Aktion*, my mother instinctively could see the dangers we were facing. She decided that in order to survive, we must all hide.

My parents approached a farmer, Josef. He had a great deal of respect for my father who had befriended him in the past by extending loans of money and treating him well in the restaurant. Both my parents knew that they could trust him. But hiding Jews was risky for non-Jews. My parents' offer of the building, property, and business convinced the farmer to hide us.

Before we were scheduled to leave to farmer Josef's house, rumors started flying that a second roundup was coming, which prompted us to leave sooner. Mother woke us up in the middle of the night and told us to get ready to walk to the farm. I put on my lace shoes, my pleated skirt, and took my grandmother's shawl. I can remember that the evening was extremely dark. I followed mother, who was holding on to each of the boys. It was a long, tiring walk. Father stayed behind to cover for us, explaining when asked that we had gone to grandmother's house in a neighboring town.

The farmer's family—his wife and three daughters—were nice to us. We hid in a cellar with a false brick wall, which had to be entered through a board in the kitchen floor. After several weeks, they told mother that they had been warned of an inspection to take place and that we had to leave. Mother suggested that if a hole could be dug away from the house, then no one could find us. She pleaded desperately and was determined. The farmer and family agreed to this plan.

A pit was dug underneath a stable. The entrance was at an angle. To enter, we had to slide down, feet first. The entrance was covered with stones, earth, and a board with nails that matched the rest of the stable floor. The hole was just big enough to lie down or sit; one could not stand up. We sat quietly, listening to whatever might be audible.

We remained silent in the darkness and though I could not write, I occupied myself by creating poems and committing them to memory. The poems were about our situation, my pain, and my yearnings. I longed for light, for sun. After a few months, father joined us in the hole. We remained there for two years, only able to come out twice.

I lack the words to describe our suffering. Urine from the pigs leaked down on us. We were overrun by vermin, lice, and roaches. Once a day we deloused ourselves by picking our clothes and dropping the vermin into the burning kerosene lamp. In the spring the lamp failed to burn due to the lack of oxygen. Our own breathing became difficult, at which time farmer Josef inserted a thin pipe from the outside into the hole. Every couple of days the hole was opened and we were handed some bread, soup, water, and news about the world outside.

In the early winter of 1944, the farmer told us that his family, like many other Polish families, was leaving for western Poland. Another family took over the farm. They knew about our hiding and they continued to help us with water and bread. That family also left and another took possession of the farm. They were not aware of our existence under the barn floor. We had no food and no water. Mother took chances of being discovered as she slipped out at night to get some water.

The front was moving closer. The Germans were retreating and the Russians were advancing. We could hear the bombs exploding all around us. We heard German voices. Then we heard Russians. Yet, we were afraid to come

out. We were desperate—being without water and food for days—so with great difficulty we crawled out of the hole. The twins and I could not walk. The twins had to be carried. We gathered some of our clothing from the farmhouse—my grandmother's shawl, the pleated skirt, and my shoes, which were too small by now—and returned to our apartment in town. My pleated skirt was made into a dress and my new shoes were made out of wood with leather tops from the seats of our dining room chairs.

Bobrka became a tragic place to be in and we could not remain. We left for Lvov, where we discovered that our cousin Herman had survived. My brothers and I attended school for several months. In the spring of 1945, just before the war ended, we went on a cargo train to Krakow, where cousin Herman brought me a gift, a violin, which I carried throughout my travels. It is still my treasured possession, as is my grandmother's shawl.

From Krakow we crossed borders to Prague, where for the first time in years, I slept in a comfortable bed. I remember jumping on it. We continued to Germany, where we were hoping to contact mother's brother in America. We came to St. Ottillien, a convent and monastery in Bavaria, where I made many wonderful friends. My brothers and I stayed there while my parents left for Fohrenwald, a displaced persons' camp, and we were later reunited. There I learned to ride a bicycle, and attended lectures and concerts performed by concentration camp survivors who had been great musicians before the war.

We arrived in the United States in May 1946. Then a new reality and very difficult times faced us. The United States was still recovering from the war economy. We had to learn a new language and my parents had to find employment. I began attending Washington Irving High School in Manhattan and graduated with honors in June 1948. During the summer months, I worked at different jobs. I continued my education at Hunter College, majoring in biology. After graduation in 1952, I began working at New York University Medical Center as a serologist. Years later, I worked at Good Samaritan Hospital in Suffern, New York.

In July 1952, I married Norman Pearlstein. We raised three children and today have seven grandchildren. My brothers continued their education and are commercial artists. One retired and lives in Manhattan and the other is renowned for his Judaica art and lives and works in Israel.

When I learn about other people's suffering during the Holocaust, I consider myself the lucky one. We survived because of my mother's instincts to be able to foresee the dangers ahead and to carry out a plan. Though I think myself lucky, the suffering and our losses can never be forgotten. I still have nightmares.

Return to Dedication for Good

by Sam Ron

One hundred Jewish families resided among a population of 3,000 thousand Poles in Kazierza Wielka, which was located a short distance from Krakow. This is where I was born in 1924 and lived with my younger brother, Israel, and parents. My father, Joseph Rakowski, was a successful businessman and a Zionist of liberal leanings. My mother, Zelda, was from a religious family and held on to traditions. My family had a comfortable life and owned their own spacious home, which was rare for the community. My father ran a successful lumber business, which provided a good life for us and where I helped out when I got older.

I attended the Polish public school for seven years, earning a standing of best student. At the same time I attended the cheder (Hebrew religious studies) and again excelled. Although anti-Semitism was rampant, I had good relations with my fellow students and neighbors.

On Friday, September 1, 1939, at six o'clock in the morning, planes began flying over the town without any resistance from the Polish forces. Two days later, thousands, especially men, began fleeing east, not knowing what they were running from. Many died from their ordeals in Siberia, many were never heard from again, and some survived and returned after the war.

On Wednesday, September 6, the German army marched proudly into our town, without encountering any resistance. The first shock of occupation was the mobilization of all men 16 and older to report for work. Cleaning streets, removing from the roads dead people and animals who were killed in the bombardments, and other hard menial labor became the daily ordeal for the selected.

The only synagogue, situated close to Polish homes, was ordered to be torched. The gentile residents dismantled it physically, so that their own homes would not catch fire.

Daily existence was under the mercy and domination of German administrators and German police, who were assisted by the Polish police. Life took on a grave and fearful face. The edicts were numerous and presented hardship and persecution. A curfew was enforced. No Jew was allowed to travel or leave town. The wearing of white armbands with a blue Jewish star was mandatory. All furs had to be turned over to the German authorities. Every Jewish business was taken over by Germans or the Poles. All these and countless other edicts were enforced under the penalty of death. People lived from day to day, with the hope that the Germans would be driven out and normalcy and decency would resume.

The Jewish population of Poland was gathered into ghettos where the will and dignity of life was reduced to only a struggle for daily existence. In 1942, deportations to the mass-murder killing camps started in Kazierza Wielka and in all nearby communities. Many ran away to escape the unknown. This action prompted my family to go into hiding; but we had to leave our 94-year-old grandmother behind, knowing that the hardship of hiding would be too difficult for her. Seven family members hid at a business associate's barn, where we stayed until September 1942. We soon learned that the morning of deportation, my grandmother was shot and 300 men, women and children who had returned from their earlier escape where taken into a nearby forest clearing and shot.

With the approach of winter, my family decided to smuggle us into the Krakow ghetto. Fourteen people squeezed into two tiny rooms of our aunt and uncle. My mother and I worked in ammunition factories, while my brother, aunt, and uncle worked for Oskar Schindler of "Schindler's List" fame.

When the ghetto was liquidated on March 13, 1943, people were marched to the Plaszow concentration camp, where the men were separated from the women. The evil, depraved commander, Amon Goeth, was in charge of the camp. His recreation was to shoot and kill Jewish people who passed in the vicinity of his rifle's scope. Life was a suffering existence, without any idea of what tomorrow would bring or who would be carried off to be buried.

In October 1943, I was among 3,500 inmates who were moved to Camp Pionki to work in an ammunition factory. Separated from my entire family and in a stunned state, I was unable to question or comprehend the daily suffering. It seemed that this was the natural state of being as one moved with the fellow sufferers, avoiding any confrontation.

Around July 1944, as the Russian army was getting nearer, the Germans evacuated most of the laborers to Auschwitz. Miraculously, and for no known reason, I was picked along with 350 other Jews to dismantle the ammunition factory and to rebuild it in the vicinity of Sachsenhausen concentration camp. Many non-Jewish political prisoners from many countries, and homosexuals, criminals, and even those accused of the plot to assassinate Hitler, populated this camp. Here, my group was quarantined with very little food, and threadbare clothing. People died from hunger and the strenuous life. Croatian SS militia guarded us. Finally, those who survived the isolation were released and were sent as a labor force to Glewen, where for several months we rebuilt the ammunition factory and lived and worked in the most inhuman conditions.

In February 1945, we were returned to the main Sachsenhausen camp, where by this time the barracks were packed with inmates from many liquidated camps and had been brought by the death marches to this locale. A space meant for one was occupied by four. The grueling slave-labor work, under the most severe conditions, included work at the grenade factory, making bricks destined for the grand facades of Berlin, repairing damaged railroad tracks, and digging up unexploded bombs. Many workers died.

Talk began to circulate that the Jews were to be separated from the gentile population and would be taken away. A friend, David, whom I met on the death march, and I became each other's watchdogs, taking turns at rest and protecting each other. We pulled off the yellow triangle from our uniform and passed for Polish prisoners by using only the red triangle emblem.

Twenty thousand to 30,000 men of all nationalities were marched out of Camp Sachsenhausen, among them the Polish prisoners and my friend and I. We were handed a slab of fresh bread, which was an unexpected bonanza. This was the last food that I would have for a long time. It turned into a death march of three weeks and took many lives, both by shooting and starvation. We were lead into a forest clearing, where over 2,000 men were gathered without food, water, and or sanitation. People ate the bark off the trees in an attempt to appease their hunger.

On May 2, 1945, in the middle of the night, all guards disappeared. My friend and I, with many others, walked out of the forest towards the main highway, which was clogged with thousands of German troops escaping from the Russian front (they preferred to be captured by the Americans).

Meeting up with American soldiers lifted my spirits, and for the first time in many years I felt a sense of safety. My friend and I had no desire to live in any barracks or camps even if we were free to live in DP camps, which were supported by the UNRA. (United Nations Relief Agency). We managed to get housing on the outside and continued to rebuild our lives.

After returning to health and regaining the sense that we really had a meaningful future, we returned to Krakow to search for family members who might have survived. On one of my searches, I discovered my mother's name and address on a list of survivors. Guardedly, I went to see her and to this day I cannot express my emotions or find the words to describe that aching reunion. Much later, I learned that my younger brother, Israel, had died in Mauthausen, while my father survived. Father was a skeletal version of a human being—a frame only covered with skin. He was hospitalized for close to a year to bring him back to health.

When I secured my freedom, I had a burning desire to punish the oppressors and the vile people who betrayed their responsibility to fellow citizens and their religious teachings, but somehow I regained my humanity and turned my intensity to do good.

In 1945, with great determination, I joined the *Bricha*, an organization that facilitated the transfer of survivors to Israel. I used my energy and dedication to smuggle thousands out of the Eastern Europe countries into the DP camps in Germany and on to what was then called Palestine (or, as the survivors referred to it, Eretz Israel [the land of Israel.]).

In 1946, I accompanied 110 orphaned children to Israel. There, I continued my life by devoting my energies to help build the country. In 1948 I served in the Israeli aArmy and was wounded in the War of Liberation the following year. I married Bilha Zehori, a *Sabra* (Israeli-born native). We were devoted citizens and builders of the Jewish State.

Because my parents immigrated to the United States in December 1947 to be reunited with father's brother who came to Canton, Ohio, at the turn of the century, in 1956 Bilha and I and our children moved to Canton, where we built a good life with our three children.

From Cell Seven to Life

by David Rosenblum, as told to Caryn Rosenberg

The Early Years: 1925–1939

I was born the youngest of 13 children in Krakow, Poland, on May 13, 1925. My birth name was Shmuel David Rosenblum, but my family called me "Dolek," the Polish derivation of the name. My father, Nehemiah Zev, was a tailor and my mother, Tzurtl, helped him run his shop. In the years before I was born, six of my brothers and sisters died of various childhood diseases, including the influenza pandemic of 1919. So, when I arrived, I was treated like a little prince by my mother, our nurse, and by my sister, Rose, who was 13 years my senior. My relatives said that all of the other children would grow up and move away, but that I would remain home with my parents. I was my mother's prize.

I had three older brothers and three older sisters. Jacob was the elder sibling—16 years older than I. When I began attending *cheder* at the age of four, Jacob was already a furrier's apprentice. Rose was my eldest sister and did a lot in helping my mother to care for the rest of us. Next in line was Luzer. He was a tall, dark young man whom I came to admire greatly because he studied hard and became a dentist. After Luzer came Nusek—a strong, athletic young man who preceded me by about 10 years. When I started school, if anyone tried to pick on me, Nusek was there to fight my battles. Following him

177

was my sister Hinda. She had beautiful, long, dark hair, out of which she fashioned two braids, one encircling each ear, as was the style in Poland at that time. The "glint in her eye" bespoke strength of character, as well as a fierce hunger for life. Hinda was an incredibly talented violinist, and we often gathered around our radio when her sweet tones were broadcast over the airwaves. Next came Hanka, who was beautiful in her own way. Her light brown hair and blue eyes struck everyone who saw her and could well have saved her life in the ensuing years when a German soldier fell in love with her and wanted to marry her. But, like her sister, Hanka proved herself a determined soul and refused to leave her family.

We all lived in what at the time was considered to be a nice building in a traditionally Jewish area of the city. The apartment that I shared with my parents and sisters consisted of a large area that served as a parlor and kitchen and two bedrooms. I slept with my parents in one bedroom, while the girls shared the other room. My older brothers, who were practically adults when I was born, occupied their own apartment in the same building.

When I was four, my mother's Siberian nephew, who had immigrated to the United States, stopped in our town on a trip to visit his family in Russia. He found himself enchanted by my sister Rose—and she by him. By week's end, they were married and ready to embark on a new life in the United States. I would not see Rose again until 1933, when she and her husband returned to visit with their young son. They gave me a gift of an American cowboy outfit, marking the beginning of my ongoing infatuation with anything American. It also marked the last time that my sister would see her native home.

Attending cheder for my Jewish education, I joined other young Jews and Poles in public school. We learned side by side, in harmony. But, during the days leading up to each Christmas and Easter, we Jews were cast out of our classrooms while Polish priests took over, teaching a catechism about these two holidays. Usually, the priests taught our schoolmates that the Jewish people had killed Jesus Christ and were responsible for other unjust murders in religious lore. So, after the priests' tenure, we returned to school and unjust beatings.

This pattern continued until 1939, when my eldest brother Jacob left Poland for the United States. He settled in Queens, New York, near our sister Rose, and planned to work in the U.S. to earn enough money to bring over the rest of the family. However, the events of that autumn would preclude that. At the time, I was 14. On the night of August 31, 1939, I peeked outside the house. The sky was red—blood red. The next day, Germany attacked Poland and life as Jews had known it in Europe for hundreds of years changed forever.

We'd heard that Warsaw had fallen with barely a fight. Four days later, my friends and I stood at the bridge overlooking the Vistula River near my home as German tanks barreled through the borders into Krakow. Life under German occupation was hard. My father's business was taken from him. We Jews were forced to wear yellow armbands bearing the Star of David, and were considered property for the Gestapo to use as they pleased We heard about neighbors who had been snatched from the streets by the elite troops and disappeared. One day, as I walked along the road, with my Star of David visible, a German car stopped and ordered me inside. I was whisked away to a police station, where I sat alongside other Jews who had also been kidnapped. Our eyes focused on a door at the far end of the room, from which a man emerged, at various intervals, with blood and pieces of clothing all over his hands. Minutes became hours, as, one by one, another of us was called into that room. No one returned. I was sure that, when my turn came, I was going to die. Finally, I was called inside. The door slammed behind me. Blood covered the floor. The man was holding a knife. When he gave me an apron, I looked around and saw chickens in the room. I realized that he was slaughtering poultry. He ordered me to take his fresh kills and pluck the feathers. A few hours later, he let me go; I was sent out another door into the street. My family had been frantic with worry about me, and everyone heaved a deep sigh when I opened the door to my apartment. But my father knew that he had to do something to make sure that this kind of scare—or worse—would not happen again.

The Ghetto

I did not look like a Jew—at least not the way that the German propaganda had stereotyped us. I had light brown, almost blond, hair and light hazel eyes. My nose was short and turned up; I could have easily passed for a non-Jewish Polish teen. My father bought me the papers of a 15-year-old Pole named Romek Zarembowicz. These documents became the key to my family's safety over the next few years. Always in hand, they allowed me to remove my star and mingle among the general public.

As the war continued, the Jews in our city were forcibly moved to the Krakow ghetto and crowded in with German Jews of Polish ancestry who had been deported from Germany. Only those who were healthy and of working age had the "privilege" of living in the ghetto. This posed a great problem for my grandmother, who was very old—almost 100 and ill. So, the women in my family took my grandmother and sneaked to Szydlowicz, the small village, or "shtetl," from which my ancestors had come. Though some miles away from Krakow, Szydlowicz had always been predominantly Jewish. Generations of both my mother's and father's families had lived there for centuries.

Because I was young and possessed my false papers, I was the logical choice to act as "'messenger" between the men in Krakow and the women in Szydlowicz. Each week, I took money or some other object of value from my father, removed the Star armband from my clothing, and made my way out of the ghetto. I assumed the role of my alter ego, Romek Zarembowicz, and traveled to the shtetl where I again donned my star, hid my fake papers, and delivered my stash to my mother and grandmother so they could trade it for food and other items they needed to live. If I were caught, I could be killed. It was a dreadful pressure for a fifteen year old, but I was the only one who could do it.

Things quickly got worse for Jews in the Krakow ghetto. German Gestapo began to evict Jews from their homes and banish them from the city to the east. We didn't know where they were going, exactly, but people were scared. The Storm Troopers came for my brother Nusek, but he had already run away to join Jewish partisans who were doing what they could to fight the Nazis from their "stations" in the forests of the east. Still, my father decided that the rest of us should move to Szydlowicz. There, I lived in a small house with my parents, two sisters, one home-dwelling brother, and my elderly, sick grandmother, even as the reality of the Final Solution seemed to be engulfing us.

One September morning, in 1942, I awoke before dawn. Since supplies and food were scarce, it had become my job to travel, on foot, across town borders and stand on line for bread and supplies. I headed out before sunrise that morning, finally obtained the food, and walked back toward our village. Drawing near, I heard a commotion—loud voices, dogs barking—and screams. The closer I came, the louder it got. I reached the edge of town and realized that the Gestapo had chosen this day to "collect" the Jews of Szydlowicz and bring them to the train depot to be taken "east." We'd heard that the German military was killing Jews in the east, but no one wanted to believe it. We hoped that the Germans had been honoring their word about resettling us in working communities until the war was over.

I raced to my family's house, yelling for my parents. There was no reply. I ran from room to room and saw no one. "They must have packed the maximum fifteen- pound bags and been marched to the train," I thought. Then, I peered into my grandmother's quarters. My heart stopped. There she lay—my beloved 100-year-old bubbe—shot to death in her bed. Evidently, she had been unable to walk to the depot. So the Gestapo had just shot her there. The horror stifled my screams. I was jolted back to the present by the sound of trucks and dogs outside.

I knew that I had to get to the train station if I wanted to see my family again. I clutched my fake papers and ran toward the station. Hundreds of my Jewish neighbors sat on the ground or on suitcases. Holding the snarling canines, Storm Troopers paced above their captives, guns cocked and ready. I spotted my father and the rest of my family. I wanted to run straight to them, but I knew such an indiscretion would have resulted in all of us being shot. My father's eyes met mine, and in that moment of knowing silence, we agreed on what I had to do. Fighting back tears, I approached the Gestapo officer in charge of those guarding my family. I showed him my papers and, pointing to my father, cried: "THAT Jew owes my father money, and if I don't get it, my father will beat me to death!" After scrutinizing my face and credentials, the officer ordered the Rosenblum family to step forward. He turned to me and asked: "Is this the Jew that owes you money?" Before I could answer, my father "acknowledged" that he owed the money. His eyes locked with mine, my father and brother slid gold rings off of their fingers and handed them to the officer as payment. The officer handed the rings to me and told me to leave. My father and I continued to absorb the sight of one another, as we both knew that it would be the last that we would have. We knew that my family was not heading to work somewhere. I longed to say goodbye; to say I love you—but I literally bit my tongue, knowing that one word, or gesture of endearment, would end it, right there, for all of us. As I backed away, clutching the gold rings, I saw my father, Nehemiah Zev; my mother, Tzurtl; my brother, Luzer, the dentist; my sister, Hinda, the violinist; and my beautiful, devoted sister, Hanka, shuffle up the plank and disappear into the dark confines of a cattle car.

On The Run

I was seventeen years old, all alone, with nowhere to go. I couldn't go back to our house, now only a tomb for the blood-stained shell of my grandmother. If I stayed in Szydlowicz, someone would recognize me as a Jew. Wanting to stay close to my family, I followed the train tracks, sleeping in nearby gutters on the way to . . . wherever. They led northeast; I trailed behind, ending each day with the train in sight until it entered the gates to Treblinka, a camp outside of Warsaw. Standing on the outside of the fence, I heard guards shouting at the Jews to get off the trains, herding and prodding them to another part of the camp; I could hear screams coming from there. I didn't know it until later, but that day my greatest fears were realized: my family had been sent to that area directly upon exiting the train; they would find out then that there would be no hope of working, or of somehow, saving themselves—not in a gas chamber.

I had to warn someone that the horrors we had imagined were coming to pass. From Treblinka, I set out toward Warsaw, where I had an uncle. When I arrived at that ghetto, I put on my armband bearing the Star and found an entrance in the surrounding walls. In the ghetto, the Germans put some Jews in charge of implementing their edicts. Those in charge were often the first to be fed and the last to be deported. When I told these Jewish police what I'd witnessed at Treblinka, they shunned me. They refused to believe that Jews were being slaughtered like animals. Surely, they insisted, the resettlement to the east would allow their comrades to live in peace. After all: Jews were receiving postcards from their friends and family who had been "moved" before them and those cards said that things were good. They didn't understand that the Nazis would force Jews to fill out those cards as their last action before entering the gas chambers. I wasn't the only one who had returned to the Warsaw Ghetto with such stories—and while many refused to hear, eventually others understood what lay in front of them and planned an uprising several months later.

In early 1943, the Nazis came to liquidate the Warsaw Ghetto, marching up and down each street, ridding the buildings of their inhabitants and sending them to any number of horrors that awaited the trains. With my fake identification papers, I was able to sneak outside the ghetto walls just in time to watch as the uprising began. It went on for weeks until the last Jew was taken. I watched as flames engulfed the ghetto, melting away any remnant or echo of life.

For the next several months, I wandered the area between Warsaw, Szydlowicz, and Krakow, again sleeping in gutters and finding food where I could. I came to a monastery and told a monk that I was an orphaned Pole. In exchange for work, I received room and board and participated in church services. One day, as I assisted the priest in giving communion, a young man looked up at me. I recognized him as a former Polish schoolmate of mine. He said "Dolek, what are you doing here? You are Jewish." Everyone stopped and stared; I'd been found out. I dropped the tray I'd been holding, doubled over as if in great pain, and galloped out through the back door of the church.

Ducking from one hiding place to the next, I discovered two partisan groups: one Russian, one Jewish. I joined them for a short time, helping to blow up railroads and secretly fighting against the Gestapo and the Nazis. However, when I heard that my long-lost militant brother, Nusek, was still alive in the countryside, I left the partisans to look for him. My impassioned search was aborted when a former neighbor spotted me. At that time, Hitler's political policy mandated that Poles who assisted Jews be executed; those who turned a Jew over to the Nazis received a bottle of vodka and a loaf of bread. Before I knew it, this former co-habitant was hunting me down, finger pointed, yelling "Jew!" to anyone wearing a swastika. Soldiers held me at gunpoint as I protested that I was not a Jew, but rather the Polish citizen, Romek

Zarembovich. I showed them my papers, but my ex-neighbor persisted in his pursuit of vodka and bread. So a soldier demanded that I pull down my pants. I complied, and they saw that I was circumcised—marking me, unmistakably, as a Jew.

I landed in cell #7 at a prison called Montelupe where I awaited punishment for my twofold crime: being Jewish and daring to impersonate a Pole. My execution date approached and as it drew closer, I became unable to fathom the idea of being alive one minute and dead the next. However, I knew that my end was at hand, at merely 17 years of age. I'd lost my home and family; soon, hopelessness began to outweigh fear. One day, in my despair, I found a utensil and etched my name and the date into the wall—a lone, enduring testament to my existence. Now resigned, I removed my belt and attempted to hang myself. As the strap tightened around my neck and I began to dangle, the door to my cell opened and they pulled me down. I had crossed the bridge to a new dawn. Later, I would realize that this was the moment that I embraced life, in truth, and resolved never to let go.

Auschwitz

In July of 1943, 563 prisoners were transported from Montelupe to Auschwitz-Birkenau. Thirteen of us were Jews. I remember seeing the gates of the concentration camp with the words *"Arbeit Macht Frei"*—"Work Will Make You Free"—posted above the entrance. We went in to the receiving depot where we saw other trains comprised of those telling cattle cars. Nazi soldiers, joined by Polish and Jewish Kapos, were yelling, *"Macht Shnell!"* German shepherd dogs strained at their leashes, barking and growling at prisoners who piled out of cars where many had survived a number of days without food or water. The dazed people, mainly Jews– young, old, men, women, children— tried to acclimate themselves to the tumult. The soldiers poked and prodded them to turn left or head to the right. If anyone moved too slowly, that person was shot on the spot, as was anyone who tried to help him. Women shrieked in protest as their children were ripped from their grasp. In answer to children who asked where their parents were, soldiers pointed to the smoke stacks that could be seen in the distance.

The military men barked abrupt orders, all the while grabbing people and shoving them in one direction or another. I will never forget what I saw next. Apparently, a young woman had given birth in a cattle car and was cradling her newborn in her arms. A Nazi yanked the infant from her and, as she screamed, took one of the baby's legs in each hand and jerked them in opposite directions, ripping the tiny body in half. The young mother shrieked and fell to the ground, sobbing and writhing in horror. When she finally looked up into the Nazi's eyes, he returned the stare, then raised his pistol and shot her between the eyes. In other places along the depot, women's screams drew my own disbelieving stare to other babies being tossed in the air and used for bayonet and target practice.

These heinous murders of children threw me into a state of shock; I became numb and followed orders without feeling, walking, oblivious, wherever I was sent. Among a group of men who were designated for work, I heard someone tell us that we were infested with lice and had to be showered with disinfectant. However, some men were sent in another direction, to a "shower'" a distance away. Told to strip out of their "dirty" clothes, they were then herded into the showers as upbeat music played in the background. It was in these communal showers, after the doors had been shut and locked behind the men, that poisonous Zyklon B gas poured from the shower heads. At first, the occupants trapped inside screamed and tried to climb over and on top of one another to escape. Then they scratched at the ceiling. Within 20 minutes, they had all suffocated and camp workers pulled their bodies out to be burned in the crematorium.

Those of us sent to work were also sent for delousing, but in this case we were given real showers. First, however, our heads were shaved. Then we showered and were given striped uniforms. Then I lost my identity: another prisoner "inscribed" my left arm with the painful brand that transformed me from Dolek Rosenblum into "#153004."

The ensuing months saw us awakened before sunrise from four-tiered bunk barracks. Forced to run outside in the main area as our captors took a head count, we were fed water—with a piece of potato floating in it—and a stale piece of bread. Sometimes, someone wouldn't run quickly enough, and he'd be beaten or shot. Eventually, we went off to work in a factory, making tools or ammunitions for the German war effort. We didn't return to the barracks until very late at night. We never really learned the names of those with whom we shared our living space; often our roommates starved to death overnight and would be replaced with a new person. In this case, many became human vultures, pecking at the dead man to find a morsel of food that he might have saved or a piece of warmer clothing on his body.

I lived in the first barracks of my section at Auschwitz; in order to use the latrines, our group had to walk down several rows of bunkers. Camp guards stationed at these bunkers shot a prisoner if they didn't approve of his gait. Noting this, I decided to forego the walk to the latrine when the urge descended upon me one night; instead, I chose to relieve myself at the side of my barracks. However, a guard witnessed this transgression and wrote down my Prisoner I.D. number. Those caught breaking the rules were brought to the front of the camp to serve as examples of consequences wrought by misbehavior. I was to be the example this day. I did not know what to expect; but I had seen the "guilty" hanged before the throng of unwilling onlookers.

Paraded out onto a platform, I was ordered to unfasten my pants; they fell to my ankles. Then, I was told to bend over a short table; I felt the first lash of the whip. They ordered me to count aloud each crack of the whip against my skin. I found out that fifty lashes had been applied. I had fallen unconscious before number fifteen.

I was brought to another block to await the gas chamber; but another inmate signaled the block leader, and for some reason I was spared. A few weeks later, I was transferred, along with 5500 other inmates, to Warsaw where we were charged with the task of cleaning up the rubble after the liquidation of the ghetto. We worked there for the remainder of 1943 into 1944, clearing out the buildings and streets—sometimes finding bodies in the ruins.

I was nineteen, and the tide of war had turned against Germany. Russian soldiers crashed into Warsaw, and the Nazis evacuated all 5500 of us on a 140-kilometer death march without food or water. Those who fell behind were executed. People were so desperate for water that during the few periods of rest, they dug into the ground, praying to find it, in any form. They came upon the precious resource; it bubbled up from the ground, and they purified it by straining the liquid through their clothes, again and again. But, only 1500 of the original 5500 marchers survived the journey to the next concentration camp.

Dachau

At Dachau, I worked building F-2 airplanes. However, when we worked under anything but the utmost scrutiny, we made sure to leave out components imperative to the function of the airplanes. It was our way of giving our lives meaning and declaring our pride, even under such dire circumstances. We constructed machines that, most certainly, would not work against our own people. This practice continued into 1945 when the Americans were closing in on Hitler's forces. The Germans realized that the consequences of their own unspeakable actions would be more severe if there was any concrete evidence telling of what they had done to European Jews. So they set out to exterminate the remaining "evidence"—us—in the mountains. In April, 1945, we were hauled into cattle cars and shipped in the direction of the Swiss Alps. Hundreds of people packed each cattle car but not an ounce of food or water accompanied us. Men died on their feet as our bodies were huddled so tightly against one another that nary a one could fall to the floor.

We stopped for fuel and for the soldiers to refresh themselves. During one of these brief interludes, two fellows and I noticed that the rear high venting windows in our car might be sufficient to allow our bodies through them in an attempt to crawl out of the car. This was our chance to escape certain death that lay ahead. The soldiers' attention seemed to be focused on the other side of the train, permitting us to crawl out and down the back of the cattle car. Beyond the motion-detecting barbed wire, I saw a meadow that ran into a deep forest. Hope lay within the deep brush of that forest. But, if any of us touched that wire, the Nazis would be alerted, and we'd be dead. I was the first to try. I managed to crawl on my belly without touching the barrier just above me. As I ran into the meadow, the second man popped up on my side of the horizontal fence. The third fellow began to crawl, carrying in the tiny space between his back and the wire all three of our lives. Suddenly, guards began to fire their guns. I felt bullets whiz by me as I neared the forest. I heard the dreaded thud of my comrade hitting the ground behind me. I turned to see my other partner fall, and then a bullet grazed my temple. That horrific sensation sent a shiver of adrenaline through my body, electrifying my pace toward the shelter of the trees. I sprinted for about a quarter mile into the green thickness before conceding a bit of speed.

I didn't know where I was or if I was still being chased. So I climbed a tree, in whose leaves I nestled for days. Without food or water, I dared not move from my perch, lest I draw attention to myself. For the first time since that pivotal day in the Montelupe prison, I pondered the possibility of hopelessness. I was exhausted to an extreme where I sat, wide-eyed, and I felt parched beyond anything I could have imagined. Light evolved to darkness and back again. I was completely bereft, in every conceivable way; I would be twenty years old in a month—but I couldn't take it anymore. It was time to surrender.

So, when I saw the unfamiliar insignia on the Army tank rolling ahead below, I decided to turn myself in. Climbing down from the tree, I walked toward the tank, hands in the air, expecting to die at any second. The tank stopped and the hatch opened. Speaking my native Polish, I offered myself as a prisoner to the soldier who emerged.

The man looked at me, and in his best Brooklyn Yiddish, told me that I had just surrendered to the Americans and that I had been liberated. I told them where the remainder of the Dachau trains was headed; they told me to stay behind as they went ahead to liberate the passengers of those trains. "No way," I told them. I was going with them. I climbed to the top of the tank as we forged onward to free the survivors of the final march to the mountains. It was May, 1945, and, in commemoration of my twentieth birthday, I was free.

Liberation

The war was over. We survivors were left to try to make some sort of future for ourselves. I had been only fourteen when it had all started. Now I was twenty. My parents were dead; my brothers and sisters in Europe also were gone. I was alone, homeless, and adrift, with no direction. After beating the Nazis and the other members of the Axis, the Allies, including the United States, Great Britain, and the USSR, put us into Displaced Persons camps. I was assigned to an American run camp near Muhldorf, and from there I was to try to rebuild my life. I never found my brother Nusek and learned that he had survived the war only to be murdered in a pogrom upon his return to Poland.

The Allies and the Red Cross were hard at work, trying to reunite families; I posted a notice on their board with my name and the names of my sister and brother who lived in Queens, NY. I prayed that the reunification efforts would be able to help me find my family in America.

Meanwhile, I made plans to move to Palestine. I became a Military Police officer at Muhldorf. This position allowed me to access resources toward helping displaced persons find their way to Palestine. However, due to the restrictive practices of the British, Jews had to sneak into their own homeland.

In America, my brother and sister searched, unyieldingly, for any relatives who might have survived the Holocaust. Late in 1945, I received a letter from them via the Red Cross. Rose and Jacob, with the support of their families, were busy making plans to bring me to the United States to live with them. Inspired by rekindled joy and hope, I replied to their letter, initiating regular correspondence. Periodically, I would receive CARE packages from Queens with letters reminding me to steer clear of any kind of trouble so that my immigration to the U.S. would go smoothly. I was also admonished to "brush my teeth" and to use the toothpaste they'd sent. When they packed these boxes, they would roll dollar bills into the toothpaste tubes and so, as I dutifully cared for my teeth, I garnered enough cash to maintain my health while I waited to come to America.

I boarded the second ship bringing refugees from Germany to the United States. We departed in May, 1946. So fervently did I want to purge myself of the horrors that I had left behind that, negligent of the fact that the sea journey would be a long one, I hoisted my suitcase overboard; so, all I had were the clothes on my back. Still, I was eager to start my life anew in America.

On May 24, 1946, my ship docked in Manhattan. I was one of the first to leave the ship. As I walked down the gangplank, my eyes found my beloved sister, Rose. She had last seen me as an eight-year-old boy during her final visit to our pre-war home in Poland. But she recognized the twenty-one year old man rushing toward her. She addressed me in Polish, asking if there were any other family members who had survived. I shook my head in sadness; Rose fainted into my brother Jacob's arms. The scene was immortalized on the front page of the May 24 edition of the *New York PM*.

America

I lived with Rose, her husband Jack (who became my surrogate father), and their two teenage sons in their home in the Astoria section of Queens, NY. My brother, Jacob, his wife, Bernice, and their two young children lived down the block. Jack was a barber in the neighborhood; Jacob, a furrier in Manhattan. My family offered me everything I craved—a home, Brooklyn Dodgers games, even an education—but I was restless. Perhaps after being imprisoned for so long—and now, as an adult—I needed the freedom to roam as I pleased. I bought a car and decided to experience the full breadth of this new, beautiful country; my travels brought me to San Francisco.

Settling there for a time, I kept busy with various jobs, ranging from door-to-door salesman for Fuller Brushes to shoe salesman. But after a while, I began to miss my family and decided to move back to New York. I had many friends who were also Holocaust survivors, and some of us rented a flat in Manhattan. I became Jacob's partner in J&D Rosenblum Brothers manufacturing furriers. It was a partnership that lasted fifty years.

I lived in America for eleven years before meeting my wife, Sandra Litman, a young woman from New Jersey. We married in 1958 and moved to Newark, and later, to Bloomfield. Our daughter, Caryn Hinde, was born on June 28, 1960. Her Jewish name, Tzurtl Hinda, commemorated my beloved mother and sister, Hinda. My son, Steven Howard (Shepsel Nehemiah), came along on November 3, 1962 and he was named for my father.

Life in America was good. My new country offered me much opportunity and rewarded me for hard work. But, I could never escape the memories of the hell I'd lived through in Europe. At night, the past would haunt my dreams. Sometimes they were coming after me; often, they would be coming after my children.

I had few photographs of my parents and siblings who perished during the Holocaust, but they were displayed prominently in every home I inhabited in the United States. Once, my daughter told me that she saw me sitting alone at the table after a Passover Seder, clutching one of those photographs. She said it appeared that I was looking so deeply into their faces that it seemed as if I were trying to pull them back to me—or me back to them. Caryn said that she could actually feel my yearning.

Unlike many of my fellow survivors, I talked about the Holocaust; what I had gone through, personally; and the effect that my experiences had on my life. I never withheld these things from my children, and when they reached school age, I went to each of their schools to tell my story: I believe that it is imperative that our young people learn about what happened to Jews, and all those who were persecuted because they were different from the majority. By learning about what can—and did—happen, I hope that young people of this, and future generations, will ensure that nothing like that crime against humanity will ever happen again, anywhere.

After living a full life, David Rosenblum passed away on November 7, 2005 at the age of 80—an age that he never thought he'd see as he sat in Cell #7 in the prison at Montelupe.

Survival and Justice

by Jack Rubin

The appearance of the cattle car train frightened me. I was 15 years old and had to load on to the train the treasure which had been gathered from Jewish homes. Gold, diamonds, jewelry and scores of valuables were stripped from all who were gathered in the Brick Factory Camp. The faces of my own mother, father and sisters, who I had to beg to part with all their valuables, remain a dreadful memory.

As a child and young man, I had to face a new order and become a survivor in the evil world that befell me, my family, and all the Jews of Europe. I was born in 1928 in Vary, Czechoslovakia, a lovely, fairly modern small town of 3000. Forty-six Jewish families lived there for generations and were well-treated, respected, and regarded as equals. A democratic way of life offered good opportunities for advancement in business, trades, education, and many professions. I was the adored youngest child with two older sisters who created a circle of love and pleasure.

My father, Fishel, an attractive, immaculately dressed man, who always wore a white shirt and tie and sported a close-shaved beard, was esteemed both for his leadership and his knowledge of Jewish law, prayer, and history. He graduated Yeshiva at the age of 18 and could have been a rabbi. But when he married my mother, his father-in-law installed him in a business, a department store, which served the town and the surrounding farming communities. It became very lucrative and provided a very comfortable life.

My mother, Rozal Rosenbaum, was an attractive and accomplished woman. She enjoyed performing classical music on her xylophone. She was educated in the progressive school systems, which reflected those modern times.

My sisters also were given the opportunity to learn about the modern world. Father would say, "What is to God is to God and what is to people is to people."And so my home had a flavor and life of both worlds, and of an observant family.

My father served as the president of the synagogue. Each Sabbath was a celebration. His children were his cherished family whom he blessed each Friday night upon returning from synagogue. He never failed to bring home guests, who traveled through town, and remained with them over the Sabbath in special quarters that he had built for their comfort.

In 1938, when Hungary was designated the legal government over the territory of Czechoslovakia, things started to change. The first repression that was enacted was that no Jew could own a business. Father turned over his store to a gentile friend and neighbor to run it for him. Life took on a new phase. Hooligans roamed the streets, broke windows and abused Jews at will.

By 1939 the Nazi influence became more oppressive and harsh toward Jews. The gendarmes flitted about to carry out a variety of edicts against the Jews. No radios; no traveling on trains without permits; no higher education for Jews. Without their normal means of maintaining their families, many went to work for farmers or to any job just to get by. Life was difficult, but no one felt any threat of severe violence or death.

In March, 1944, when the Germans entered Hungary, Jews were forced out of their homes, and ghettos were established, mainly in brick factories. With the cooperation of the chief of police, we were able to remain and celebrate Passover in our home. The day after, we, too, were forced out to a town school yard with one small valise each, where we spent three days. A professor, a respected acquaintance, offered to take me and my sisters and hide us deep in the center of the country away from danger, but my parents declared that we would stay together. We would not be separated.

Trucks took the Jews of Vary and many other small towns to Beregszasz, where we were housed in a brick factory. Conditions were harsh, but they had food kitchens run by Jewish agencies. After four weeks, we were crushed into cattle cars, over 100 in each car. Without food, water, or any provisions for personal bodily needs, we barely kept our sanity, especially as we saw people dying around us. We did not know our destination; we only knew that we were being transported to labor camps. It was the end of May, 1944.

After two-and-a-half days, the train came to a stop in the darkness of night. In the morning, the doors were opened to the glare of daylight, the hysterical shouts of "*Auf gahen!*"—get off. The first thing we saw were the Germans, in their perfectly pressed uniforms holding German shepherd dogs, who were straining to attack at a moment's command. The beating and painful shoving by the kapos brought us into a state of complete submission, especially after the dehumanizing experience and suffering of the train journey. The kapos gloated that the smoke rising above the chimneys was the destination of many. We were at Auschwitz!

I recall the unemotional expression of Dr. Josef Mengele as he motioned us with his crop to the left or right, designating whether one was fit for labor or the gas chambers. They marched my line to rooms where we were undressed; all hair was cut off speedily, without care if a piece of flesh was snipped. We were marched through a liquid disinfection pit where the nicked flesh burned with pain. We were thrown striped uniforms and clogs and marched into barracks where we were packed like sardines for the night.

Early the next morning we were given questionnaires asking what our professions were and what kind of work we did. I wrote that I was a student with aspiration of becoming an electrical engineer. My father, being a businessman, was separated from me and we were housed in different barracks. We were given two postcards and were directed to write to two neighbors declaring that we were well treated, working on a farm, and eating well.

After four weeks in Auschwitz, 500 inmates with mechanical and engineering background were sent to Thiel in France at the Elcas Lorraine. This was a copper mine, where in the interior belly of the mines, operation shops were installed producing airplane parts. I was one of the 500.

We were there from June to September, 1944, and were treated fairly. We were allowed to shower once a week, were even given clean clothes, and no one died from starvation.

When the Allies succeeded in landing in Europe, the labor force was transferred to the Kochendorf Concentration Camp in Germany, where many inmates from other labor camps and concentration camps were gathered. Here the shops were hidden in the caverns of the salt mines, where Italian and German workers produced the parts, while the Jewish prisoners had to dig additional shops in the salt corridors. The conditions became severe. We never saw daylight, working from 3 am to 9 pm. Beatings, hunger, disease were the norm. I was wounded by grenade shrapnel and spent close to eight weeks in the dispensary where a doctor, a friend from my hometown, treated and protected me from returning to the killing labors. We remained in Kochendorf from September to March 1945.

The approach of the Allies forced the Germans to move the prisoners. The nightly death marches killed many and brought the survivors to Dachau at the end of April, which at this time housed not only Jews, but Poles, French, and other prisoners as well. Within weeks, the Jews were ordered to step out in the big plaza, where we were given civilian clothes with "KL" (Camp Lager) imprinted on the back. We were told that we would be taken by train, this time in passenger cars, to Switzerland. The effort failed because of the bombed-out bridges, and on April 30, 1945, while still in Germany, an SS motorcycle squad arrived. The ruthless shouting, beatings, and shootings kept all of us in a state of terror. People were dying. And just as suddenly that night we found ourselves without guards.

I was very sick, with a high fever and had just about given up my efforts to keep going, when, on May 1, 1945, we saw American jeeps and tanks. With our arms up in surrender, we heard a voice coming from the top of a tank, saying "Are you *Yiddishe Kinder* (Jewish children)?" These words still resonate to this day with relief and tragedy. Tears and a mournful cry escaped my whole being. Within half an hour a field hospital was set up with doctors and nurses who provided excellent care. I stayed for two weeks.

I settled for a short time in Mittenwald, and then was transferred to Pilsen. I soon discovered that my mother's sister, Aunt Esther, had survived, and had been liberated by the Russians. After many inquiries, I was reunited with my sisters. But our hometown held no attraction for me. All was gone; only memories existed. I decided to get into a Displaced Persons' camp near Munich, where I restarted as a free human being.

In August, 1947, I entered the United States and settled in Connecticut, where I married Shirley Cricow. My three children, Michael, Lynn, and David, have been the foundation of rebuilding the Rubin family, and my four grandchildren, Joshua, Daniel, Cara, and Jared, are the blessings which allow me to pronounce with a strong voice, "I am the richest man in the world!" In 1999 Shirley and I moved to Boynton Beach, where we have remained. I am an active member of the Anshei Shalom Synagogue as well as the Child Survivors/ Hidden Children of the Holocaust organization.

As much as I have loved my new country, when I learned that the "Gold Train" had been captured by the American army and was never acknowledged or returned to the Hungarian survivors or Jews in need, I was ashamed that my great country ignored this travesty. And so I joined the class action suit to bring attention to not only the stolen wealth, but to the fact that my beloved America would consider holding on to it. I knew that the "Gold Train" was not a fairy tale. I gathered a carload full of valuables. I loaded these valuables. I was forced to strip the jewels from my own mother. I stood firm to have the United States do the right thing. The United States stands for moral and ethical laws. It stands for justice. It must never do less.

And Then There Was Silence

by Katherine (Rosenbaum) Sattler

The small city of Uzhorod, located in then eastern Czechoslovakia, got its name from the Uzh River, which divides the city into two halves, the old and new sections. The 1939 census stated that the Jewish population was 7,357. This is where my parents, my brother Andy, my sister Gabriela, and I, Katerina *Katoka* (my nickname), spent uncomplicated, comfortable, and happy young years.

My handsome, blond, blue-eyed father, Kalman, who had a sweet and kind disposition, was man admired by both the Jewish and non-Jewish community. As a young man, he had hopes of becoming an attorney like his brother in Berlin, but his dream came to end when he had to take over the long established, lucrative wholesale/retail grocery family business when his father died suddenly. He married my beautiful mother Julia, the eldest of six siblings who was adored by her Orthodox religious father, who even approved that mother not cut her hair and wear a wig as was the Orthodox custom when a girl got married. My family followed the Jewish traditions, holidays, and kept kosher, but enjoyed a more modern life and pleasures. My father's charitable contributions to the synagogue and to the poor rabbis of the city was a weekly duty that I and our maid performed every Friday afternoon, delivering package of foods for the Sabbath.

In the pre-war years, our house, which still stands and is now used as government offices, in the pre-war years provided a life of comfort and much pleasure, especially the walnut tree in our back yard which served as a canopy surrounded by benches and tables around it. My girlfriends and I spent many happy hours playing games and being young girls entering the teen years.

In March 1939, Hungary annexed our part of Czechoslovakia, and their Nazi loyalty brought with them a virulent anti-Semitism, which became a daily occurrence against the Jews. During this time, my brother Andy was away in Budapest learning to become a baker. Father did not like such a career, but mother convinced him that it was better than doing nothing.

One day my father asked me to accompany him to the cellar, where he showed me some bricks behind which he had hidden jewels and valuables. I was both awe struck at my father's ingenuity and his trust in me, the youngest of his children.

On March 19, 1944 the Nazis occupied Hungary and our city. I remember one morning being intruded on by a tall German soldier who talked to mother. She soon came into my room and told me that I must move my things to their room. I objected, asking, why I had to do so. Mother answered me with a stern voice, which I rarely heard; she told me not to question but to obey, and I did. A number of German soldiers took over our house, and the four of us had to use my parents' bedroom and the kitchen.

And so life became more fearful and difficult. All Jews had to wear yellow stars sewn on to the front and back of our clothes. Jewish children were not allowed to attend public school; all businesses were taken away or were closed. Edicts established in other countries against the Jews were enforced here too. Father's statement, "It does not look good," became a line that was heard often. I could not understand such a concept: what does "not good" mean?

One of the soldiers showed some sympathy to our family and even sat with us at our table when mother made stuffed cabbage, which reminded him of his home and his children. He once said to me: Remember, when asked for volunteers, step forward and volunteer.

The night before Passover, April 16, 1944, mother told each of us to pack a little suitcase, while she packed a box of food. Soon shouts of "*Heraus*"—"Get Out"—were heard throughout our avenue. We lined up outside and were assembled along with my grandmother, extended family, and many other families, and were walked to a fenced in lumber yard. When we got through the gate, the first thing I saw was three soldiers, one Hungarian, cutting off clumps from the beards of the religious men. Seeing this spectacle brought me to tears and now father's statement, "It does not look good," had a new meaning. The ache and misery was etched on everyone's face. The imprisoned Jews numbered a few hundred and each day more and more people were brought into this wretched place where we were housed in sheds without any sanitary facilities in miserable conditions.

After about one week we were again gathered and walked a distance to a brick factory. The conditions got even worse there because we had no access to food and were not given any when our own meager supplies ran out. One day, the German soldier who lived in our house spotted me through the fence and gave me a bread. He was the one who told me to always volunteer.

After about two weeks we were again told to line up and were marched to a train, which was parked on a track outside the town. Father's health and stamina were weak and he could not move fast enough, according to the over-seer's demands. A Hungarian soldier hit father with a rifle, which sent him reeling. Seeing my father so abused, my state of mind became fragile. When mother saw that my courage was fading, she urged me with a determined voice, "Be strong my child!" We then helped grandmother into the cattle car, scrambled up ourselves, and avoided being knocked over by the crush of people who were being prodded to get in along with us.

Our car housed about eighty people, with a pail of water and another to serve as a toilet. All doors and windows were locked from the outside. We were in darkness and only discerned day from night from a crack in the ceiling of the car. Everyone seemed in shock. There was standing room only and after a while people sat on each other to find some sort of comfort in this entombed space. My sister was overcome with all this. Father tried to bring hope, saying that they were taking us to a place where we would be able to work and have improved conditions. It could not get worse than this.

We traveled for two or three days; I could not tell for sure how long this trip was. Finally the train came to a halt. The doors clanged open and with shouts of *Heraus*—out—and with abuse, we got down from the cars. We were blinded by the morning light and were in a state of confusion. We were told to leave everything on the train or on the ground. Clutching my sister and mother, we got to the ground and saw a number of bald men in striped clothing milling about on the landing. They looked at us with big, unfocused eyes. I was sure that we had arrived in a place for the insane. Suddenly, an SS soldier pointed to the three of us to go to the left, while father, grandmother and other members of my family were pointed to the right. This was the last time we saw our dear ones. The scene was surreal. Everyone was quiet except for the crying of the little children. We never said goodbye.

Our group of women was told to move forward and we were sure that they were taking us to work; we never knew what awaited us at our destination. This was Auschwitz. I don't remember how I got there; I felt as if I was out of my own body, just hanging on to my mother and sister. We were marched to a building where we were ordered to strip down, leaving our clothes and shoes at a distance. The line brought us to shaving stations, where all our hair, including our body hair, was shaved. Then we were marched into the showers, coming out wet and without towels to dry off. We were thrown gray uniforms, without consideration for size, and were instructed to take shoes from the pile, but were unable to look for the right size. All the time I kept mother and Ella close to me. As we looked at each other, we could not help but laugh at the caricatures of humanity that stared back at us. Our appearance brought us to laughter; it was our last for a long, long time.

We were told to form rows of three across. My sister and I put mother between us to support her. They took us into a large barn. Within ten minutes SS women asked for volunteers and, of course, I remembered the German soldier's counsel to always volunteer. I dragged my sister and told my mother, "Step forward, you are volunteering with me." Twenty-four women were taken to a huge building, which was equipped with three tier shelf-like bunks. Here we were turned over to a woman Kapo. I asked her where the factories were where we would be working, and what were they manufacturing there. She glared at me and said, "You see those flames shooting up into the sky? That is where your father is coming out from. He has been killed and is being burned there." With shock and disbelief I hid this information from my mother and sister; I said to myself that this could not be real, The Kapo was trying to frighten me. Yet my whole being was shaken. I don't know where I got the strength or determination to encourage mother and Ella every day: "We will stay strong."

As the Kapo walked us to an unoccupied bunk, she warned me not to tell anybody that my companions were my mother and sister. "This is where you will stay and sleep." Six of us took the middle level stunned by these conditions. Later that day, we were ordered to line up five across. A bowl of some sort of soup was passed around from person to person; each took a sip and passed it on to the next person. We were so hungry that we did not look or care what was in the bowl. I vowed that I would do everything to survive; I must live and be strong for my mother and sister.

Every morning, in the bitter cold, in our threadbare dresses, we were lined up for an "*Appell—Tzeil*," a selection-count. We stayed in the camp for about a week and a half. Then, one day, a German doctor came and chose about one hundred and twenty women, including my sister and me to go to one side. Mother was not among us. When he was distracted I pulled her to my side. We

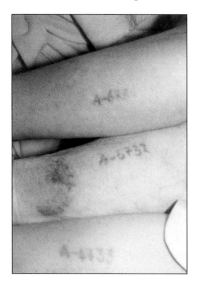

were then taken to a barn for tattooing. I justified the burning pain and demoralizing treatment by believing that we would be working in the same place. My sister was assigned number 6731, mother was 6732, and I 6733. I cannot say for sure, but later I was told that we were the only three with successive numbers who survived.

The next day we were given white kerchiefs for our heads and red polka dot dresses (some got blue), and we were taken to work at another camp, where we filled big sacks with straw. We were told that we would be living here, close to the crematoriums of Birkenau (Brezhinka). Something was different here; the air was not the same—the smell of burning flesh was a constant reminder of what was happening to the transports, to our families, to our people.

The next morning we were marched to a curved building close to our sleeping quarters. We were astonished at the mounds of thousands of clothing reaching to the ceiling. We were assigned to sort the clothes—men's children's, women's. Then we were told to open up any covered buttons where gold coins might be hidden and place them in a box. We were instructed to open the lining of handbags and clothing seams and hems where we might find diamonds and jewelry. We worked at this day in and day out. The amount of valuables was immeasurable. These items were the calculated hope of our people to survive—a hope which was taken away as soon as we were placed in the cattle cars.

As I looked at some of the elegant jewelry, which was a symbol of our desperation for survival, I instructed mother to bury some in the ground when the guard was not looking. Of course, we could not benefit from this act, but morally I felt that this was an act of defiance. One day I came across a jacket that shook me to the core; it was my father's. Touching this garment burned my hands as I handled it with tenderness and yet wanting to get it out of my sight. I did not want to believe that our father was one of the crematoria victims. I had to stifle my screams. I could not share this with mother and Ella and did not tell them until liberation when we were searching the lists of survivors. Keeping this truth, this burden to myself, was beyond endurance, but it made me grow up fast, especially as a protector of my mother and sister. My mantra, that I repeated with a sense of confidence often to strengthen their will was, "We will get out of here!"

Compared to the survival of other inmates, our squad had some benefits. We were obliged to shower every couple of days because the Nazi thought it was important to keep the clothing sorters clean so as not to contaminate the shipments of goods back to Germany. The reasoning was beyond our comprehension because we had to wear the same dresses—full of lice and dirt—without washing them during our entire captivity.

Getting sick in Birkenau was in itself a death sentence if one sought help at the infirmary. No one ever got well—or at least no one ever came back from there. When I got sick, my sister tried to steal a potato and unluckily got caught and was beaten mercilessly. She was made to kneel on a sharp gravel ground for twenty-four hours and was shaved again of her new growth of hair. I don't know how I managed to pull through from my illness but I did; I again became the driving force and voice to keep strong, even though our Kapo Manci informed me: "You will never get out of here alive, you saw too much, you know too much." I heard these words, but did not give in to defeat.

Smelling a continuous noxious odor, our Kapo told me that they were eliminating the Gypsies. And so it was on many other nights, when the gay prisoners and the transports from Theresienstadt were the victims of this murderous evil. The piercing cries and yelling tore me apart, but what hurt me to the core was when there was silence—I knew that that was the end of the people brought here.

The transports started to slow down. At one point, we were lined up and I was sure we were destined for the gas chambers. But for an unknown reason we were taken back to our camp quarters. We learned later that the arrival of a new transport took our place. Every day we reported for the "tzeil"—count and selections. Keeping my mother and sister at my side, I pinched mother's cheeks to give her a healthy glow, and it worked. In my heart of hearts I was so afraid, but I could not show it to mother.

At the end of November, 1944, an SS soldier walking by at one of our line-ups, stopped in front of us and stated, "A mother and two daughters. I have two daughters at home like you;" he then walked away. With disbelief I said to mother, "I am starting my third life. The first is when I was born, the second is when the new transport took our place for the gas chambers, and now, this is the third, the SS man did not select us."

When the news came that one of the crematoria had been sabotaged and slowed down the murder, we became emboldened and a sense of hope sprang up from our exhausted bodies. On January 18, 1945 we heard planes flying overhead and the sounds of exploding bombs at a distance. We knew that the Soviet Army was advancing. With urgency, the German guards and Kapos ordered everyone out of the barracks. I managed to steal a jacket as we were herded out to the announcement by Kapo Manci, "We are getting out of Camp."

And so the "Death March" began. As we now know, it was the Germans' method and intent not to leave any witness behind to accuse them of their methodical murder. The march was another way to kill. We were marched at a grueling pace, without food or water and wearing only our threadbare dress uniforms in the cold winter weather. Our group was composed of about 100 women. People were shot if they slowed, stopped, or dropped. We ate grass and snow. Looking back now, I cannot believe that I was part of this evil and the evil that continued. Corpses scattered on the sides of the road from previous marches showed us where our own road was leading. The SS, with their growling German shepherd dogs, showed no pity; they were killers. I was ready to give in to this torment. But Mother, seeing my despair, slapped me on my face to keep me from giving up. My parents never hit us, and this slap has become a symbol of the great love that was expressed to save me.

As I look back at those final days, I cannot imagine how we managed to stay alive. Many from our convoy died or were killed. Mother was at a stage of not being able to put one foot in front of the other. My sister and I dragged her and we arrived in Ravensbruk, a concentration camp for women, where we were housed with non-Jewish Russian women, who beat the Jewish arrivals. We stayed at Ravensbruk about four days and then we were put on an actual passenger train and were taken to Neustadt-Glewe a labor concentration camp near Hamburg. We were housed about seventy women in an empty room, without mattresses or blankets. We were a labor force digging anti-tank trenches and unloading box cars filled with potatoes. We could not hide even one since we were watched very carefully and the punishment was a beating or death. A soldier, who was from Yugoslavia, asked me where I was from and when I told him that I was from Czechoslovakia, it evoked some sense of pity in him and he occasionally gave me extra bread.

Here my sister became very ill. There was nothing I could do to help. I was desperate and I remembered that when I was a little girl sitting on my grandmother's lap, she told me about a remedy of little black pills and honey which was good for the stomach. I dared to ask the Yugoslav soldier to bake me one potato and burn it to charcoal, which he did. I crushed it and fed little pieces to my sister. I had to beg her to eat it, pleading, "Please do it for me." Mother thought I was crazy but it worked. The next day my sister felt better.

Again planes were flying overhead and the sound of bombs could be heard at a distance. We started to hope that this time we would be freed. And my proclamation was, "We will be liberated for Ella's and my birthday." Our conversations of hope focused on the kind of food we would cook. Early one morning, I saw out of the window that the soldier's barracks had been abandoned, and on May 3, 1945 we saw familiar faces—our guards—who were wearing civilian clothes. I said to my mother and Ella that May 4 would be our liberation day. And so it was. Through the gates of the camp we saw Russian tanks. The soldiers could not believe the spectacle of suffering humanity. They threw food to us.

We knew we were free, but what now? We broke into the food storeroom and got bread and margarine. We smeared the margarine twice as thick as the slices of bread. The next thing we did was to take possession of the German soldiers' barracks and their beds. To sleep on a bed was not real anymore, but somehow seeing others enjoying this luxury made the dream become real for all of us. Our next venture was to get clean clothes and my mother's dream was to cook a chicken soup for us. My girlfriend and I went to the nearby village and stopped at a farmhouse to get clothing and a chicken. The farmer, seeing two bedraggled girls who did not resemble humans, threw us out. We were shaken with his abusive treatment of us. As we dejectedly walked away, we met up with some Russian soldiers who asked us what we were doing here. I told them who we were and where we came from and how the farmer would not help us. One of them said to come with him. He confronted the farmer ordered him to stand aside. He told us to take anything we wanted. We took a pillow cases and I stuffed clothes for me, my mother, and Ella. Walking out, we heard chickens cackling in a barn. We caught one and stuffed it in the pillow case. We found some carrots and vegetables and rejoiced that we would be able to fulfill mother's dream. We found a man who killed the chicken for us. We plucked it clean and mother made us a most wonderful chicken soup. All the chicken soups after this did not taste as great as the one my mother cooked for us right after liberation.

Two days after we were freed, we decided to go to Prague. Twelve women and two girls walked together and wherever possible sought out the Red Cross to help us. Our journey was long. We walked and on occasion got a lift and finally got to Prague by truck. As we stepped off the truck, we looked at each other questioning, "What are we going to do here?" We again found a Red Cross relief station, where we were fed and directed to the Jewish organization, HIAS. They helped us with living quarters and mother and Ella were hospitalized for malnutrition.

My mother's constant search for father and Andy finally brought me to the point where I had to disclose my secret of father's death. Eventually we did locate Andy, who survived Mauthausen and many labor camps. Needless to say our reunion was full of tears. We returned to our home and I went down to the basement hoping that the hidden valuables would still be there, but every stone, every brick from the walls and floors, were gone. When we were looking at the list of names searching for survivors, we met an American soldier from Los Angeles. We told him we had two uncles living there. He helped us contact our family, and he advised us to register at the American Embassy. Following his recommendation, we got to the Embassy at 4:30 in the morning— we were first in line.

And so our return to a more normal life began when we arrived in Los Angles in 1946. We were met by our dear family, who provided us with an apartment and declared, "This is your home." I attended school at night and worked days for a designer, Athena, translating sketches into patterns. Eventually I enhanced my skills in fine tailoring and worked for a major movie studio in the production of costumes for films. I met my husband, Carl, and we were married in 1949. We have three children, two boys and one girl, and five grandchildren, who have enriched our lives and our family.

After many years of silence about my Holocaust life, I found my voice in 2008 when my daughter invited me to speak to her class. I know that what we went through and our losses were beyond words, beyond anyone's imagination, but as best as we can, it must be recorded and remembered. "We will be strong," is a motto I lived by during the hellish era and that I am living by now. It is the legacy I have left my family.

A Boy of Many Names

by Allen Spak

Sometimes I have to stop and think, what is my real name? Is it Avrum, Avrumele, Slavik, Allen? I have sounded each one, and have come up with different reactions of memories and lost memories. The only connection to my very early years is by my names; my very early memory is veiled and difficult to bring forth as real.

Avrum was my biblical designated name, by which I knew I was blessed to be a Jew. Avrumele was my loved name, evincing gladness and appreciation of being of the family. Slavik was my Polish name, which tied me with the country of my birth on May 20, 1940 in Lutsk/ Łuck, Poland (Soviet Union); Allen is my chosen name, one of freedom and a childhood that I can recall with pleasure and gladness.

My mother, Basia Barr, came from a landed Jewish family, dating back generations. They operated two mills, raised and milled wheat and other crops, and enjoyed a prosperous farming enterprise. Grandfather Shaya ran a successful business, had personal and good relations with the administrators of the area, and treated his workers with fairness and generosity, which earned long term loyalty and admiration of our family.

Mother's older brother, Reuven, was destined to continue in our family business and so chose to study agronomy. Her sister, Masha, was also given modern opportunities as the family had the means. Mother pursued her interest in fine sewing, embroidery, and tailoring, which served her well later on.

The family followed Orthodoxy but in a more modern form, while still keeping kosher, observing the celebration of holidays, and honoring the Sabbath each week. While studying in Lutsk, mother met my father and they married in 1938. Lutsk was comprised of 39,000 people, about 17,000 of whom were Jews. The greater surrounding area had a population of more than 300,000 people, mostly Ukrainians, Poles, Jews and a small number of Czechs and Germans

On February 5, 1939 the *Molotov-Ribbentrop Pact* gave the Soviet Union the freedom to annex the eastern part of Poland, including Lutsk and eastern Volyn. On September 17, 1939, a couple of weeks after the German attack on Poland on September 1, the Soviets came in with their armies, meeting no resistance.

For the oppressed Jews of Poland, who were treated as outsiders and were discriminated against, the Russians offered a feeling of safety, opportunity, and equality. Of course, the gentiles looked at Jews as traitors; but the Jewish people, who had suffered discrimination for decades under the Poles, saw the Soviets as the salvation to their hard lives. gentiles and Jews who were landowners and wealthy were called *Burzhuis*—Capitalists—and were deported to Siberia if they objected to having their properties taken over by the Communists or could not accept Communist life. Most of the people who accepted the new ways came from the poor population.

Life changed. Those who were able to remain in their homes subsisted on their meager gardens or sought jobs that were meted out by the bureaucrats through favors and knowing the right people. The world I was born into was a world turned upside down; it was full of upheavals and uncertainty. On June 22, 1941, Germany broke their pact and attacked the Soviet Union and, of course, our area. This was not a mild entry, as the Soviets had done in 1939. Planes and bombs were flying, and the population was confused about how to keep safe, and what to do. The locals, who felt betrayed by the Jews' acceptance of the Soviet regime immediately aligned themselves with the Germans, rounding up many of the Jews and killing them. It was a heartless massacre of young and old. Other family members who had left for America urged the extended family to get out and escape, but they could not be moved. They felt that they could not leave their homes. By this time, the refugees who were escaping the German atrocities from the center of Poland brought with them stories of evil that was headed our way. My parents, in danger of being taken for slave labor, decided to get away from the approaching threat. They contacted a gentile family, with whom they had good relations, who let them stay with them for a few weeks.

One day they heard that the Ukrainian collaborators were searching the neighborhood, looking for Jews. Father immediately ran and hid in the attic of the adjoining barn; mother hid under a bed, and I, a toddler, was stashed away in a woodpile next to a hot stove. Hearing the havoc the intruders were creating in the house and fearful of being found, mother dashed out through a rear window, barefoot, and hid in the forest, while father was discovered and killed. I was not found out. I did not make a sound, even though it later was discovered that I had suffered a severe burn on my elbow, which left a scar for life.

When mother returned and learned father had been killed, she decided to take me away from this dangerous neighborhood and approached a poor Ukrainian woman with a few children to take me in and raise me as her own if mother should not survive. She gave her many gold coins as payment to help with my upkeep and so we were separated. I cannot remember any emotional partings; I really cannot remember much. I know that mother provided me with a wonderful lady, Lisa, who sheltered me. She was a strong, big-boned woman, with dark hair and a round high cheekbone face who welcomed me as her own. It was easy for me as a little boy to attach myself to and find comfort with my Ukrainian mother. She was my mother. I never knew that I did not belong nor that I was Jewish.

I don't recall a man being about, but there were several children who were my companions playing games of hide and seek and catch. The one resentful and unhappy memory was not being allowed to swim with the other boys. Now, of course, I understand, since all swam in the nude and I was circumcised, which would have been a giveaway that I was Jewish. I recall a garden, many chickens and ducks, as well as cows and goats which apparently provided good nourishment.

While I was with my Ukrainian mother, Lisa, my mother never came to see me. I was safe and never felt that I did not belong. I had lost all memories of my toddler life and assumed that Lisa and her family were mine. During this time, mother—tall of stature, self assured, and fluent in Ukrainian, Polish and Russian—passed as a non-Jew. With false identity papers, she drifted about from locality to locality subsisting and not trusting or making any connections to anyone. By the time the Soviets succeeded in overcoming the Germans in the Russian territories and liberating our area, it was the summer of 1944. I was 4½ years old. After a time, a woman appeared who embraced me with an ardor that almost squeezed my breath away. She came to take me away; she said that she was my real mother. The confrontation with Lisa, who did not want to give me up, gave me hope; but after mother pleaded and warned and offered her a generous money payment, I was handed over to this stranger. I was very angry with my Ukrainian mother. Why she would let this stranger take me away. Wasn't I a good boy? What did I do to deserve this? I refused to go with this unknown woman no matter what she promised. But with much coaxing, a promise of a train ride and being physically compelled, I was led away from my Ukrainian family to join strangers.

We traveled by train to the city of Lodz, where many survivors settled. Mother led me into a beautiful, fashionable apartment with a balcony overlooking the street. Compared to my humble cottage at Lisa's, this was a palace. Soon a man entered who was introduced to me as my father. He greeted me with warmth and welcome. Actually, this man was my stepfather and this fact was not disclosed to me until I was sixteen years old when he passed away; of course, I was very disturbed by this hidden truth and felt betrayed. But I could not stay resentful long because my own father had died when I was so very young and I did not remember him or even know his name.

I was encouraged to speak Yiddish, to which I countered bitterly that I didn't speak the languages of *Zhyds*, a derogatory name for Jew. Of course, I recognized that somewhere in my stay with my Ukrainian family, *Zhyd* was used as a disparaging term against Jews. I struggled for a long time to accept my identity, my Jewish family.

We stayed in Lodz about a year. After dealing with the tragic fact that the entire family, except for one cousin, had been murdered, Poland had become a graveyard; in addition, it was a dangerous place for Jews. Beatings and killings were a frequent occurrence. All survivors were leaving—most to the American Occupied Zone of Germany.

Another family and ours hired a truck and with a payoff of cigarettes and vodka, we crossed into Germany, the American Zone, and finally were accepted, and were registered in Fernwald, a DP Camp in Munich. Our standard of living was spartan, but we learned to enjoy our freedom and a life without fear.

And so, at the age of six I finally had to accept myself as a Jewish person. I made friends, started school, learned Yiddish and Hebrew, and after many people commented that I looked like mother, I finally accepted this fact and I learned to love and appreciate my mother and value her strength and the sacrifices that she made for me.

I found great satisfaction joining and participating in a children's Zionist group and learned to understand Jewish history and culture along with establishing a yearning for Israel. The inspiring message from our leaders lifted our spirits and self-esteem. Mother and I were all for going to Israel, wanting to be united with my hero, the one surviving cousin who settled there, but father insisted that his family in America was where we needed to go. He said that we had enough of suffering and struggles; he wanted to come to the land which was always described as the "Land of Opportunity."

Our crossing the Atlantic on a military ship was an adventure intermixed with seasickness, but my first taste of America was Coca-Cola and I decided that I liked America. We arrived in New York in June, 1949. I was nine years old and again had to face adjustments and again learn another language.

We were met by a cousin whose parents had immigrated to the States in the 1920s. We were received with kindness. After a couple of days we were taken to Baltimore, Maryland, where father's family received us with open arms in order to repay the goodness of my grandfather, who had paid for all their travels and helped them establish their lives in the U.S. In turn, they helped my parents establish a grocery store (with an apartment above), where my parents worked long hours but managed to make a living and helped me take advantage of all the benefits that this great country offered.

My school years were happy ones and I managed to play every sport and partake of any opportunity to fit in. I became an American boy.

After father passed away in 1956, mother and I were left alone. By this time she had become less self-assured and needed me to help her both emotionally and with running the store. And so we continued together. Mother made it possible for me to continue my education, and I first became a pharmacist and then a dentist. It was a hard road, but together we made it.

During my high school years, I became reacquainted with my elementary school crush, Ellen Sachs, which turned into love and a permanent attachment. We married on August 8, 1963, and were blessed with a family of a son, daughter, and four grandchildren.

As I look back at my life, I know that I have learned a great lesson: the love of one's mother is unbreakable. Her perseverance and will to survive, to reunite with her child, showed me an example of strength to overcome my own health hurdles and value my own children as a blessing.

I have found that I do have another name and that is, Child Survivor of the Holocaust. I also know that evil and hate must be erased from this earth.

Escape from Nazi Austria to Shanghai

by Erica Liebermann Spindel

As I try to pass on my Holocaust experiences, I strive to remember what I witnessed, suffered, and survived as a little child. I was only five years old when the frenzy of the evil reached my street, but a clear image of that time remains in my memory.

My home in Vienna, Austria, on Mariahilfer Strasse—6th District—brings images of my life with my parents. My father, Max Liebermann, a slender, attractive man had a serious way about him. He and his parents came to Vienna to escape the hard, discriminatory life in Poland. He worked as an electrician, which provided a decent living. My mother, Sidonie Jaegendorf, statuesque and on the plump side, was self-assured and had a good sense of humor, but that did not deter her from being the disciplinarian. She was well-educated and was employed by the court as a secretary. She also loved to create embroideries and needlepoints.

A mutual friend's introduction led to my parents' marriage. They were a compatible couple. They shared an apartment with my Jaegendorf grandparents, and all created my safe world when I was born on February 11, 1933, the year Hitler came to power in Germany.

Mother's family, parents, and grandparents transplanted from Poland to Austria well before the Second World War, while mother and her two brothers were native-born Viennese. One of her brothers settled in Switzerland and the other immigrated to the United States before the Hitler era.

Life for us was uneventful. As an only child, I enjoyed being the center of attention and was indulged with many toys. I began kindergarten at the age of five, but my memories are very vague since soon after, Jewish children were excluded from the public schools. Out of our apartment window I witnessed a dramatic scene of an hysterical outpouring. This picture is etched in my memory. It was March 12, 1938, a man, with outstretched arm, was greeting an ecstatic gathered crowd on either side of the street yelling "Heil Hitler." Hitler inched along in an open top black limousine, surrounded by an entourage of cars, as he beamed with pleasure at his warm reception. This was the day of the Anschluss, the annexation of Austria by Nazi Germany.

The evil against the Jews was manifested in brutal beatings, countless oppressions and arrests. On November 9-10, 1938, the night of broken glass, Kristallnacht, about 6,000 Jews were sent to Dachau. My father was among them.

Within a few months of the annexation, my uncle took me away to live with his family in Switzerland. He wanted to get me away from the upheaval of the hateful oppression against the Jews and to make it easier for my parents to escape Austria without worrying about me. I lived in Switzerland for one year and immediately learned to speak French and lost my fluency in German. I was provided a good life but missed my family terribly and had to contend with the fact that I was not an only child here; I had two older cousins who at times I would defy.

Father was held in Dachau and Buchenwald for nine months. With great courage and determination, mother traveled to Berlin and proved officials with ship-passage tickets out of Austria to Shanghai, for which my uncle had paid. In May, 1939, father was released, emaciated and a beaten man. His will broken, he relied on mother to make all decisions. She hastily packed a couple of trunks with necessities for our survival in China and forwarded them to the ship waiting in Marseilles. In the meantime, my uncle prepared me for travel, accompanied by a cousin, who was returning to Paris. I had one suitcase, a packed lunch, and an identity tag with name and destination that hung on my chest. At the age of six, I was both scared and full of adventure. My destination was Lyon, France, where I would be reunited with my parents.

I was met by my parents at the station with hugs and kisses. I recognized mother, but my father was not the same man. His suffering in the concentration camps broke him and he never truly recovered. In addition, I lost the ability to communicate in German, spoke only French, and my parents did not know this language. We had barriers to overcome to become a family again.

We boarded the ship SS Athos II in Marseilles and started our long journey to Shanghai, through the Suez Canal, Egypt, Indian, Singapore, Indochina, the Philippines, and Hong Kong. We arrived in Shanghai in June 1939, 30 days after we started. This journey again offered a new world to which I had to adjust. The weather, the many languages heard, and the confined quarters were an adventure; at the same time they were difficult for all travelers.

Shanghai was an internationally controlled city and the only city in the world that one did not need a visa or financial guarantee to enter. It became a safe haven for Jewish refugees from Europe who could afford a ticket during the late 1930s and early 1940s.

By 1941, nearly 25,000 European Jews from Nazi Germany, Austria, Poland and Lithuania found shelter in Shanghai; we were among them. Getting off the boat, we were greeted by a member of the Joint (American Jewish Joint Distribution Committee) and were transported to a camp and deposited in a room with 20 other arrivals. Our small space had bunk beds and little table; we draped the space with sheets to have some privacy.

The sanitary conditions were beyond barbaric. Using a bathroom was a torturous experience. We had access to cold water only. To get hot water, we had to buy it from a vendor and use this luxury in a basin to wash dishes, wash ourselves, and do hand laundry. The winters were brutally cold. We had no means to heat the rooms and so we bundled up and somehow survived. Mother acquired a small kerosene burner so we were able to have hot soup or tea. All in all, we had no choice, so we adjusted to life. We were not alone trying to maintain life. Mother was able to get a job as a cook at the yeshiva (religious school) and managed to bring home better food than was handed out in the mess hall.

As bad as the living conditions were, the Jewish community, with the help of the long well-known Persian and Iraqi Jews in China, established a good school for the children. This is where I began my education and continued in acquiring additional languages, including English, Hebrew, and Japanese, when we came under their occupation.

Japan had attacked China/Manchuria in 1937, but after they attacked Pearl Harbor on December 7, 1941, their military forces took control of Shanghai, including all foreign sections, and made our lives wretched. Germany and Japan were Allies, so the Germans asked that the Japanese set up concentration camps in Shanghai and promised to supply all equipment to help kill Jews. In 1942, Joseph Meisinger, the "Butcher of Warsaw," came to Shanghai to force the Japanese to impose the Final Solution on the Jews. By all accounts, the plan was to liquidate the Jewish inhabitants by rounding them up on Rosh

Hashanah (the Jewish new year), load them onto ships, send them out to sea, and starve them or sink them.

The Japanese did not support Nazi racial policies and were not interested in the plan. As a concession, the authorities declared on February 18, 1943, a "Designated Area for Stateless Refugees," ordering all undocumented refugees, including the wealthy ones who had lived outside the ghetto, to move into the one-square-mile area in Hongkou district, establishing the Hongkou ghetto. The Jews were not allowed to leave without government-issued passes.

At the beginning, day passes were handed out relatively freely, but as time went on they were limited, cutting off most of the Jews from any possibility of working on the outside and helping themselves to provide better nourishment. The Japanese stepped up restrictions; a curfew was enforced, the area was patrolled, and food was rationed to a near-starvation existence. Conditions in the ghetto were appalling, especially during the summer months. Lice, bed bugs, fleas and mosquitoes found their victims in the refugees. It was impossible to maintain cleanliness. The population was beset with all kinds of diseases, including typhoid, malaria, cholera, diphtheria, dysentery, small pox, and scarlet fever, which were treated by the limited medical facilities that the refugee Jewish doctors could provide. The will to live weakened for many.

The Japanese ghetto boss, Goya, a little nasty man, showed off his authority by ill-treating the residents. Without cause, he would slap a passerby or shout a rude remark, depending on the day and his mood. But looking back at those 10 years, it is clear that most people maintained a sense of humanity about themselves and community. People prayed in makeshift synagogues, home talent theatres offered diversions, some American films were a special treat, and even some coffee shops and a version of night clubs was available for the light-hearted. For the children it was a way of life. We did not question. We grew up without toys or the carefree fun that should be a child's life

As the Allies became more successful in their fight against the Japanese, and with the end of the war in Europe, the American front finally reached Shanghai with numerous aerial bombardments. There were no bomb shelters or even basements in Hongkou. The sirens blaring sent everyone running for safety. We hid in a jail until the all-clear siren screamed its double blare of all clear. The most destructive raid took place in July 17, 1945, when 31 refugees were killed, 500 wounded, and 700 left homeless. The Japanese, hoping that the Americans would not bomb the district inhabited by foreigners, had a radio transmitter and stored ammunition and oil in the restricted area.

On August 15, 1945, the Japanese surrendered in Shanghai. The Japanese military remained in the city maintaining order until August 26, when a small landing party of American Marines arrived. The appearance of the Americans was a liberating and uplifting event. They recognized that we were abused, had suffered starvation, and needed to be helped. They were generous, handing out chocolate bars and candy. Their open, smiling faces seemed to act as a kindling to the revival of hope.

At this time, the Joint Distribution Committee, UNRA (United Nations Relief and Rehabilitation Administration) and Jewish charitable organization stepped in to help revive us. With this help, mother, father and I—like many others—were finally able to get jobs away from the ghetto compound. I was now 13 years old. I continued school, taking business courses of typing, shorthand, and bookkeeping and helped out by working part time in a newly established leather manufacturing business run by a fellow refugee.

Father's suffering in Dachau and Buchenwald, our hard life and limited medical care finally broke father's endurance. His failing health reached an end and he died in 1947. The happiness of being free from the war was short-lived for us. Mother and I were left alone, in our desolate loss, without family to comfort us or give us support.

We soon learned of the personal loses to our family by the Nazi killers and of the murder that was committed against the Jewish people of Europe. We remained in Shanghai until 1949. Our options of where to go and how to continue were not clear to us or easily available. The shocking reports of what happened to the Jewish people in Europe left most refugees without any choice of returning to their homes of birth. In addition, the turmoil of the fighting between the Communists and the Nationalists convinced most to leave China. By 1948, people resettled in many countries, but for most the destination was the newly declared independent state of Israel.

In the meantime, at the age of 15, I graduated high school—just when we were able to leave for Israel. The sailing was a long one, with a stop in Naples, Italy. My mother's brother, my uncle from Switzerland, met the ship and with much negotiating and guarantees, he was able to get us off the ship and join him in Zurich. Our reunion was joyous and tragic. It took me some time to adjust to the Western world. The modern sanitations fulfilled my often wished for luxury. I experienced it all with awe, relearning how to enjoy life and laugh with pleasure.

My mother's yearning to come to America was of long standing. We were sponsored by relations in California, and in January 1952, we once again boarded a ship and sailed to New York. The skyline of the skyscrapers and the outstretched arm of the Statue of Liberty mesmerized me. I almost had to pinch myself that we had survived and arrived at the gates of a free country, to live life without fear. We were met by my American uncle, who convinced us to remain in New York.

Since I had the facility of the English language and had office skills, I got a job as a secretary for a lingerie company on the 53rd floor of the Empire State Building. I had to overcome my fear of these lofty heights, which I did, and worked for this company for four and half years, reaching the status of bookkeeper.

I continued to live a life as a free American, but did not taking anything for granted. I met my husband, Joseph Spindel, also a Holocaust survivor from Poland, and we married in 1958. We are blessed with two wonderful sons and daughter-in-laws and four adorable grandchildren.

For many years I looked at myself as a refugee, but as I learned more and understood what I saw with my own eyes, what I had experienced and lost, I came to realize that I am a survivor.

I feel lonely for my grandparents, who were in my life for such a short time. I feel a great loss that my dear father had shattering experiences that shaped and destroyed and shortened his life at a young age. And I am saddened that my mother had to see her only child suffer and lack the glee that a child should have. But as I got older, I found my voice to speak of the Holocaust and present another pane into Jewish oppression and suffering.

Four Years in Hell

by Hanna Temel

Brno, the second-largest city of Czechoslovakia, is a place of happy memories for me. I was born there on March 13, 1930, the only child of Dolly and Karl Spiegel. My father was a successful wholesale merchant of fine woolen textile, while my mother helped with the accounting.

My father was a kind and selfless man who gave comfort and open-handed charity to the needy, whether Jew or Christian. He believed that every human being, even the oppressors, must have a shred of decency. He was trusting and generous and would share the last slice of bread with those he believed to be hungrier than he was. My mother was a statuesque and elegant woman. She had a no-nonsense attitude, did not expect anything from anyone, and relied on her own strength. She was an adoring parent and I felt guarded and rejoiced in as a precious jewel.

My maternal grandfather, Hugo Berger, and grandmother, Ida, owned a store where grocery products, produce, and delicatessen were sold. It provided a good life for us, and in general the entire family was well situated. Our family leased a spacious apartment in a modern suburb where Jewish life was unhindered. I excelled in my studies, and skipped fifth grade because of my abilities and effort. After the Nazis took over the country, Jewish life was curtailed and at that time I continued my high school studies at a Jewish school where again I enjoyed learning and had success in my studies.

Under German occupation, life took on a different and shocking phase. The hardships and regulations decreed against the Jews—confiscating properties, businesses, autos, furs, jewelry, bank accounts and anything of value—left the community in a daze. Jews were forced to move from buildings owned by Germans, which originally had been taken away from the Jews. Our lives became a nightmare, which turned into an even a more horrendous reality when, on November 27, 1941 (my mother's birthday), my parents, grandmother Ida, aunt Grete, and I were ordered to report to a high school, bringing only one suitcase and a duffel bag per person. The humiliation and mistreatment was just the beginning. Within three days, our transport of 1,000 Jewish men, women and children was loaded into a train. The train ride was slow, but suddenly was diverted to Theresienstadt. Men were separated from women and children and locked into separate ancient military housing. Ours was the second transport to arrive at the newly opened concentration camp.

After six weeks, 500 people from Brno and 500 from the first transport from Prague were assembled again, and after a slow and difficult train ride of three days and nights without food and water, the train arrived in Riga, the capital of Latvia in northeastern Europe. Unbearable cold greeted our arrival, as we had to march for about an hour to the ghetto from the station. Those carrying duffel bags were lucky because all luggage was confiscated. Most of us were left with just the clothes we wore.

Riga, a city with a once-thriving Jewish community of 30,000, now was the gathering place that overburdened a deplorable life for the local Jews and those who were brought from the smaller communities and from other countries. When my family arrived in the ghetto, they found that almost the entire Jewish population, including several transports of Jews from Germany, was decimated. Only 3,000 young men and about 100 women and teenagers who stayed hidden were spared. Our transport was probably diverted and spared—for the time being—because the murderers had too many bodies on their hands.

People were packed into two ghettos, which were in the worst part of the city. The Latvian men were in the small "Latvian ghetto" and Jews from Germany, Austria, and Theresienstadt—now called "Group Prague"—were gathered into the "German ghetto." The housing was primitive and crowded, but at least families were able to stay together. My parents and I slept together in one twin-size bed. At least our body heat kept us warm. The shock of this life did not leave time for anger or answers. One had to determine a will to live. One had to learn to adapt and survive.

The weekly rations of mildewed bread, tiny amounts of margarine, marmalade, grits and some frozen potatoes and shriveled-up carrots were never in sufficient quantity to fill our hunger. The anguished hunger of those who were unable to leave the ghetto for work or did not have anything to trade was even more dire. Many soon died from their weakened conditions.

During Passover of 1942, Adolf Eichmann appeared at the ghetto. All who did not work, including children, had to stand in rows of eight for hours. Those who seemed old and sick or were unable to work were "selected" to the left. My grandmother Ida and Aunt Grete were among this group, as were small children and mothers with infants. They were told that they would be sent for less strenuous work in another camp. Of course, the truth was that they were gassed in the transport trucks.

My mother at first worked preparing the vacated housing for the new arrivals from Austria and Germany. They cleaned and sorted the abandoned clothing. The daily search of the workers uncovered that a woman took a tiny ball of wool. The entire working group of 40 was lined up and every fourth woman was shot. My mother was among the survivors who returned to the ghetto, dazed. After this work, mother, along with many other women, was assigned to shovel the snow off the streets. Those who had something to trade were lucky to get a piece of bread or butter. But even this was a great danger. The women were frisked often, and if caught with any unauthorized item were immediately hanged. The sight of the gallows was a surreal picture that could be seen from my window. This almost became my mother's punishment when she was discovered smuggling food into the ghetto. By a miracle, her hair was shaved instead and she was made to stand at the gate as a deterrent for the returning workers.

My parents and I spent two years in the ghetto, where our lives were at constant risk. We were all subject to the whims of the SS, who for fun harassed the inhabitants with brutal edicts or death. During this time, thousands of inhabitants disappeared, never to be heard from again. On one occasion—I cannot fathom where I garnered the bravery—I hid a Jewish Latvian policeman who was one of many planning a revolt and were betrayed. Fifty were shot near the gallows as I trembled with each salvo of the rifle shots. When my parents returned from work that evening, I disclosed my deed, hardly able to speak. Father liberated the man from his hiding place and he left immediately. We never heard from him again. He may well have been shot too, because soon an additional 200 Latvian Jews were captured and shot.

Mornings, I attended a makeshift school, and in the afternoons I worked in a tailor shop in the ghetto. My mother worked in a carpenter shop in the port of Riga and father in the shoe depot for Feldbekleidung of the German Air Force—Luftwaffe—in Riga, where they sorted the shoes and clothes from the battlefields. On some rare occasions, father succeeded in smuggling a pair of shoes, hidden in his clothes, while mother, knowing that it would be a death sentence, took them to her workplace and bartered for food.

In the fall of 1943, the ghetto was liquidated. The Luftwaffe asked for its trained workers by name, adding families to the list, which saved my mother and me. We certainly would have been of the thousands who were killed. We were sent to a newly built concentration camp, Kaiserwald—which was run by criminals—where we were chased off the trucks and herded into the camp. Here the families were broken up. Men were separated from the women in camps surrounded by a double row of barbed wire fencing. A similar eight-feet-tall fence ran around the perimeter of the camp. Only the SS guards could walk in between the fences. Guards with rifles were stationed on raised platforms, which overlooked the entire camp.

The women, the labor force, were taken to the bath barrack, where they were deloused. The humiliation of having to undress and march in front of the SS men who inspected them for head and body lice, and being shaved of all hair, only made some feel more defiant since they did not want to succumb to the Nazis' design to break their spirit. All meager possessions were taken away. We were lined up, five women to a row, and were counted and harassed by both male and female SS for over five hours and finally were packed into the barrack blocks. Mother and I were assigned to Block 3. It was a long bare room constructed of boards. German women prisoners took up the places along the walls and underneath the windows. The floor in the middle was for the Jews, where straw-filled sacks barely accommodated two prisoners and did not suffice for all the captives. The German women prisoners were either criminals (who wore green triangles), political prisoners (red triangles) or asocial prisoners, mainly prostitutes (black triangles). Later, the German prisoners got better, separate housing, "because they could not be subjected to share the barrack with lowly Jews." Within three months, three-leveled bunks were built and steadily more and more women were brought in and crowded together.

As horrible as the women's camp was, the men's camp was even worse. Not only did the guards and the entire array of SS harass the men, but three criminal prisoners ran the camp. They were Nazis and in cahoots with the SS. It was hard to tell who was worse. The stories about men sweeping barracks with hairbrushes and even toothbrushes are, unfortunately, true. Men were dunked in latrines, where they drowned. The severe labor condition and bitter cold precipitated father's rheumatism in the sites of his old injuries. The unbearable pain resulted in his walking with a limp. This was a dangerous handicap for a Jew who was evaluated by his ability to work.

The slave laborers loaded and unloaded bundles of uniforms from trucks and had to sort them in stacks in warehouses. Torn and bloody things were sent to be fixed and cleaned in Germany. The laborers were ordered to ship reasonably clean and undamaged uniforms to the front lines, but much of the stuff became damaged in their hands. Things that could have been repaired they tore even further and added to the unsalvageable pile that had to be scrapped. They got some satisfaction of revenge by contributing, even if symbolically, to the Germans losing the war. Although they were struggling to survive, they chose to walk a thin line, since the punishment for sabotage was death.

In the summer of 1944, the Germans were already evacuating Riga. The food was bad and there was not enough of it. The coffee not only resembled dirty water, but it was poisoned with nitric acid. My father lost his job at the *Feldbeklaidung* and was left behind to work menial jobs at the camp. He became weaker and was beaten frequently. When they were selecting who was to leave Riga on the boat, his limp gave him away and he was taken with the other men in his group into a barrack on the outskirts of the women's camp, behind a fence next to my barrack. We knew that the people who were weak and sick were to be killed. I was able to get close to the fence to speak to father. I approached an SS officer, who after the war was tried in Nuremberg for war crimes, and pleaded that he transfer my father to the working men's barracks. "I am sorry," he said. "I cannot let him go, but you may join him if you wish." Suddenly the whole thing was eerie. I wanted to be with my father and I felt that life wasn't worth living. But I also knew that they separated men and women and I would not be with him. I answered the SS officer that I had to ask permission from my mother. Then I went back to the fence and told my father what the Sturmbandfuhrer said. "Don't you dare," said father. "My only hope is that you and your mother stay alive. . . . Go back to the barrack and stay away from me. Don't ever come to this fence again." That was the last time that I saw or heard my father. We were told that his group was sent to Buchenwald. This was another lie. They were all taken and shot in the infamous Birkenick forest near Riga.

In August, mother and I and the people who were sent to the "right" were shipped to Danzig. A tortured trip, which lasted three days, brought us to the concentration camp in Stutthoff. Stutthoff was 50 times worse than anything we had experienced before. Two thousand women were crowded in a barrack that was too small for 500. We spent the days standing in the August heat. At night we were standing too, as there was no place to sit down. The rooms were filled with standing women. One couldn't fall; all one could do was lean on a neighbor. After some time at Stutthoff, at a very meticulous selection, when each woman had to file naked, wearing only shoes, before a selected group of Nazi SS men, I was selected to the left and my mother followed me. We said to each other, "What are we going to do now, we don't want to die." Because of a miraculous intervention by a friendly Kapo, mother and I were able to be shifted to the women selected to the right that were transported to a working camp in Poland. And again we lived in tiny plywood huts where the conditions were dreadful and hunger was great. The menial work of carrying bricks and digging trenches was backbreaking.

The camp was made up of 500 women guarded and harassed by SS women and guards led by *Sturmbardfuhrer* Schultz, who was the boss. As the Russian front was getting closer, Schultz announced that even though he had orders to abandon the camp, the people who didn't feel like going should stay behind and welcome the Russians and give a good word for him. My mother desperately tried to convince everybody to leave because by then we knew that one should never stay behind with the weak and frail. Sure enough, after we marched a few miles, Schultz rode back in his motorized vehicle and shot everybody.

We marched, clad in minimal prisoner clothing in the wet snow, which was sticking to our wooden clogs. One had to shake off the weighty burden every few steps. No food or water was provided. We were hungry and ate dirty snow to quench our thirst. Sometimes we slept on the road and at times we were taken into a barn. If we were lucky, we were able to steal some roots or other fodder. After the short stay, the march continued again. Ivan, as the Russians were referred to, was everywhere. The retreating German populations were driving covered wagons with all their possessions inside.

On March 9, 1945, at about 10 in the morning, my mother looked out of the barn and didn't see the usual guards. She dared to venture out and explore a distance, where she spotted Russian tanks roll by. She called me to come out. When we discovered that there were no Germans in sight, we ran back, embraced, and kissed everybody. The Soviet army in their forward march did not take prisoners. They shot every German in uniform including Schultz and his cohorts. The Jewish survivors were liberated on March 10, 1945, just before my 15th birthday.

The poor, bedraggled, emaciated survivors pillaged the abandoned German wagons. Many became violently ill after gorging on the rich foods. Mother and I were prudent and started with plain bread, but regardless, all got sick eventually. We remained in an abandoned house with the group of women until the end of April when we returned to Brno. Every street of the city was in ruins from the bombings. Not one person survived from our family. I was the only child of my age group—or younger—from the Jewish school who survived the hell. What used to be our property was destroyed and what was left the Czech government took over from the Nazis. My mother was told that the government didn't have to return our possessions or homes since they did not take it from us. Friends who guarded some of my mother's and grandmothers' jewelry returned them to us. On the whole, our prewar good friends returned most of the things they held for safekeeping. We even got back some money, which was held for us.

I resumed my schooling and made up the years I missed. After finding ourselves alone, without family and no sense of belonging, mother and I left Czechoslovakia for Bogota, Columbia, in 1946. We were reunited with my aunt and family who had settled there before the war. Here I renewed my life, grew to adulthood, married, and established a family of three children—Charlie, Sofia, and George—and six devoted grandchildren. In 1963, we moved to Florida, where I earned a degree in Liberal Arts. In 1997 I lost my husband Max, who had been my dear partner.

I have been a committed speaker on behalf of the Holocaust for many years. A vicious killer starts with a stranger and in the end finishes off his own family. The Nazis started with the handicapped, mentally deficient, Jews, Gypsies and gays. Then they went against the Slavs, French, and Dutch and were out to conquer the world. They would not have stopped once the Jews were gone. They would not have shut off the crematoria once they were working at full blast. They would have found someone—and like the Hangman story, who knows who the last one would have been?

Saved By the Quakers

by Richard Weilheimer

I was born in Ludwigshafen, Germany, in 1931. My father was a businessman and my mother operated her own kindergarten. The rise of the Nazis and their anti-Semitic laws had a devastating effect on our family from my early years on.

Twelve days short of my seventh birthday, on the night of November 9, 1938, a time in a boy's life when he should be laughing and playing with children his age in a secure environment, Kristallnacht took place. The events of that infamous day became etched in my mind. Kristallnacht, often referred to as "The Night of Broken Glass," was the first violent Nazi mass action against Jews.

Our family was awakened shortly before dawn by the sounds of destruction, shattering glass, and euphoric shouts by a sea of humanity gone berserk on the street below our windows. Mobs of hooligans smashed Jewish-owned shops and looters felt free to claim whatever merchandise they coveted.

As frightening as these scenes were to me, they were eclipsed by the sight of the monsters who climbed the stairs to the apartments where the store owners lived. They dragged out helpless, bewildered people, forcing everyone, including children and elderly parents, out to the street. The barbarians beat some people with clubs or whatever was in their hands. This image of bloodied children and their families will never leave me.

Before we had a chance to react, mobs of thugs stormed into our apartment. They wore no uniforms, were unknown to us; they were just hordes of people out of control with hatred for Jews. They grabbed my father and arrested him. We had no idea where he would be taken or why, but there were no laws protecting Jews and no explanation was required. Days later we learned that he was shipped to Dachau, the first Nazi concentration camp.

Taking hold of my brother Ernst's and my hands, our mother fled from the house. Our destination was the synagogue where grandfather was the cantor. As we approached, we could see the flames from a distance. We were not close enough to determine if the fire came from inside the house of worship or from the heaps of sacred objects tossed and torched on the sidewalk. To witness the firemen standing idly by their trucks, smugly satisfied that the fire from the synagogue would not spread to adjacent Aryan property, was very puzzling to me.

We decided to return to our home to retrieve some sweaters. The sight that greeted us at the apartment is still embedded in my mind. Our home had again been violated and all our possessions were trashed. The intruders, with axes and sledgehammers, demolished the entire contents our home. Every piece of furniture was decimated into splinters; dishes, knickknacks and life's little treasures lay in fragmented heaps. Clothes and linens had been dumped in the center of the rooms and ink, paint and molasses poured over them.

Almost two years later, on the morning of October 22, 1940, the notorious, brutal Gestapo came to our home. We were given one hour to pack and told that we were being relocated. A lone guard watched us stuff the single suitcase each of us was allowed to take while his partner posted himself at the front door. An entire celebration of life, memorabilia and cherished possessions had to be forsaken: photographs, family treasures, books, musical instruments, and irreplaceable heirlooms.

Together with my mother and father (who had been released from Dachau after five weeks), Ernst and I were loaded on one of the trains—old passenger cars with seats ripped out, and windows shuttered and sealed from the outside.

We were on the train for three days and nights, often sidetracked for hours. The only food we had during the first two days was what we had brought from home. On the third day we pulled into a station where the shutters, which had kept us in dimness, were opened. We then knew that we were in Pan, a city in southern France. There were civilians on the platform with rice and water for us. They were representatives from the American Friends Service Committee, a Quaker organization. We soon continued to the town of Oloron St. Marie, just north of the Pyrenees. We were then released to stand on the station platform in pouring rain. Our meager possessions were piled in the mud and we did not know if we would ever see them again.

Thus the Nazis began their ugly mission to rid Germany of its Jews. Camp de Gurs, near the Spanish border, was the largest camp in France. No one suspected that this place was merely an anteroom of death—a way station to hold us until the extermination camps in Poland were ready.

The camp had inadequate drainage and the mud was deep and so sticky we had to remove our shoes because the suction made it almost impossible to walk in that quagmire. Gurs consisted of compounds separated from one another by barbed wire, with sentries patrolling the outer perimeters reinforced by guardhouses at the entrances. In addition, the whole camp was surrounded by more of this wire fortification. Men and women were quickly separated and assigned to different compounds with the young children being relegated to barracks in the women's section. We slept on the damp, bare ground as there were no mattresses or blankets available. Hatch covers swung over openings on the sides, but most were not operable. Light and sufficient air could get in only when they were propped open with a stick. With much rain and cold temperature, they were mostly closed despite the dank air and darkness. A single low-wattage light bulb was turned on for an hour in the morning and evening leaving people at either end of the barrack in darkness.

Sanitary conditions were crude. Rows of wash basins stood at the perimeter of each compound where once or twice daily cold water was available. A person could wash in the open, in full view of other inmates and guards. Primitive latrines were located alongside the barbed wire. Prisoners had to climb several steps to reach elevated platforms of wooden planks with rounded holes cut into them under which sat steel drums. One can hardly describe the sickening smells that permeated the camp. Before long almost every inmate was afflicted with dysentery.

Food was near starvation level. Twice daily, we were allotted a "soup" consisting of hot water with a few turnips and occasionally other vegetables such as carrots or beets and—rarely—shreds of meat. We also received a slice of bread so small that every crumb counted.

The Vichy authorities had eventually managed to obtain straw for us to sleep on and then provided sacks to stuff so that we had "mattresses." It turned out that the straw was rotten and infested with vermin. Our parents did everything possible to assure us that our confinement would be temporary. Most adults truly envisioned their eventual resettlement, free from Hitler's ever-extending reach. But inmates died every day, particularly the very young who could not be protected and the elderly who could not adapt to this terrible depraved life.

Of the various aid organizations actively involved in alleviating our misery, the Quakers were the most successful. They eventually located LaMaison des Pupilles de la Nation, an orphanage in the southern French town of Aspet, and negotiated for the release of some children from the camp to fill the vacant beds. We did not know then that none of our parents would survive the Holocaust. All 48 of us children would soon be orphaned. It was during our 16 months' stay at the orphanage that Ernst and I learned of our mother's death at Camp de Gurs at the premature age of 39.

Eventually the U.S. State Department authorized entry visas for a few "refugee" children and once more the Quakers selected Ernst and me. The escorted us to Marseille, where we awaited our rescue ship.

Some events defy explanation. Our father was able to obtain a safe conduct pass out of Gurs. He met us at Marseille and we were able to spend one day together prior to our departure. In anticipation of his arrival, I had walked the streets, picking up cigarette butts from sidewalks and gutters. I stripped them, collecting the tiny bits of unused tobacco so that I would have a farewell gift for my father. He had learned to roll his own cigarettes. We could not possibly have imagined that this would be the last time we would see each other.

We received the following letter from father after Ernest and I landed in America:

Friday, June 16, 1942

My cherished children!

> *I hope this finds you well, as is the case with me. Although I was allowed to spend a nice day with you on Wednesday, it was sadly much too short. You sailed out to sea yesterday, Thursday, June 25 about 4 p.m. They would not allow me near the steamship. I would so much have loved to see you and speak with you once again. I went in the afternoon to the jetty on the harbor and saw the Imerethie II anchored there. But I could only come to the gate, some 100 meters away from the ship.*

> *At 4 o'clock, I saw the gangplank retracted and another pulled, and shortly after, your ship was towed out by a small tugboat. People stood at the pier waving and shouting their good-byes. Tragically, I could not be with them and soon the boat was out of sight.*

> *My thoughts were with you. So my dear, good children, I again wish you all the best and above all, good health. Travel with God. May he protect you and keep you well. May he provide you with a joyous future filled with good luck and may he allow you to grow into healthy, Jewish youngsters who can stand tall among men in this difficult world. You are so good, loved and upstanding and you will endear yourselves and be welcome.*

> *I send regards from all the people here who know you, and they wish you everything good. I will be glad when you are among our loved ones and once again have your own good home. I hope to join you; that is what dear mother wanted. We will*

never forget her. She would have loved to travel with us but God wanted it different.

I pray to God daily for you and your voyage, which will hopefully be good. Take care of yourselves, especially in the heat, and you my dear Richard, always look after dear Ernest. All will become right with God's help. Stay happy, cheerful and good. I don't want to make a lot of words now. Travel with luck. I hope soon to be with you again and stay with you.

My beloved boys, stay well, and write to me often as it is my greatest joy and only wish to hear from you soon again.

Regards and kisses, your loving father.

I believe we were on the last ship out of occupied Europe. Five days after we sailed, the infamous Adolf Eichmann arrived in Paris demanding immediate implementation of the Final Solution for the Jews in France. I never heard from my father again. He was shipped to Sobibor on convoy #50 and, like the others in the cattle car, gassed on arrival.

Richard Weilheimer passed away on November 27, 2009

Rekindled My Hope–My Heritage

by Murray Weisman

My father, Ben-Zion, married my mother, Sara Brown, when he completed his education. They moved to Lodz, Poland, where he obtained a position as a Hebrew teacher. My mother, who came from an Orthodox family, was the driving influence on our lifestyle, and cared for our house and her family with affection and compassion.

I was born in Lodz in 1930, the youngest of five children; I had two brothers and two sisters. We lived a modest life, guided by mutual respect, responsibility, and love for each other. *Shabes*—Sabbath—and the holidays, were the central focus of our lives; we counted the days with impatience. This was a time when we enjoyed our new clothes, shoes, the holiday festivities, and the aroma of wonderful foods that filled our home.

At the age of three-and-a-half, I was enrolled in a *cheder* where I learned Hebrew and Yiddish and where the repetitious teaching and learning embedded the lessons for life. I began Polish public school at the age of seven, where most of the students were Polish, as were all the teachers. The daily threat of abuse and beatings by the non-Jewish students is still a disturbing memory for me. Anti-Semitism was an all-pervasive reality in Poland, going back hundreds of years, and was supported by the religious teachings in the schools—blaming the Jews for killing Jesus—which spilled over against even little children like me.

In the summer of 1939, the world's two most ruthless dictators, Adolf Hitler and Josef Stalin, aligned, signed a pact, invaded, divided, and occupied Poland. The Russians occupied the eastern half of Poland. The Germans occupied the western part of Poland, including Lodz. Within the first few days after the German invasion, the Polish army collapsed. With the German anti-Jewish influence that filtered in even before the war, thousands of Poles took to the street and broke into Jewish stores, taking whatever could be removed and as much as they could carry. *"The moment of joy finally arrived, we got our share of revenge from the rich Jewish exploiters,"* was often heard as justification for the plundering of Jewish property.

On September 8, 1939, the German Army entered and occupied my hometown, Lodz, which had a Jewish population, estimated at 230,000, living throughout the city. From the first days of occupation, the Germans began issuing order after order designed to restrict and control and destroy Jewish life. A dusk-to-dawn curfew was imposed under the threat of death for any violators. Regardless of age, sex, and status in life, all Jews were required to wear an armband and later a yellow patch in the shape of a Star of David with the word *Jude*—Jew—inscribed in the center. These patches had to be sewn onto the left chest of the coat for easy identification.

The Poles eagerly collaborated with the Nazis, helping to identify Jews, particularly the rich, the educated, and the prominent leaders. These Jews were picked out immediately and arrested. The detained Jewish elite became hostages, with extremely high ransom payments demanded for their release. But once the ransom was paid, the captives were not released; instead, the Germans killed them.

Abducting Jewish people from the street was a daily occurrence. Within a few days following the occupation, all three major synagogues were destroyed. The Altshtatishe synagogue was within walking distance of our residence. One day we saw the Gestapo unloading black hundred-gallon barrels and placing them in and around the synagogue. That very evening we heard explosions and through our windows saw huge red flames consuming everything inside. I felt that a part of me had been destroyed—my voice silenced from my participation in the choir every Saturday.

Reports were circulated that the Nazis would take away all children under five. They told us that they would place them in institutions where they would be fed properly with adequate milk, which was not available in Lodz. Not trusting the Germans, and thinking that in a small community the little ones would be safer out of the reach of the Nazis, my family decided that my oldest sister, Rivke, should take her two children, Sara, four, and Esther, two, to a small town, Klimantov, where our grandparents lived and had trusted Polish friends who would provide shelter and protection for them. I learned later that these Polish protectors murdered my sister, but the fate of the two little ones I never discovered; perhaps they were raised as Catholics and may still be alive somewhere.

The Nazis established a *Judenrat* (Jewish Council), appointing Mordechai Chaim Rumkowski as the head of the council. He appointed Jewish police to keep order in this horrible, chaotic, and miserable environment. He later issued ghetto paper money as the official currency, and postage stamps. He rode around in a horse-and-buggy coach, making speeches on the street corners, transmitting orders to us that the Germans required of him.

When the ghetto was about to be liquidated, a Nazi, Hans Biebow, took control of administering the ghetto. He spoke fluent Yiddish and gave orders to Rumkowski. He requested that all Jews over 12 years of age assemble the next morning at the public square. Rumkowski threatened that if we didn't go voluntarily, the Gestapo would come and take us by force. Biebow spoke in Yiddish, complimenting and pacifying the Lodz population that they were famous for their skills and excellent work and that the German army needed their productivity. He told them that the German government wanted them to come to Germany and work in the factories. He said they would be treated well, with adequate food, clothing, and shelter. Whatever they might need would be provided. At this point, many Jews were dying from starvation and epidemics of typhus, fever, cold, and overcrowding. We saw no other way to survive. Many chose to believe what Biebow promised, and the next morning went to the railroad station.

My parents debated what to take and what to leave. Valuables, such as jewelry, they thought would be safer to hide in the house, so they would be sure to have them when they returned home. At precisely 6 a.m., we heard lots of noise and commotion. The Nazis kept screaming: "*Raus, raus, schneller raus*" (out, out, faster, out), followed by gunshots. The commotion was coming from the buildings next to our block. Suddenly, a neighbor rushed in jumping for joy, shouting they had enough people and our block would not be deported. "Thank God, we were saved this time. A real miracle from God," said my mother.

In February or March 1940, on a cold winter morning, I was on my way to the bakery to buy bread. As soon as I stepped into the street, I saw Gestapos with guns in their hands, positioned directly across the street from me, gathering people for their selection. As I tried to explain that I was just out on an errand for bread, a guard hit me with his gun on the left side of my head. He pushed me into the waiting truck, which was filled within a half an hour. A caravan of nine trucks, loaded with abductees, traveled for an hour before reaching the destination of rail cattle cars. We were forced into the cars that were slammed shut, locked, and sealed.

After many hours, the train finally stopped in a wooded area not far from Selchow, a small town in the eastern part of Germany. In the early morning, the doors of the cars were opened to a landscape covered with snow with a dense forest on either side of the tracks. A large contingent of military in dark blue uniforms, backed up by civilian guards, all equipped with guns, clubs, and whips, was stationed at the door of the railroad car. I was very frightened, freezing, thirsty, and hungry. I was confused and disoriented; I didn't know what was happening to me.

Stepping off the cars, a cruel ritualistic inquisition began. Nazis, some with

226

guns, some with sticks accompanied by a few vicious dogs, yelled obscenities at the abductees from Lodz. We were commanded to form lines, five people abreast, and were marched into the camp where we were ordered to empty our pockets and throw any possessions we had—including rings, wallets, watches, and pencils—into an empty barrel. We were punished with beatings for infractions of camp rules we did not know existed. These infractions included keeping your hands in your pockets; not taking off your hat when a Nazi approached; not standing at attention when the guard talked.

We were inspected and counted before going to work in the morning and again in the evening when we returned to camp. I was small and a Nazi asked how old I was. I told him that I was 14, instead of 10, and also told him that I was a carpenter. These answers were my lifesaver throughout my camp life. The first job I was assigned to do was to trample the snow in the woods. After that, we had to cut trees in preparation to building a highway. We worked in freezing, hot, or rainy weather conditions. The Nazis' aim was to inflict as much pain as possible.

Our daily food was an inch-thick slice of bread and a ladle of ersatz coffee in the morning, and in the evening a bowl of watery soup. I was conflicted whether to eat the piece of bread at once or divide it into two or more portions: one for the morning, and the other for midday. I opted to divide it into two portions. Hunger was a permanent condition of our existence.

As time went on, the daily suffering had a devastating physical and emotional impact on the inmates, including myself. After about three or four months, which felt like forever, many inmates began to weaken, physically, spiritually, and mentally. They were ready to give up life. The difference between life and death was negligible. The consequences of going to the health center was to be marked for liquidation. The sick inmates were isolated, and taken away by truck to an unknown place. They never returned. I, too, became ill. My body would not move, my hands and feet refused to bend, every muscle in my body became stiff and I developed a high fever. One prisoner, a doctor, diagnosed my medical problem as a *hexenschuss*, which is caused by overburdening and stretching the muscles too much. His medical advice to me was a period of rest and warmth. Rest and warmth were hard to come by. After suffering for two days, the aches gradually subsided and the movement of my limbs caused less pain.

The exhausted and abused inmates were to build a highway running from Berlin to Moscow in 5-mile stretches. Once a section of the road was completed, the prisoners from the Selchow camp were moved to a new location, Grunow. When the second section was completed, the prisoners were moved to a third camp, Christianstadt. All the camps had the same programs designed to decimate the inmates through hard work, starvation, and torture—all leading to death.

At the work site in Christianstadt, I met a Polish war prisoner, Henry, from a nearby prison camp. We became good friends and gained mutual trust in each other. We decided to escape by taking a train to his hometown, not far from Lodz. Unfortunately, the train inspector checking my ticket asked me for identification, which I told him I had lost. He arrested me and handed me over to two Nazis waiting for me at the next station. I do not know what happened to Henry. The next two days I was subjected to extreme punishment. Finally they dragged me to the barrack for more punishment. It took me weeks to recover from the savage torture inflicted on me. It was a miracle that I was able to stay alive after this ordeal. Several months later, Christianstadt camp was liquidated and we were transported to Auschwitz in the summer of 1942. I was 12 years old.

The indescribably long train trip to Auschwitz finally came to a halt. The railroad cars were unsealed and the doors opened. Dozens of SS with machine guns formed a semicircle as we disembarked from the train. There was another transport of Jewish men, women and children, who were exhausted, frantic, and frightened. This second transport carried baggage, bundles, and suitcases. It was a deceptive Nazi tactic to allow deportees from shtetls—little towns—to take some belongings with them. At the roll call, everybody was ordered to step forward and leave their belongings behind. One woman refused to part with her suitcase, which was made of rushes or twigs. A Nazi with a revolver in his hand stepped toward the woman and kicked the suitcase with his heavy boot. The suitcase opened and a bundled up infant fell out. The Nazi stepped forward and trampled the infant, then he shot the woman and the infant. This scene destroyed my sense of reality, and I became numb.

Our processing into Auschwitz began in the first section, where we were ordered to undress completely and put our clothes in piles. Next was the painful cutting of all hair, executed with dull clippers, which pulled the hair more than cut it. Then I was tattooed on my left arm with the number 142558. This was my new identity. The final insult was a body inspection to make sure that nothing was hidden anywhere. After this we were given a blue white canvas uniform made of wood fibers.

The sheer enormity of the place with the gas chamber, crematorium, the gallows, the mass execution site, and the nauseating smell of burned flesh had a debilitating effect on all inmates. At this stage of Auschwitz, the gas chambers and the crematorium were not quite operational. Big trenches were used to burn the victims. Some of the victims were still alive, even after being shot and driven to the trenches to be burned.

At the end of 1942, there were about 50,000 prisoners. The great majority were Jews from all over Europe, interspersed with some German political and criminal prisoners who, even here, spewed anti-Semitic sentiments against the Jews.

The routine was similar to the one in the previous forced-labor camp. We were awakened before dawn by a tormenting, screeching whistle and, if we did not jump out of the bunk immediately, we received a flying object on our heads known in the camp language as a telegram. The long latrines, with about 20 places cut from wooden planks to serve as toilets, emitted an unbearable smell and served about 500 hundred inmates on one side. To use the limited facilities was a struggle; there was a scarcity of water, no towels, no toothbrushes, no toothpaste, or toilet paper. Breakfast was the same as in the other camps: an inch-thick piece of black bread, a ladle of artificial coffee, and a watery soup for supper.

My first work assignment was unloading cement or coal from freight cars and putting it into trucks. The cement sacks were heavy for someone as small and weak as I was, but under the terrorizing, brutal Kapos brandishing whips, somehow I struggled to carry these sacks. Unloading coal without gloves or face and eye protection was even harsher. At one point, my left eye began itching terribly from the coal dust. I stopped for a moment to try to wipe my eye with the corner of my jacket. The sadistic Kapo saw me stop, became wild, and started to hit me with his whip. One strike landed over my left eye, which permanently damaged the sight in that eye. I did not feel the other blows over my body, just the eye, which was excruciatingly painful. Years later I had to have corneal transplants, which proved not to be successful, and I never regained sight in my left eye.

On the next job I hauled stones from one pile to another. I was only a child of 12 who had to endure the harshest life without anyone offering a helping hand or a word of kindness. In December 1942, in freezing-cold weather, I was selected along with others who appeared completely without energy to go to one of five waiting trucks destined for Birkenau. I was terrified and thought once again that this was my end. While the SS were looking in the other direction, I jumped out of the truck into a crowd of elders who were guarding the prisoners on the truck. Among the group was the elder of my barrack, whose room I cleaned each Sunday. The barrack elder apparently took pity on me and covered me until I was able to return to the barracks.

About a month later, an SS asked for carpenters at the morning roll call. With distrust and apprehension, I stepped forward. From 50 volunteers they picked only 20, and I was among them. Again a truck was waiting for us, but this time it was a manufacturing company truck. A few hours later we found ourselves in Auschwitz III, also known as Buna/Monovitz; and so ended my tormented tenure at Auschwitz.

Buna/Monovitz was a smaller camp with a prisoner population of between 20,000 and 30,000 and did not have any crematoriums. It did have several mobile gallows, which were used frequently. During one roll call, in the middle of July 1943, the Nazis discovered that five inmates had escaped—two

Jews and three Poles. A week later one of the Jewish escapees returned to camp. He told us that the three Polish companions killed one of the Jewish escapees and were planning to kill him too. A few days later the three Poles were caught, brought back to the camp, and were hung. Justice was done.

At Buna, the same brutal system of skimpy food rations and the customary practice of twice-daily roll calls was maintained. Marches were played while we were going to and leaving work. Weekly selections and brutal beatings were the norm. The vicinity outside of Buna had dozens of factories at various stages of development by different German and non-German companies producing a whole range of military equipment. The most notorious factory was the IG Farben Industry with several facilities designed to developed and produce synthetic rubber. Civilians of many nationalities were also working in the same area. However, inmates were not allowed to speak or otherwise interact or associate with the civilians; to do so resulted in severe punishment.

I was chosen to do a carpenter's job with the others who had volunteered. We were assigned to Block 15, where the carpenters, the shoemakers, and the electricians lived. As we marched to work, we were forced to sing loudly. When the Kapo noticed that a prisoner did not sing loudly enough, he became a target of severe beatings. My first assignment was to build scaffolds to insulate pipes outside the IG Farben installation. I joined a dozen other carpenters, all Jewish, who, like me, had been deported to Auschwitz III. My work was to climb up a ladder, carrying a 10-foot-long board, four inches thick by eight inches wide, to set up the scaffold, and tie up the board with special iron hooks, so that we could stand on it. On this high perch, we were whipped by the icy cold Polish wind, ripping through our bodies.

My supervisor, Shloyme, had a big heart in proportion to his size. He whispered to me when I came down to get a supply of insulation, asking my name. I told him I was called Motek at home. He said, "This is Mordechai, in Hebrew." Then he told me that he had a son about 20 years old with the same name, but that he had not heard from him or from his entire family—his wife and four other children—since he had been picked up in a small town, not far from Vilna over two years ago. We were able to quietly whisper to each other while trying to straighten out a pile of insulation. He handed me a package of insulation as he said, *"zei vorsichtig"* (be careful). Those were comforting words. I felt that these spoken words came from a father to his son. I started to cry, tears pouring from my eyes. I thanked him for his caring words. I had not heard such a tender expression for over two and a half years. These words were like a spark to rebuild my low spirits and morale. I began looking to the future with some hope in spite of the bleak reality.

Some time in March 1943, a transport came from my hometown, Lodz. I was eager to talk to them about my family at home. I was told that my parents had been evacuated a year before and they had been sent to Chelmo, an extermination camp near Lodz. Needless, to say, this news had a devastating effect on me. I was broken and my renewed hope to continue the struggle seemed useless. I felt alone and started to believe that my present life was how it should be. I had no family to return to if I survived.

We knew that the Russians were getting closer when they bombed some factories in Buna during the fall of 1944. One day, as the sirens shrieked of an impending attack, I scurried down the scaffold and looked for shelter. I tried to get into a bomb shelter when a Nazi stopped me from entering, saying: "It's not for dirty Jews." As the Russian plane approached, I hid in a nearby ditch. The bombs destroyed the shelter, including all the Nazis in it. I was extremely happy to have experienced another miracle of revenge and survival.

The Russian planes started to fly over us day and night. Blackouts were in effect during the night air raids. Four electricians, three Jewish and one Pole, planned to cut the electric wires so that the prisoners could escape. But the Polish inmate betrayed the three Jewish electricians, who were hanged in front of the prisoners. As the bench was pulled out from under the men, we heard their last uttered words. The first said, "*Comraden*, friends, we are the last ones," the second, "Let freedom live!" and the third one said, "Head high! The Nazis will be dead!" To discipline us before further deeds could be planned, the Nazis made us parade around with heavy, painful hearts, tears flowing to see these brave men displayed in their death.

In January 1945, rumors abounded that the Russian Army was making striking advances in our direction. The frequent blackouts and bombing of the IG Farben and other industrial installations caused mass hysteria and confusion. We heard that the Sonderkommando, those who attended the cruel work in the crematorium, and four Jewish girls who supplied the gunpowder to destroy the crematorium, had been executed. At the same time, the Lodz ghetto was being liquidated, and thousands of deportees began to arrive in Auschwitz.

On January 18, 1945, we were ordered to vacate the barracks. It was a brutally cold, snowy, and windy day when we started the infamous death march out of Auschwitz; we were ill-equipped, without food, dressed in threadbare clothes, and needing sleep. As we marched in columns of five abreast, the snow turned into a brown mush. I was almost carried along by the prisoners around me as I marched with my eyes closed, like walking to my own funeral. I had an urge to drop to the ground into the muddy snow and sleep. Those unable to continue dropped dead; many were shot in the process. After three tortuous days and two nights, over a third of the initial prisoners arrived at the concentration camp Gliewitz. The relentless hunger pains, bitter cold, icy winds, wet clothes and shoes were a miserable combination with devastating impact on our fragile weak bodies. We remained in Gliewitz for one day and one night, battling to keep the will to survive and rest. We continued the march for an hour to a railroad track, where we were loaded onto overcrowded cattle cars, which took us to an unknown destination, traveling for six days and five nights. No food, no water, no sanitary facilities. The pain from thirst was greater than from hunger. My tongue and mouth were painfully dry. I put my tongue to the wooden boards of the cattle car with the hope that perhaps the cold board would soothe the dryness and the burning sensation in my mouth. Finally, in the darkness of night, we arrived at the concentration camp Dora, a satellite of Buchenwald, near Nordhausen. As soon as we were finished with the tortuous, ritualistic roll call, I found a toilet with running water. I put my mouth under a faucet and kept drinking until my body was full of the lifesaving water.

There were no gas chambers at Dora, but there were three crematoriums and each could process three bodies at a time. These crematoriums, however, were not sufficient to accommodate the daily casualties of dead. There were about two dozen hangings daily, so they supplemented the crematoriums by digging big ditches and piling the bodies into them, covering them with wood and fuel, which were then burned in the open. The flames shot up to the sky. The terrible obnoxious odor of the burning bodies carried for miles. In addition, they had a number of gallows at different campsites; hanging prisoners was an ongoing activity at Dora. The butchery at Dora was so brutal, that I almost looked back at Auschwitz with nostalgia. Here the Nazis behaved totally wild, like hungry lions released from a cage. To survive a day in Dora, where random killing was a continuous practice, was indeed a miracle. One SS guard kept bragging that he could not eat breakfast unless he killed some Jewish inmates. One disastrous day, I happened to be the target. This murderer approached me from behind and stabbed me three times in my upper back and right shoulder with a sharp instrument. I fell to the ground and he thought that I was dead. Other inmates put some clay-dirt on my wounds to stop the bleeding, while they had to continue with their work. After work ended, some prisoners carried me back to the barracks. It was another miracle that I survived this brutal attack.

Sometime around the middle of March, at the morning roll call, the Nazis counted and separated about 25 young Jewish prisoners, including me, who appeared exhausted. We were ordered to a truck and traveled several hours until we arrived at the notorious camp, Buchenwald. I was assigned to a brick-making factory, where other young Jewish children were employed. After a month in Buchenwald, the stabbing wound had not healed. I was weak, frail, and ready to collapse. On a day, in April 1945, the Nazis called for roll call; the Buchenwald camp was being liquidated. I was in no physical condition to comply; instead I found a place behind the barrack with a pile of dead bodies. I dug myself into the pile until an American soldier dug me out. Those men who the Nazis evacuated both from Dora and Buchenwald were marched to a village, herded into a cattle yard, and the Nazis threw grenades into the hardly living gathered prisoners; only a few were able to escape and survive.

On April 11, 1945, I was liberated. I was one of the youngest to endure five and a half years in seven camps and survive. A day after the liberation, the joy of being free was not a time of celebration for me, for I learned that my entire family had been murdered.

Several weeks after, the surviving children were taken to Paris, where the OSE, a French-Jewish organization dedicated to the protection of children, received us with fine accommodations and the best of treatment. Subsequently, we were taken for three months for rehabilitation to Equi, a summer-camp-like facility, to help us adjust to normal life. We were returned to Paris and were placed into group homes, each with 30 youngsters. We were provided with the education we had missed during our incarceration. After four years, I left the group home for the United States. In 1950, I arrived in New York

My first job was menial, but I found that I could provide for myself. I attended night school to learn English and after two years I enrolled in the University of Minnesota and in three years I received my B.S. I then took a position with the Juvenile Court in St. Paul, Minnesota. After two years, I enrolled for my M.A. in social work at Ohio State University. When I finished, I took a full-time job as a social worker in Cincinnati, where I also enrolled in night school for a law degree. In the meantime, I met and married my life partner, Marianne, a young woman from Cincinnati, and continued with my education and earned my J.D. degree. I then took a position as executive director of the Dayton and Montgomery County Mental Health and Mental Retardation Board, a position I held for 10 years. Subsequently, I took a position as a civilian attorney with the United States Air Force, from which I retired in 1991.

In spite of the Nazi determination to destroy me, I have overcome and outlived them all. My wonderful family—three children and four delightful grandchildren—have rekindled my hope for my family heritage to continue.

About the Editors

by Judith Evan Goldstein

Dr. Jack Salzman

Jack Salzman received his Ph.D. from New York University in 1965. His long career in the academic world has included positions at Long Island University, Hofstra University, Hunter College, New York University, and Columbia University, where he was Director of the Center for American Culture Studies. In addition, Dr. Salzman has been a Fulbright Professor in Finland and Japan. His publications include *Years of Protest, Struggles in the Promised: A History of African Americans and American Jews,* and *Bridges and Boundaries: African Americans and American Jews.* For thirty years, he was the editor of *Prospects: An Annual of American Cultural Studies.*

Professor Salzman has a deep interest in the Holocaust and the lives of survivors. With his editorial expertise, profound dedication and commitment, he helped create a work filled with information, historical accuracy, and the essential tragedy of the war. In the work he did for this collection, as has been the case for everything he has done for the past fifty years, he has been assisted by his wife, Cecily, who has provided invaluable editorial help.

The authors, whose stories are written with tears and great sorrow, are honored to have the assistance of Jack and Cecily Salzman in putting together this book. In the name of the Child Survivors/Hidden Children organization, thank you!

Zelda Marbell Fuksman

Zelda Marbell Fuksman, born in Poland, is a child survivor of the Holocaust. She presently is chief editor of the quarterly newsletter of the Child Survivor/Hidden Children organization of Palm Beach County, Florida.

For the past ten years, Zelda has devoted her seemingly limitless time, effort, and hospitality to working as editorial chairperson of the book committee. She has feverishly interviewed members of the organization, collecting and writing testimonies, and deepening our understanding of their war experiences. She has acutely observed and concentrated on the intricate memories they have of the war and has helped them articulate these memories.

In the past, when still living in Illinois, Zelda was a charter member of the Child Survivor Organization and participated in resisting the planned Nazi march in Skokie, Illinois.

Now a resident of Boca Raton, Florida, she is an active speaker in schools and other venues, sharing her own war time experiences, and focusing on how we can make a better world for new generations to come. Zelda is a gift to our organization.

Timeline of the Holocaust Era

1933
January 30	Adolf Hitler appointed Chancellor of Germany
March 20	Dachau Concentration Camp opens
May 10	Nazis burn thousand of books

1934

August 2 — President Hindenberg dies; Hitler proclaims himself Führer und Reichskanzler (Leader and Reich Chancellor)

1935

September 15 — "Nuremberg Laws": anti-Jewish racial laws enacted

1936

July — Sachsenhausen Concentration Camp opens

1937

July 15 — Buchenwald Concentration Camp opens

1938

March 13 — Anschluss (incorporation of Austria): all anti-semitic decrees immediately applied in Austria

November 9 — Kristallnacht—attack on Jewish people and their property—many Jews murdered and 25,000 to 30,000 were arrested and placed in concentration camps. 267 synagogues were destroyed and thousands of homes and businesses were ransacked. Kristallnacht also served as a pretext and a means for the wholesale confiscation of firearms from German Jews

1939

January 30 — Hitler in Reichstag speech: if war erupts it will mean the Vernichtung (extermination) of European Jews

August 23 — Molotov-Ribbentrop non-aggression pact signed between Soviet Union and Germany—provides for partition of Poland

September 1 — Beginning of World War II—Germany invades part of Poland

October 28 — First Polish ghetto established in Piotrków

November 23 — Jews in German-occupied Poland forced to wear an arm band or yellow star

1940

May 7 — Lodz Ghetto sealed: 165,000 people in 1.6 square miles

May 10–12 — Germany invades the Netherlands, Belgium, Luxembourg, and France

May 20 — Concentration Camps Established - Auschwitz I in May 1940; Auschwitz II (also called Auschwitz-Birkenau) in early 1942; and Auschwitz III (also called Auschwitz-Monowitz) in October 1942. For the extermination of Jews; Gypsies, Poles, Homosexuals, the disabled and mentally deficient. Russians, and others were also murdered at the camp; Zyklon B gas was used in the extermination.

November 15 — Warsaw Ghetto sealed—ultimately contained 500,000 people

1941

June 22	Germany invades the Soviet Union
June 23	Einsatzgruppen begin mass murders of Jews in the Soviet Union
July 31	Heydrich appointed by Göring to implement the "Final Solution"
Sept. 28–29	34,000 Jews massacred at Babi Yar outside Kiev, 70,000 at Ponary, a forest outside Vilno
November 24	Theresienstadt (Terezin) established as a "model camp" near Prague
December 8	Chelmno (Kulmhof) extermination camp begins operations—340,000 Jews, 20,000 Poles and Czechs murdered by April 1943 and additional killings in June/July 1944
December 11	United States declares war on Japan and Germany

1942

January 20	Wannsee Conference in Berlin—Heydrich outlines plan to murder Europe's Jews—"Final Solution"
March 17	Extermination begins in Belzec—by end of 1942, 600,000 Jews murdered
May 7	Extermination by gas begins in Sobibor killing center; by October 1943, 250,000 Jew murdered
July 22	Germans establish Treblinka Concentration Camp
July 28	ZOB—Zydowska Organizacja Bojowa, which means Jewish Fighting Organization formed in the Warsaw Ghetto

1943

June	Himmler orders the liquidation of all ghettos in Poland and the Soviet Union
April 19–May 16	Warsaw Ghetto uprising
October 1-2	Danes rescue 7,200 Danish Jews from impending deportation

1944

May 15	Nazis begin deporting Hungarian Jews; by June 27—380,000 sent to Auschwitz
June 6	D-Day: Allied invasion at Normandy, France
July 20	Group of German officers attempt to assassinate Hitler
July 24	Russians liberate Majdanek killing center

1945

January 17, 25	Evacuation by death marches of Auschwitz and Stutthoff
January 27	Soviet Army liberates Auschwitz
April 6–10	Death march of inmates of Buchenwald
April 30	Hitler commits suicide
May 7	Germany surrenders to the Allies, ending the war in Europe

Financial Contributors

Mr. & Mrs. Burton Benjamin
Mr. & Mrs. Irv Beron
Mr. & Mrs. Henry Bialer
Mr. & Mrs. George Bodrogi
Mr. &Mrs. Richard Boyman
Hamilton Branford
Mr. & Mrs. Morton Brill
Mr. & Mrs. Alan Bronfman
Mr. & Mrs. Ira Cheifetz
Rochelle Cohen
Cypress Social Club—Boca Raton,
    Florida
Jeff Eichel
Mr. & Mrs. Mark Eichel
Mr. & Mrs. Norman Frajman
Free Sons of Israel - Delray Beach
    Lodge, Delray Beach, Florida
Barbara Friedman
Mr. & Mrs. Hershel Fuksman
Mr. & Mrs. Henri Galel
Gilah Inverrary Woodmont
    Hadassah
Mr. & Mrs. Leon Ginsburg
Marilyn Goldman Family
    Philanthropic Fund

Mr. & Mrs. Gilbert Goldstein
Mr. & Mrs. Harry Goldstein
Mr. & Mrs. Albert Goodman
Mr. & Mrs. Norbert Graber
Mr. & Mrs. Anszel Gun
Hillel Day School, Rabbi Adam
    Englender, Boca Raton, Florida
Mr. & Mrs. Donald Hirschorn
Mr. & Mrs. Roger J. Hochstin
Mr. & Mrs. Harold Jaffe
Helen Jonas
Hedviga Jungstein
Yvonne Kant
Mr. & Mrs. K. Kien
George Kittredge
Mr. & Mrs. John Koenigsberg
Edith Kovack
Mr. & Mrs. Robert J. Kwait
David Lachman
Elaine M. Laflamme, Esq,
    Akin Grump Strauss Hauer Feld
    LLP
Lakeridge Falls Women's Club
Mr. & Mrs. Peter Leibowitz
Mr. & Mrs. Benno Lindenberg

Financial Contributors Continued

Daniel Lindenberg
Mr. & Mrs. Marcel Lindenberg
Mr. & Mrs. Ronald Lipson
Stephy Malaga
Mr. & Mrs. Melvin Marcus
Noah Marmel
Mayim Chapter Of Hadassah
Mr.& Mrs. Walter Millard
Mr. & Mrs. Georges Miliband
Mr. & Mrs. Alex Moskovic
Ruth Nemovitcher
A. Terry Nuss
Judy Orent
Mr. & Mrs. Felix Pearson
Myron Perry
Dr. & Mrs. Henry Rabinowitz
Sherry Redler
Ridgeview Junior High,
    Pickerington, Ohio
Alan Rogers
Alan Rosenfeld
Jack Rozenberg
Jack & Shirley Rubin
Randy Sablonsky & Family
Mr. & Mrs. Israel Salzbank,

Mr. & Mrs. Israel Salzman
Fred Abbot Saperstein P.C.
Katherine Sattler
David Schapiro
Seymour Shapiro
Marilyn Schwartz
Seligman Family Foundation
Jesse & Wilma Bulkin Siegel
Mr. & Mrs. Robert Solari
Mr. & Mrs. Lewis Solomon
Erica & Joe Spindel
St. Jude School, Boca Raton,
    Florida
Mr. & Mrs. Arthur Tannenbaum
Top Flight Entertainment Ltd.
Mr. & Mrs. Arnold Turok
Mr. & Mrs. Clifford Viner
Mr. & Mrs. Bryan Wasserman
Harriet Webber
Mr. & Mrs. Richard Weilheimer
Joyce D.Weissman
Wilf Family Foundation
Willard Bear Audrey Bear Trust
Women's American ORT—
    Huntington Point Chapter

List of People on Back Cover Collage

(left to right)

Top Row. John Koenigsberg, Katherine Sattler, Joe Eckstein,
Mary Eckstein, Pierre Chanover, Cecilia Pearlstein

Row 2. Cecily Salzman, Jack Salzman, Sam Ron, Erica Spindel,
Riva Bernstein, Georges Miliband

Row 3. Richard Weilheimer, Zelda Fuksman, Hershel Fuksman,
Judith Evan Goldstein, Helen Jonas, Leon Ginsburg

Row 4. Cynthia Glazier, Murray Weisman, Frieda Jaffe,
Norman Frajman, Magda Hammer, Michel Jeifa

Row 5. Morris Friebaum, Hanna Temel, Max Markovitz,
Jack Rubin, Benno Lindenberg, Marcelle Bock

Row 6. Rosalyn Haber, Rachelle Bashe, Andrew Hartman,
Alex Moskovic, Rosette Goldstein, David Rosenblum

Row 7. Regina Glinzman, Maureen Marullo, George Bodrogi,
Judy Freeman, Allan Spak

240